A London & North Western Railway

Engineman At Work

The Diary of Thomas Baron

Frontispiece: 'Crewe Single' No. 500 Menai outside the Southern Division shed at Rugby about 1868. It was built at Edge Hill in 1847 as No. 169 Huskisson, was sold to the Lancaster & Carlisle Railway and on return to the LNWR became 500 Menai. It still has its original boiler and fittings, but is in typical Ramsbottom condition, with castellated chimney top, standard green livery with black lining, hook-type front coupling and six-wheeled Ramsbottom tender. The Menai on which Thomas Baron worked was not this one but 'Crewe Goods' 2-4-0 No. 206 built in June 1848. The location of this photograph was much discussed for many years and generally agreed by such authorities as S. S. Scott and F. E. A. Eades to be Stafford but was finally placed as Rugby in an article by Harry Jack in the LNWR Society Journal, September 1995, Volume 1 Number 8. Off-camera to the left was a long radial shed with space for one or two engines on each of its twenty roads – see plan of Rugby shed on Page 16. The 'Bloomer' on the left, originally No. 247, was the first of the class, built by Sharp Brothers in August 1851, renumbered 847 in April 1862 and rebuilt at Crewe between 12.1867 and 5.1868 – its Crewe-style smokebox with its distinctive flap-type door is evident here. No. 1435 on the right was built at Crewe in July 1865, and Menai lost its nameplates in December 1872, which dates the picture accordingly.

A London & North Western Railway

Engineman At Work

The Diary of Thomas Baron

1855 – 1862

Edward Talbot

Preface and Acknowledgements

Some years ago, probably on my first visit to the Public Records Office, now renamed for some unaccountable reason the National Archives, at Kew, I searched the catalogue and came across 'Diary of Driver T. Baron' (reference RAIL 1015 4). The document itself was full of interest, but as it would have taken a long time to copy it, either by hand or by photocopying, and as I had other priorities, I just made a mental note to look at it again some time in the future.

When I returned some years later, things had changed considerably. Fortunately, those who run the National Archives pursue the enlightened policy of constantly improving the facilities for the greater convenience of researchers. When laptops became available, they allowed them to be used in the reading room and installed power sockets on the tables, and when digital cameras were introduced, they not only permitted them to be used to copy documents but also provided camera stands to prevent camera shake. Thus, I was able recently to copy the 'Diary of Driver T. Baron' on digital camera and to type it out at home in my own time.

When I was able to look at the diary at my leisure, I soon realised that it is not really a diary in the conventional sense at all, in which the writer records events and often makes personal comments on them, but is very largely a concise account of Thomas Baron's daily work, recording the date; the driver's name; the name of the engine; and usually the destination, type of traffic and mileage run. Occasionally he records things which happened outside this routine, but not often and even when they are tragic and distressing, always briefly and succinctly.

I also soon realised that it was of great interest not only to members of the London & North Western Railway Society but to anyone with an interest in the railways of the 1850s. If it were to be published, it would be best for it to be accompanied by an explanatory commentary and other relevant information. I sent copies to Michael Bentley and Harry Jack, and both reacted with great enthusiasm and offered to contribute to the text. As an engineman by profession, Michael offered a study of the working conditions at the time and Harry locomotive details and a biography of Thomas Baron, as well as making valuable suggestions about content, captions, the selection of photographs and so forth. Later I showed it to Martin O'Keeffe, who also made a valuable contribution, especially with information relating to the Black Country canals, iron works and the railways connected with them on which Thomas Baron once worked.

Thanks are also due to the National Archives for permission to publish the diary, to David Deakin for liaising with James Arnold of Harris Museum, Preston, who kindly gave permission to publish pictures of Preston station by Robert Pateson; to David Viewing, modeller extraordinary, for loan of drawings and interesting discussion of early locomotive details; to John Boyle, Marc Dobson, David Keay and Mike Norris; to Gaye Blake-Roberts, Richard Ball and David Patrick; and finally to Dr Jon Coe, a descendant of Thomas Baron, for encouragement and much family information.

Edward Talbot
Gnosall, Stafford
2018

Figure 1: *Drawing of 6ft 'Crewe Passenger' 2-2-2 No. 279* Stephenson *as built at Crewe Works in December 1851 - with one exception. At that early date LNWR nameplates seem to have had the name only, with none of the additional inscriptions such as the date, the company's name and the place where built. The photographs of 'Problem' No. 229* Watt *(pages 13 and 86) and the nameplates of* Cornwall *are evidence of this. So the draughtsman might seem to be in error in this respect. But see Plates 27 and 28, which seem to show that early nameplates with the name only were later modfied with one-line inscriptions as here.*

Contents

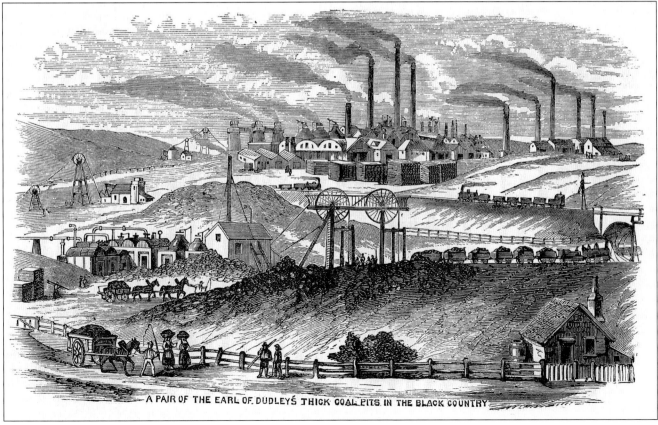

A PAIR OF THE EARL OF DUDLEY'S THICK COAL PITS IN THE BLACK COUNTRY

Introduction

The Diary of Thomas Baron is an extremely rare and valuable document, quite possibly unique. It is a record of the daily work of an engineman on the London & North Western Railway from 1855, when Thomas Baron started as a cleaner at Preston shed, to 1862, when he became a driver on the Abergavenny branch. It may seem strange that he kept a diary continuously from 1855 to 1862 and then stopped for no apparent reason. Why he stopped is unknown - the diary contains no explanation - but possibly at Abergavenny each day's work was the same, or at any rate almost the same, and he decided that it was not worth keeping a daily record of it. In 1877 he became Night Foreman at Abergavenny shed.

Baron's diary provides a glimpse of the operating of the LNWR only a quarter of a century after the opening of the Liverpool & Manchester Railway, in the 'Dark Ages' or 'Lost Years', as it were, of railway history, and only ten years after the formation of the LNWR itself.

The Liverpool & Manchester Railway is the subject, quite rightly, of numerous books and articles, and the history of the early companies, such as the Grand Junction Railway, has also been the subject of well researched histories. Similarly, the work of the locomotive engineers, such as Trevithick at Crewe and Ramsbottom his successor, is well documented, and from about 1870, when photography became widespread, these subjects are also very well illustrated. But documentary evidence providing an insight into the work of enginemen and railway operating in this early period is so rare as to be almost non-existent.

For the whole period of Baron's diary, engines were made almost entirely of iron – cast-iron, wrought-iron and iron plate – copper and brass. Steel only became readily available from 1864, when Crewe first had its own steel works, and was in general use only from the late 1870s. Rails too were of iron, and any lighting at night depended on oil lamps, which were better than nothing but provided only feeble illumination. Engines had no cabs, only weatherboards, to provide protection from the elements (the first cabs on the LNWR were introduced in 1872 by F. W. Webb), and so the men were exposed on the footplate - rather like the drivers of the road coaches that preceded the railways - for many hours in whatever weather conditions prevailed, day and night, at all times of the year, and what is more, as the diary shows, working hours were long, fifteen hours a day being common, and longer not unusual.

Engines were not fitted with brakes of any kind, and enginemen had only two means of stopping at their disposal: 'powing' as it was called, that is, putting the engine into reverse with the lever reverser (the screw reverser was as yet not invented) and applying the hand brake, which forced wooden brake blocks against the wheels of the tender. Brakes applied by the power of steam or air pressure or vacuum had not been invented. The only means of putting water into the boiler, once steam had been raised, was by means of feed pumps driven off the piston rods, and so when the engine had remained stationary for some time, it had to be run back and forth in a siding or on some other suitable length of track, so that the pump could do its work and raise the water level in the boiler. Sidings were installed at Victoria station in London, for instance, so that engines could run up and down to top up the water level in their boilers while waiting to leave with a train.

In *The Locomotive Engine, A Practical Treatise*, first published in 1857, G. Drysdale Dempsey describes the use of pumps: 'The boiler is supplied with water by two feed-pumps, which are worked by the engine. One is sufficient to supply the necessary quantity of water for the boiler, and the other is thrown out of action; but two are furnished on the engine, in order that if one should fail, the other may take its place without any delay being caused. On forcing the water into the boiler, it checks the generation of steam by its coldness, and the effect of the engine is also diminshed in consequence of the power required to work the pump. For this reason, the action of the feed-pump is generally suspended when the engine is ascending an inclination, and requires its greatest power, and the supply of water is made up by working both pumps on a succeeding level or descent; this is an additional advantage in having duplicate pumps. A small cock, called the pet-cock, is fixed in the pipe leading to the boiler from each pump, and a long handle is fixed to it, extending to within reach of the engineman standing behind the engine. The cocks are opened occasionally to ascertain whether the pumps are working properly, when a stream of water should be forced out at each stroke.'

Baron records his first acquaintance with an injector on 11th March 1861 when he has 'DX' 0-6-0 No. 548: 'New engine to Coppull, trying her injectors'. He then worked on that engine until October. But just because injectors were invented and introduced during the early 1860s, it does not mean that feed pumps were quickly replaced. It is obvious from photographs that engines such as the 'Crewe Types' (known at one time as the 'Old Crewe Types') retained pumps for many years.

Thanks to Baron's record of his daily work, it is clear that some of these engines were running over three thousand miles a month, which seems amazing, especially in view of the slow running speeds. Equally amazing is the fact that only once in the whole diary is an engine recorded to have 'failed', and that is not a 'Crewe Type'. Those engines may have been small and primitive by modern standards, but among the men who worked on them they had the reputation of being indestructible, which is supported by Baron's account.

The diary records: the date; the name or number of the engine; the name of the driver; the mileage run; and 'Remarks', usually their destination. If it was a passenger train, there is usually no further comment; otherwise, it might say 'Goods', 'Coal', 'Mineral', or whatever.

Baron himself introduces the diary at the top of the first page in the following words: 'Dairey from the year 1855. Acount of Work don, name of Engine I whent with and the Drivers I Fired for and places runt to from Preston. Comenced Cleaning at Preston June 1855.' The spelling 'dairey' for the modern 'diary', 'don' for 'done', 'whent' for 'went' and 'runt' for 'runned' (meaning 'ran' in modern English), as well as 'comenced' and 'acount' and the absence of punctuation, suggests at first that Baron was not well educated or indeed hardly educated at all.

Though he was certainly not highly educated, another influence on his spelling seems to be that it reflects the pronunciation of the Lancashire dialect rather than a consistent national standard irrespective of dialect as is thought desirable nowadays. So he writes 'shead' for 'shed' and 'cavy' for 'heavy', and records that an engine was 'of Road. Fireman Killed. Driver harm of' instead of 'off Road' and 'arm off'.

On the other hand, however, his hand-writing is clear and stylish, and his spelling, though not 'correct' by modern standards, is usually consistent in itself. Moreover, he had the tenacity to keep a diary for more than five years, despite doing hard physical work for long hours daily and with only occasional days off, and so was clearly a man of intelligence and character.

Whatever the explanation, so as to facilitate easier comprehension in the version which follows, the spelling has generally been altered to current modern forms. Baron's spelling has been retained only for the heading on the first page of the diary and for the final page which contains personal notes. An exception is his spelling of dates, which presents no difficulties. Baron does not give the days of the week but they have been added here, as they help to make clear the amount of work he did and was expected to do. His use of capital letters is also generally retained - for instance, when he refers to the 'Driver I Fired for' and 'My Mate' – because it shows the style of the day without hindering comprehension and perhaps also his respect for his driver, and so gives some insight into his attitudes and personality. In the last two pages also the original spelling is retained for interest.

In general the modern forms are obvious enough and it is only in the case of certain engine names that difficulties arise. Most names in the diary are in fact spelt as they are now believed to have been spelt on the nameplates and many of those that deviate from this do

Plate 1: *Enginemen dressed for whatever the Lancashire weather could throw at them. The engine is a Bury-type 2-2-0, originally of the LNWR/L&YR joint Preston & Wyre or North Union railways, by this time in Lancashire & Yorkshire Railway stock. The location has been described, incorrectly, as 'Manchester Road, Burnley' but is almost certainly Blackpool. A photograph of a similar engine with what looks like the same crew was taken 13 miles away, at Kirkham, the birthplace of Thomas Baron's mother-in-law. This is on page 126 of John Marshall's* The Lancashire & Yorkshire Railway, Volume 1, *published by David & Charles in 1969. Both photographs seem likely to have been taken in the early 1870s.*
LGRP 17733

so only slightly (though it is not impossible that the spelling was changed on later nameplates); in a few cases, the spelling at first defied understanding for a time but all the intended names are now clear: 'Elvellyn' for 'Helvellyn', 'Fewrry' for 'Fury', 'Hardwick' for 'Hardwicke', 'Minotur' for 'Minotaur', 'Delemere' for 'Delemere', 'Comodore' for 'Commodore', 'Mizappa' or 'Mizapa' for 'Mazeppa', 'Frier' for 'Friar', 'Caradock' for 'Caradoc', and 'Willington' for 'Wellington'. 'Belia' is presumably 'Bela', 'Tarrier' 'Terrier', 'Meneia' 'Menai', 'Meator' 'Meteor' and 'Serrious' 'Sirius'. 'Wenenington' is presumably a mis-spelling of 'Wennington'.

As a general point, of course, Baron was not an enthusiast going around with a notebook and concerned to get every minute detail written down correctly. Most probably he kept his diary at home and wrote it up in spare moments after work was finished, when he was tired, and remembered the engine name but not necessarily how it was spelt. Nor of course was he writing for publication. His diary was a record purely for his own personal interest.

Generally he records the engine name rather than the number, and in most cases where he records the number, it is for the obvious reason that the engine had a number but no name. In several cases, however, he records the number of an engine that is known to have been named. The best example of this is on 30th August 1862 when he writes '49', and yet on many days in the subsequent September he records the same engine as 'Columbine'. In some cases it may be that the engine had lost its name, unknown to the compilers of modern-day lists, but it is probably unsafe to read much significance into such variations, as again Baron kept his record purely for his own interest, not as a definitive record to satisfy the needs of enthusiasts.

Finally, there have been two main problems in producing this book, which readers need to be aware of and bear in mind. Perhaps the greatest difficulty in presenting Thomas Baron's diary has been the problem of illustrating it adequately. Very few photographs exist of LNWR engines in Ramsbottom livery, painted green with black lining and with his distinctive 'castellated' chimney, but even they are late for the period of the diary. John Ramsbottom became locomotive superintendent of the LNWR in 1857. He introduced the 'DX' class 0-6-0 in 1858 and the 'Problem' or 'Lady of the Lake' class in 1859. Photographs survive of some of the earliest examples of these classes and appear in this book. But in 1855, when Thomas Baron started

work at Preston shed, none of the engines he encountered, whether standard Crewe types, 2-2-2 passenger or 2-4-0 goods engines, or the variety of machines from companies absorbed by the LNWR, looked as they were in Ramsbottom's day, with castellated chimneys, though at least they were painted Northern Division green. Unfortunately, few if any photographs from these early years exist.

So readers need to bear in mind that photographs of engines in Ramsbottom condition are not typical of the early years when Thomas Baron was writing his diary but are used here simply because they are the most appropriate available. The same applies - but to an even greater degree - to photographs of engines in Webb's black livery with his type of chimney: they must have been taken at least ten years after the period of the diary, the earliest examples having been introduced in 1872. Fortunately, artists have long found this early period fascinating, as have modellers, and we are greatly indebted to them for their diligence in researching the period so thoroughly, for their skill in recreating it in their chosen forms and for their willingness to allow their work to be used in this book.

The other great difficulty is deciding where best to put background information. When I first came across the diary and began to read it, I had no commentary or background information whatsoever to help me to understand or appreciate it. I just started at the beginning, and the awareness and excitement that I was reading a unique document gradually came to me and built up as I read. The same applies to the other two authors - they both began to read the diary 'cold', as it were, without any preparation of any kind, and became aware of its fascination as they read through it.

In the pages which follow, Baron's diary is set out on a left-hand page, with relevant commentary, photographs, drawings and such like on the opposite right-hand page and in some cases on following pages also. At the end of the diary, there is more detailed information about various aspects of the book. There is a biography of Thomas Baron, details of his family and of the engines on which he worked; a commentary on the diary by a modern engineman who has studied the working conditions prevailing in the nineteenth century; a nineteenth-century account of an engineman's working life; reports of the explosion of the boiler of a 'Crewe Goods' 2-4-0 at Edge Hill in May 1857; reports of an accident at Harrow in 1870; and other material relevant to the period.

Abbreviations

GJR	Grand Junction Railway
L&C	Lancaster & Carlisle Railway
L&M	Liverpool & Manchester Railway
L&Y	Lancashire & Yorkshire Railway
LNWR	London & North Western Railway
M&B	Manchester & Birmingham Railway
ND	Northern Division, LNWR
NED	North Eastern Division, LNWR
SD	Southern Division, LNWR

L. Barons.

Diary from the year 1855,
Account of Work done - name of Engine Worked
with and the Drivers & Fireman -
and places went to from Preston -
Commenced Cleaning at Preston June 1855 -

Date	Name of Driver	Name of Engine	No of Miles	Remarks
1855				
Sept 5	J Booth	Chillington	20	Coaling for months on top
1856 Jan 2	J Goodman	Ribble	108	to Crewe with Cattle
March 3	C R Booth	Ribble	48	to Parkside Ballasting
Sept 9	J Booth	Vision	80	to Bemdal Excursion
Oct	J Worthington	Eden	148	to Liverpool night goods
Oct 16	C Gregory	Barronet		
17	C Gregory	Baronet		
18	C Gregory	Baronet	180	to Springs Branch Wigan
31	R Worthington	E.U.R.	74	to Liverpool night goods
Nov 5	J Booth	Brooke	24	to Bradley
6	J Booth	Sapphire	60	to Britannia and round
10	J Booth	Griffin	60	the Curve to Standish
26	C Gregory	Hoskins	60	to Springs Branch
Dec 2	R Worthington	Eagle	48	to Preston Boys Fishing Tarn Turn
				& Manct Coy night mail run
25				J Manct Coy Bklast Somerting
26	J Read to Hurst		108	J Read Somerton Bklast Somerting
1857				
Jan 5	R Bernd	Castor	108	to Crewe Engine from Wks
12	J Lanham	Leyton	132	to Liverpool & Warrington
14	J Gough	No 5	8	to Broughton Trying Engine
15	J Hands	No 5	184	to Carlisle with Goods
17	R Malt	Ellwellyn	59	to Warrington for Mail
19	W Morris	Earnest	713	to Liverpool & Warrington
20	W Morris	Earnest	94	Lpool & Lancaster all night
21	W Morris	Earnest	94	to Liverpool from Lancaster

Plate 2: *The first two pages of the diary. The right-hand page is the first of many which follow the same pattern in recording Baron's daily work.* Martin O'Keeffe

Grand Junction Railway 2-2-2 Dragon with a down train near Penkridge about 1840.
From a painting by Gerald Broom
Less than twenty years later Thomas Baron passed this way with iron ore for the Black Country.

Scene at the south end of Stafford station in the 1860s. An up express, hauled by Ramsbottom 'Problem' No. 28 Prometheus, has stopped on the through line to change engines. Its driver watches from the footplate as his firemen prepares to uncouple the engine, while a Southern Division 'Bloomer' waits to take over. Having uncoupled, Prometheus will run forward and probably turn on the turntable south of Newport Road overbridge on the up side. It will then return to Crewe, if the procedure outlined by Thomas Baron is followed, but whether it will run light engine or haul a train is unclear.

From a painting by Gerald Broom GRA

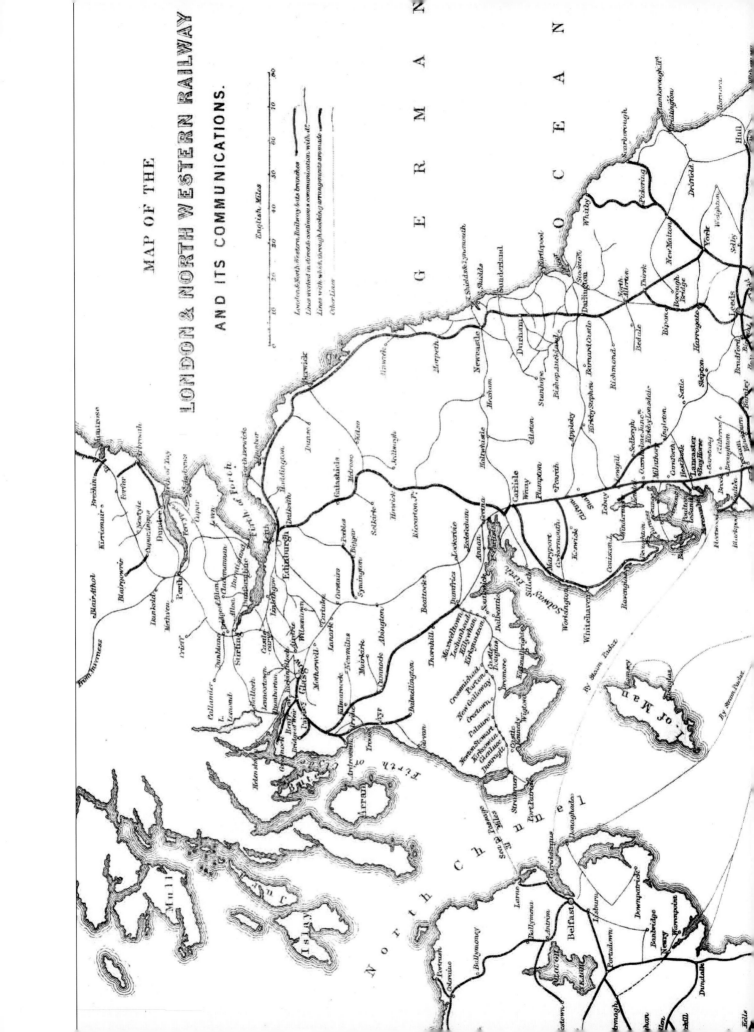

MAP OF THE
LONDON & NORTH WESTERN RAILWAY
AND ITS COMMUNICATIONS.

English Miles

London & North Western Railway & its branches
Lines worked in direct continuous communication with it
Lines with which through booking arrangements are made
Other Lines

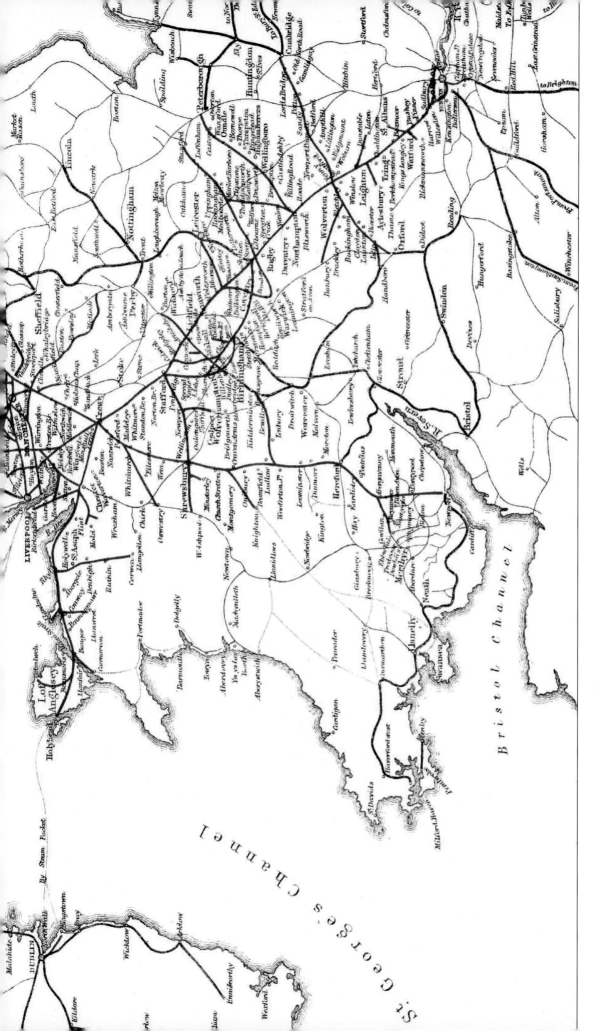

Map of the London & North Western Railway from the July 1865 Public Timetable.

In the 1865 timetable the maps are printed in colour, as reproduced here, with railway lines in red and black, and a cream background.

In the 1861 timetable the maps are in black only on white paper, now brown with age.

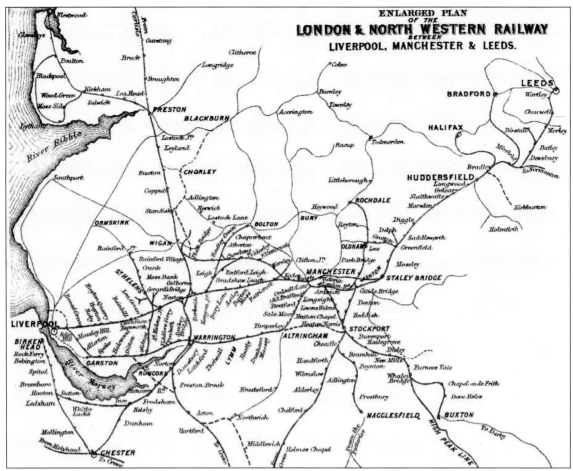

Map of the Liverpool and Manchester area from the July 1865 LNWR Public Timetable.

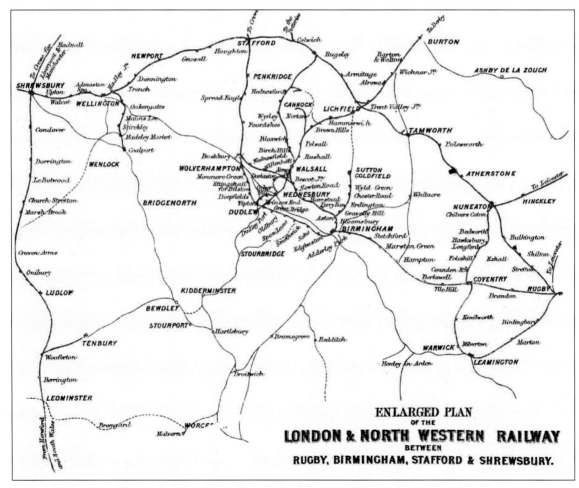

Map of the West Midlands from the July 1865 LNWR Public Timetable.

'Crewe Goods' 2-4-0 No. 159 *Adjutant near Tipton on the Stour Valley line in the 1850s.*
From a painting by Gerald Broom

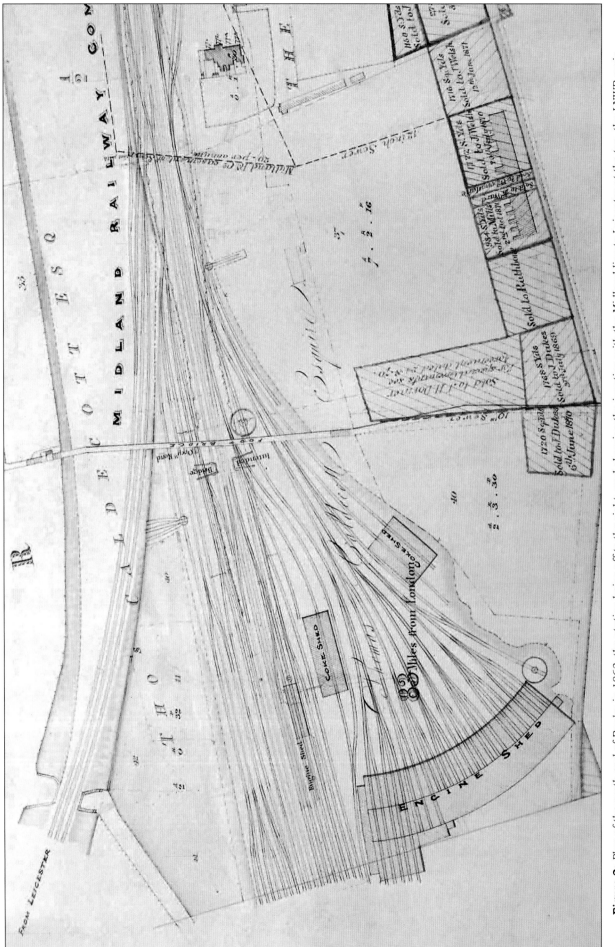

Figure 2: *Plan of the north end of Rugby in 1863, the station being off to the right, and showing the junction with the Midland line to Leicester at the top, the LNWR main line to Birmingham and Stafford going off to the left and the Southern Division shed in the bottom left-hand corner. This shed preceded the large Webb-style shed which was built later on the east side of the station and which was closed in the 1960s. The location can easily be identified by the long footbridge which crosses all the tracks roughly at the midpoint of the plan, the latest version of this bridge being put into position in 2015. The photograph of No. 500 Menai, which is the frontispiece of this book, was taken outside the five-road straight shed nearest to the main line, at the east end of the semi-roundhouse labelled 'Engine Shed' in the bottom left-hand corner of the plan, while the photographs of 'Small Bloomer' No. 602 and 'Problem' No. 804 (Plates 3 and 4 opposite) were taken with the engines posed against the background of the 'Coke Shed' parallel to the main line.*
Courtesy National Archives, Kew

Plate 3: *'Small Bloomer' No 602 by the coke shed on the north side of the tracks leading to the engine shed at Rugby in about 1868. It was built at Wolverton in 1858, rebuilt in August 1869 and named* Caliban *in 1872. It was scrapped in 1881.*

Plate 4: *'Problem' No. 804* Soult *at the same location as the previous photo, probably on the same occasion, so probably before August 1869. But what has happened to Soult's tender? Cleaners often used to work a pattern into the cleaning tallow or oil or whatever. But something seems to have gone wrong in this case. Or has Soult's previous tender developed a fault and been replaced with one that has been neglected?*

The Diary of Thomas Baron

Dairey from the year 1855. Acount of Work don, name of Engine I whent with and the Drivers I Fired for and places runt to from Preston. Comenced Cleaning at Preston June 1855.

Date		Name of Engine	Name of Driver	Number of Miles	Remarks
1855					
Dec 5	Wed	Chillington	T. Booth	20	Coaling for Smiths one trip.
Dec 12	Wed	Elk	G. Godment	108	to Crewe with cattle.
1856					
Mch 3	Mon	Ribble	T. Booth	48	to Parkside, Ballasting.
Sept 9	Tues	Ixion	T. Booth	80	to Kendal, Excursion.
Oct 13	Mon	Eden	J. Worthington	74	to Liverpool, Night Goods.
Oct 14	Tues	Eden	J. Worthington	74	to Liverpool, Night Goods.
Oct 16	Thurs	Baronet	C. Gregory	60	to Springs Branch Wigan.
Oct 17	Fri	Baronet	C. Gregory	60	to Springs Branch Wigan.
Oct 18	Sat	Baronet	C. Gregory	60	to Springs Branch Wigan.
Oct 31	Fri	Elk	R. Worthington	74	to Liverpool, Night Goods.
Nov 5	Wed	Snake	T. Booth	24	to Bradley.
Nov 6	Thurs	Spitfire	T. Booth	60	to Victoria and round the curve to Standish.
Nov 10	Mon	Spitfire	T. Booth	60	to Victoria and round the curve to Standish.
Nov 26	Wed	Starling	C. Gregory	60	to Springs Branch.
Dec 2	Tues	Eagle	R. Worthington	48	to Newton Bridge Assisting train in Snow.
Dec 25	Thurs			108	to Winwick Quay, Night Mail run off road, Fireman
Dec 26	Fri				killed, Driver arm off, went to assist.
1857					
Jany 5	Mon	Castor	R. Bond	108	to Crewe. Engine from Works.
Jany 12	Mon	Sefton	T. Smallman	132	to Liverpool & Warrington.
Jany 14	Wed	No. 5	J. Coup	8	to Broughton trying Engine.
Jany 15	Thurs	No. 5	J. Mauds	184	to Carlisle with Goods.
Jany 17	Sat	Helvellyn	R. Malt	59	to Warrington for Mail.
Jany 19	Mon	Prince Ernest	W. Morris	132	to Liverpool & Warrington.
Jany 20	Tues	Prince Ernest	W. Morris	94	to Liverpool & Lancaster all night.
Jany 21	Wed	Prince Ernest	W. Morris	94	to Liverpool from Lancaster.
Jany 23	Fri	Prince Ernest	W. Morris	118	two trips to Warrington, Mail.
Jany 24	Sat	Prince Ernest	W. Morris	132	to Liverpool & Warrington Express.
Jany 26	Mon	Prince Ernest	W. Morris	59	to Warrington Morning Mail.
Jany 27	Tues	Prince Ernest	W. Morris	132	to Liverpool & Warrington.
Jany 28	Wed	Prince Ernest	W. Morris	94	to Liverpool & Lancaster all night.
Jany 29	Thurs	Prince Ernest	W. Morris	94	to Liverpool from Lancaster.
Jany 30	Fri	Prince Ernest	W. Morris	118	to Warrington two trips 3.44 Mail.
Feby 1	Sun	No. 2	T. Booth	184	to Carlisle.
Feby 2	Mon	Prince Ernest	W. Morris	59	to Warrington Night Mail 10.26.
Feby 3	Tues	Prince Ernest	W. Morris	59	to Warrington Night Mail 10.26.
Feby 4	Wed	Prince Ernest	W. Morris	59	to Warrington Night Mail 10.26.
Feby 5	Thurs	Prince Ernest	W. Morris	106	to Newton Bridge Heavy Snow.
Feby 6	Fri	Prince Ernest	W. Morris	59	to Warrington Night Mail 10.26.
Feby 7	Sat	Prince Ernest	W. Morris	59	to Warrington Night Mail 10.26.
Feby 8	Sun	Prince Ernest	W. Morris	118	to Warrington Morning Mail 3.44.
Feby 10	Tues	Prince Ernest	W. Morris	118	to Warrington Morning Mail 3.44.
Feby 11	Wed	Prince Ernest	W. Morris	132	to Liverpool 6.30am to Warrington 3.30.
Feby 12	Thurs	Prince Ernest	W. Morris	95	to Liverpool 8.40 to Lancaster 4.00pm all night.
Feby 13	Fri	Prince Ernest	W. Morris	95	to Liverpool and back to Preston.
Feby 14	Sat	Prince Ernest	W. Morris	74	to Liverpool 8.30. Sunday in the town.
Feby 15	Sun	Jason	T. Smallman	80	to Kendal all night.
Feby 16	Mon	Prince Ernest	W. Morris	95	to Liverpool to Lancaster all night.

Commentary

1855

5th December. After just over five months as a cleaner, Thomas Baron gets his first firing turn on 5th December. Smith's was one of many collieries on the main line between Preston and Wigan (see Table 1). 'Coaling' means presumably taking empty wagons to the colliery and bringing back loaded ones. Seven days later he is firing again on the main line to Crewe. No timings are given but the 1861 *Working Timetable* shows both goods and cattle trains as taking three hours to reach Crewe. Both these two trips were on 'Crewe Goods' engines. Thomas Baron's career had begun!

1856

3rd March. Baron's next trip was on an old engine of the Preston & Wyre Railway, used for ballasting and shortly to be replaced.

Trips to Bradley (see Table 1) and Victoria follow. Victoria was a colliery just south of Standish and about three miles north of Wigan; the siding is shown as Taylor's in Table 1.

6th and 10th November. Baron works on *Spitfire* to Victoria and 'round the curve to Standish' on both days. Victoria Pit was owned by John Taylor, and the sale of *Spitfire* to him for £590 was minuted on 14th November. Quite possibly *Spitfire* was similar to another Jones & Potts 5ft 0-6-0 of the same period, LNWR Southern Division No. 174, which is said to have had a 13ft wheelbase, and so it seems likely that when Baron went 'round the curve to Standish' it was to test the engine on a sharp curve before the sale was completed, there being no other sharp curves in the area.

1857

In January of this year Baron seems to be promoted to fireman, as from 19th of the month he is the regular fireman of Driver W. Morris.

14th January. Broughton is 4¾ miles north of Preston on the main line.

The 1861 *Working Timetable* shows many of the trains mentioned by Baron. Details are as follows:

'3.44 Morning Mail'. Left Carlisle at 12.20am, stopped at Penrith, Kendal Junction and Lancaster, and was due in Preston at 3.39am. From Preston it stopped at Newton Bridge 4.35am, Warrington 4.54-59, Crewe 5.34-39, and after several more stops reached Euston at 11.00am. It is clear that the Preston engine and crew were rostered to work this long-distance train for only 27¾ miles, as far as Warrington, before hooking off and working back to Preston. Why this was so, when other trains were clearly worked over long distances, is not known.

'10.26 Night Mail'. Is not shown but the 11.14pm departure in the 1861 *Working Timetable* is presumably the same train. This stopped at Newton Bridge, Warrington, Crewe and several stations south of there, before reaching Euston at 4.37am. But as with the '3.44 Morning Mail', Preston men only worked the train for the 27¾ miles as far as Warrington.

'8.30am to Liverpool'. Though not an 'all stations', it was not far from being so, stopping at Farrington, Leyland, Euxton, Coppull, Standish, Wigan (at 9.17am), Newton Bridge (9.45am), Warrington Junction, Collins Green, St Helens Junction, Lea Green, and then all stations (six of them) to Liverpool Lime Street, which it reached at 10.45am.

'4.00pm to Lancaster all night'. The 4.00pm from Preston stopped at all stations to Kendal, where it arrived at 6.5pm. On 12th February Baron worked it as far as Lancaster, spent the night there ('all night') and worked from Lancaster to Liverpool and back to Preston the following day. On some later occasions he worked it to Kendal 'and back', but the details are not clear.

Table 1
Stations between Preston and Newton Bridge

Many of the 'stations' shown in the 1861 *Working Timetable* are clearly collieries or colliery sidings.

Preston	Wigan
Farrington	Wigan Jun, L&Y
Leyland	Pearson's New Pit
Euxton	Springs Branch
Smith's	Blundells
Darlington's	Strangeways Hall
Hargreave's	Park Lane Siding
Coppull	Bryn Hall
Bradley Hall	Edge Green
Bloomfield	Golborne
Standish	Brewis' Siding
Taylor's	Bull's Head Siding
Boar's Head	Preston Jun
Rylands and Woods	Newton Bridge

Engine classes

Baronet, Castor, Chillington, Eagle, Eden, Elk, Ixion, Snake, Starling - all 'Crewe Goods' 2-4-0s.
Jason, Prince Ernest, Sefton - 'Crewe Passenger' 2-2-2s.
Ribble - Goods 0-4-0 (?) built by Bury (?) for Preston & Wyre Railway in 1847 (?) - see page 106.
Spitfire - Jones & Potts 0-6-0 built for Lancaster & Carlisle Railway in 1846 - see page 106.
No. 2, No. 5 - uncertain, see page 107.

Plate 5: *View of Preston station from above the tunnel entrance at the north end in 1862.*
Robert Pateson. Reproduced by courtesy of the Harris Museum & Art Gallery, Preston

Plate 6: *View of the aftermath of the accident at Preston on 13th July 1896, taken from Water Street West (where Baron lodged before he was married in 1857) by A. Winter, when a down Scotch express hauled by a 'Jumbo' was derailed on the curve north of the station. The station itself is off to the left, the main line to the north is straight ahead and the engine shed is lost in smoke beyond the farther signal post. Bow Lane, where Baron's wife lived before they married, is also off to the left behind lots of buildings. A similar photograph by Winter was reproduced in* Moore's Monthly Magazine *in August 1896 under the heading 'Wanted - Leading Bogies!!', which would surely have endeared the F. Moore company to the LNWR!*

Plate 7: *The earliest known view of a Ramsbottom 'Problem' 2-2-2 - No. 229 Watt, the second of the class to be built in 1857, at the south end of Preston in 1863. It is the only known photograph showing the early form of Ramsbottom safety valves without the tail rod. Or is the tail rod obscured for some reason? If a 1500-gallon tender was fitted originally, as seems likely, this is not the original tender, as it is the 2000-gallon type introduced before water troughs were adopted and can be identified by the fact that the top of the tank is higher than the footplate side-sheet. The roof in the background covers the East Lancashire Railway (L&YR) platform. Robert Pateson. Reproduced by courtesy of the Harris Museum & Art Gallery, Preston*

Plate 8: *General view of Preston looking north west across the East Lancashire Railway yard from Bulter Street about 1870. On the left is the ELR engine shed, on the right the goods shed and warehouse, and to the left of it the carriage shed; in the distance between the two latter, is the LNWR main line and engine shed (formerly North Union). Outside the shed is what might be a 'Crewe Goods', its chimney and ornamental dome over the firebox being just discernible. The containers on the wagons in the foreground perhaps come from the nearby canal.*

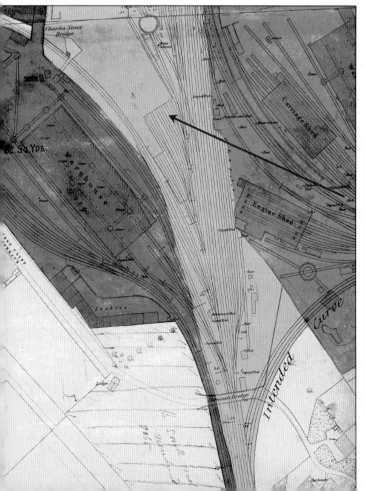

Figure 3, left: *Map showing the installations in Plate 8 above; the arrow points to the LNWR engine shed, which is believed to have opened on 31st October 1838 and closed in 1877.*

Figure 4 below: *Plan of the LNWR engine shed in the above photograph, where Thomas Baron worked.*   OS Map 1849

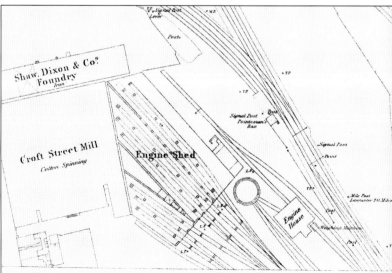

Plate 9: *A rare photograph and one which at first glance might well seem unrelated to the LNWR, yet actually shows an engine of one of its constituent companies, which came into its ownership - twice! It was originally No. 23 on the Manchester & Birmingham Railway and was delivered by Sharp, Roberts & Co in July 1842, one of four 0-4-2 tender engines, Nos 21-4, supplied by that builder in that year. They had 4ft 6in driving wheels, 3ft trailing wheels, 14in by 20in cylinders and weighed 24 tons. No. 23 passed to the LNWR in the amalgamation creating the company in 1846, was rebuilt in 1855 and renumbered 423 late in 1857. In April 1860 it was sold for £700 to the St Helens Railway, on which it became No. 2 Trent. In July 1864, however, that company was absorbed by the LNWR, which renumbered it 1364 in August 1864 as its 'cut up' number before it was sold out of LNWR stock to I. W. Boulton on 13th September 1864, becoming his No. 9. It was sold by Boulton to J. Morton at Pen-y-Bont, contractor on the Central Wales line, in 1865, and then bought back by Boulton and hired to Jas Rennie & Co at Dartford in February 1866 and then to J. Aird & Co. It was then converted by Boulton to an 0-6-0 saddle tank in 1871 and sold to the Cowbridge Railway for £800. It was again bought back by Boulton who then sold it to Chell Ironstone Mines in Staffordshire (later Tunstall Coal & Iron Co) for £850 in August 1873, after which nothing more is known about it. The photograph was presumably taken at Ashton-under-Lyne in 1864-71. On the footplate side-sheet is the plate of its owner, and the oval mark is the stamp of Isaac Watt Boulton. A drawing of the engine apparently based on this photograph is Figure 4 on page 46 of* The Chronicles of Boulton's Siding *by Alfred Rosling Bennett. Difficult to determine is the livery, the tender at least having two panels with a darker colour outside them, but a rare photograph indeed!*

As an aside, Bennett adds: 'Trent had the classic square-based ornamental dome cover which acted as the firm's oriflamme or trade-mark for so many years. It is said that these moulded brass dome covers were all made by one old workman, whose time they wholly occupied, and that when he died or retired the pattern, which required care to build up properly, was discarded in favour of a simple round-topped cover with bell-mouth. The early employment of Sharp locomotives in Germany set a fashion there of square-moulded domes of Sharp outline, although often much larger, which persisted for many years, until well on in the 1880s. Such domes were especially affected in Saxony and by the Bergisch-Markisch Railway until absorbed into the State system. Amongst builders, Borsig, of Berlin, long kept the style alive.'

The question then arises: did Thomas Baron ever work on this engine? It is not recorded in his diary but it is possible that it was one of the engines he dealt with when he was 'turning' at Preston shed. Its sister engine, M&B No. 24, was replaced in 1854, so it could have become a Ballast Engine, and in January and February 1857 Baron certainly worked on 'No. 2' and 'No. 5', whose original identities are not known, either of which might once have been No. 424. In any case, it is a good example of an unusual non-standard engine from an absorbed company still working on the LNWR, of which there must have been many, and there is every chance that he saw it during his work.

Plate 10: *Boulton's stamp from a different photograph on which it is not directly on the image and so can be read more easily: 'I. W. BOULTON, ENGINEER & C, ASHTON UNDER LYNE'.*

Date	Name of Engine	Name of Driver	Number of Miles	Remarks
1857				
Feby 17 Tues	*Prince Ernest*	W. Morris	95	to Liverpool & back to Preston.
Feby 19 Thurs	*Prince Ernest*	W. Morris	118	two trips to Warrington 3.44 & 11.15.
Feby 20 Fri	*Prince Ernest*	W. Morris	132	to Liverpool 6.30. to Warrington 3.30 Exp.
Feby 21 Sat	*Prince Ernest*	W. Morris	154	to Liverpool 8.40. to Kendal 4.00 & back.
Feby 23 Mon	*Prince Ernest*	W. Morris	74	to Liverpool 12.40.
Feby 25 Wed	*Prince Ernest*	W. Morris	118	to Warrington 3.44am Mail & 11.15.
Feby 26 Thurs	*Prince Ernest*	W. Morris	133	to Liverpool 6.30. to Warrington 3.30.
Feby 27 Fri	*Prince Ernest*	W. Morris	95	to Liverpool 8.40, to Lancaster 4.00 all night.
Feby 28 Sat	*Prince Ernest*	W. Morris	95	to Liverpool & back to Preston.
Mch 18 Wed	*Starling*	T. Booth	144	to Penrith 3.15 Goods.
Mch 21 Sat	*Minotaur*	G. Godment	74	to Liverpool 3.15 with Cattle.
Mch 23 Mon	*Menai*	J. Golding	80	to Springs Branch for Coal two trips.
Mch 28 Sat	*Elk*	T. Booth	74	to Liverpool with Cattle 4.30am.
Apl 8 Wed	*St George*	R. Anderton	80	to Kendal with Coke 10.00am.
Apl 10 Fri	*Terrier*	G. Godment	56	to St Helens. Assisting Goods. Good Friday.
Apl 13 Mon	*Pollux*	T. Booth	50	Ballasting.
Apl 14 Tues	*Friar*	T. Tyrer	118	to Warrington 3.44 & 11.15am.
Apl 15 Wed	*Pollux*	T. Booth	144	to Penrith 3.15am Goods.
Apl 16 Thurs	*Helvellyn*	R. Worthington	59	to Warrington for Old Mail.
Apl 23 Thurs	*Canning*	W. Tompson	59	to Warrington 3.40 Express.
Apl 24 Fri	*Canning*	W. Tompson	95	to Liverpool 8.40, to Lancaster 4.00 all night.
Apl 25 Sat	*Canning*	W. Tompson	95	Lancaster to Liverpool & back to Preston.
Apl 29 Wed	*Falstaff*	J. Ward	144	to Penrith 3.45am with Goods.
May 4 Mon	*Friar*	Ths. Tyrer	74	to Liverpool 12.40.
May 6 Wed	*Friar*	Ths. Tyrer	118	to Warrington 3.44 & 11.15.
May 7 Thurs	*Friar*	Ths. Tyrer	133	to Liverpool 6.30, to Warrington 3.30.
May 8 Fri	*Friar*	Ths. Tyrer	95	to Liverpool 8.40, to Lancaster 4.00 all night.
May 9 Sat	*Friar*	Ths. Tyrer	95	to Liverpool & back to Preston.
May 11 Mon	*Friar*	Ths. Tyrer	133	to Liverpool 6.30, to Warrington 3.30.
May 12 Tues	*Friar*	Ths. Tyrer	95	to Liverpool 8.40, to Lancaster all night.
May 13 Wed	*Friar*	Ths. Tyrer	95	to Liverpool 7.30 & back to Preston.
May 15 Fri	*Friar*	Ths. Tyrer	118	to Warrington 3.44 & 11.15am.
June 6 Sat	No. 14	J. Waterworth	184	to Carlisle 3.30pm Empty.
June 27 Sat	*Booth*	C. Ferguis	184	to Carlisle 6.15 Goods.
June 30 Tues	*Booth*	C. Ferguis	184	to Carlisle 5.25 Goods; at the Races.
July 7 Tues	*Redstart*	J. Haughton	184	to Carlisle 3.15am Goods.
July 8 Wed	*Redstart*	J. Haughton	42	to Lancaster for an Excursion 4.30am.
July 8 Wed	*Fly*	J. Haughton	21	to Lancaster with Excursion all night.
July 9 Thurs	*Fly*	J. Haughton	171	from Lancaster to Preston Excursion back with it at night 7.30 & the Empty Coaches to Crewe.
July 12 Sun	*Fly*	J. Haughton	40	to Kirkless Hall for Coal.
July 13 Mon	*Megatherion*	J. Haughton	184	to Carlisle 6.30, passenger train.
Aug 4 Tues	*Menai*	J. Golding	80	two trips to Springs Branch, Coal.
Aug 6 Thurs	*Wordsworth*	T. Baron	108	Piloting to Crewe, very wet.
Aug 8 Sat	*Scorpion*	T. Tyrer	133	to Liverpool 6.30, to Warrington 3.30.
Aug 10 Mon	*Saddleback*	T. Tyrer	118	to Warrington 3.44 & 11.15am.
Aug 11 Tues	*Saddleback*	T. Tyrer	133	to Liverpool 6.30, to Warrington 3.30.
Aug 12 Wed	*Saddleback*	T. Tyrer	74	to Liverpool 8.40.
Aug 13 Thurs	*Saddleback*	T. Tyrer	59	to Warrington 12.40.
Aug 15 Sat	*Saddleback*	T. Tyrer	118	to Warrington 3.44 & 11.15am.
Aug 16 Sun	*Saddleback*	T. Tyrer	59	to Warrington night mail Sunday.

15th April. The '3.15am Goods to Penrith', is probably the 3.45am in the 1861 *Working Timetable*, where it is shown as 'Man. Goods' – presumably 'Manchester Goods' – and stopped at Lancaster, Carnforth, Kendal Junction, Tebay and Shap, arriving at Penrith at 9.17am. It left at 9.22am, reached Carlisle Yard at 10.17am and the Caledonian Yard at 10.27am. It seems surprising that Baron should work this train only to Penrith, rather than through to Carlisle, but it seems certain that that is what he did, as the timetable shows the distance from Preston to Penrith as 72½ and he gives his mileage as 144.

Presumably then, soon after he arrived in Penrith, he worked another train back to Preston. The earliest possiblity is the 'London Goods', leaving Carlisle at 8.25am, stopping at Penrith 9.25-9.30, Kendal 11.15-11.23, Lancaster 12.29-12.39 and arriving at Preston at 1.45. This seems unlikely, however, as it allowed only 13 minutes in which to turn the engine, prepare it for the return journey and hook on to the train. Much more likely, especially as Baron worked through to Carlisle on several occasions later, is the 10.30am 'Goods, Friday and Saturday', which started from Penrith and reached Preston at 4.30pm. This means - allowing time for preparation of the engine at Preston before departure and for disposal on return - that he and his driver worked at least a 14-hour day and probably more.

Engine classes

Booth, Elk, Falstaff, Fly, Menai, Minotaur, Pollux, Redstart, Starling, St. George, Terrier, Wordsworth - all 'Crewe Goods' 2-4-0s.
Canning, Friar, Helvellyn, Megatherion, Prince Ernest, Saddleback, Scorpion - 6ft 'Crewe Passenger' 2-2-2s.
No. 14 - uncertain, possibly *Lion*, see page 107.

30th June. The 5.25am Goods to Carlisle is not shown as such in the 1861 *Working Timetable* but it was probably the 'Man. Goods' departing at 5.10am, reaching Carlisle at 12.5pm and the Caledonian Yard at 12.15pm. Fortunately, on this occasion Baron had time for a little relaxation in Carlisle and went to the races.

The various goods trains to Carlisle in 1861 are shown in Table 2 on page 29.

12th July. Kirkless Hall colliery was located near the end of the Springs branch. LNWR engines seem to have worked to the colliery but the colliery seems to have had its own engine also, as the following note in the 1861 *Working Timetable* shows:

Kirkless Hall Company's Colliery Engine
The above may be expected to run as under:

Leave Wigan Junc. (from L&Y) at	Return from Ryland's Siding at
7.00am	8.00am
9.00am	10.30am
11.05am	12.35noon
1.00pm	2.35pm
3.05pm	4.30pm

6th August. This seems to be Thomas Baron's first turn as a driver, though no comment is made by him, his name simply appearing under the heading 'Name of Driver'.

Plate 11: *One of the engines on which Thomas Baron worked was 'Crewe Passenger' No. 110* Canning, *which was built in February 1857. Almost forty years later, in April 1894, it became* Engineer Lancaster *and is in that guise here, outside the LNWR two-road shed at Lancaster about 1900. It now has Webb's chimney, fittings, cab and lined black livery, but still has open safety valves rather than the enclosed Webb type; and the tender has better footsteps, an additional handrail, circular buffers on the front rather than the square variety as used earlier, and also a spectacle plate for running in reverse. The engine became* Engineer South Wales *in February 1903.*

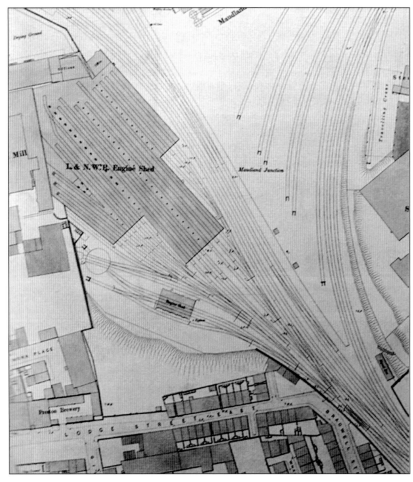

Plate 12, above: *Ramsbottom 'Newton' No. 1684* Speke. *It is still in original condition except for a Webb chimney and additional lamp socket at the base of the chimney, and a red bufferbeam with black rectangle, Webb style, in place of the green bufferbeam with painted numbers. The location is thought to be outside the new shed at Preston-see plan in figure 5 left.*

Figure 5, left: *Plan of the new engine shed built at Preston, which replaced the one shown on page 20.*

Two views of 'Crewe Type' 2-4-0s for comparison purposes.

Plate 13, above: No. 1961, a Lancaster & Carlisle Railway engine built by Fairbairn and shown without tender in Plate 15.

Plate 14, below: No. 1979, a Crewe-built engine, originally No. 105 Viscount of May 1847, which lost its name in January 1873, was transferred to the duplicate list as 1979 in June 1875 and was scrapped in July 1885. The L&C engine has a different boiler, with dome above the firebox fitted with balanced safety valves, possibly a slightly larger spectacle plate and more ornate style of driving splasher.

Both variants have coupling rods that were painted black or (perhaps chemically blackened in some way) and connecting rods and axle ends that are finished bright. Both photographs were taken in the same location, alongside the Paint Shop at Crewe Works, but photographic practice had moved on by the time of the latter photograph and the background has been removed, except for the part of the wall below the front of the engine; possibly, there was a canvas screen behind the engine, as was certainly used later to facilitate painting out in the darkroom,

Plate 15, opposite: *'Crewe Goods' 2-4-0 No. 1961 posed for the official photographer alongside the Paint Shop at Crewe Works on withdrawal in February 1879. It must have been among the earliest engines to be photographed in that location, as the Paint Shop had been completed probably less than a year earlier, in 1878, having been started only in 1876-7. The engine was originally built by Fairbairn for the Lancaster & Carlisle Railway in 1853 as No. 78 Sedbergh with cylinders 15¼in by 20in; it became LNWR No. 541 in December 1859 and No. 1961, in the 1800 series duplicate list, in January 1875. Except for a Webb chimney, it seems here to be much as built. The photograph is so sharp that it is easily possible to see small details. For instance, there is a handle on the footplate end of the boiler handrail, where the driver can reach it easily from the footplate. When he twisted this handle, a small crank, just to the rear of the smokebox, actuated a vertical rod leading down to the side of the clack valve, where it opened or closed the 'pet cock',*

a valve in the pipe connected to the pump side of the clack valve. A small pipe, perhaps ½in diameter, runs from the 'pet cock' down the sloping running plate almost as far as the boiler stay and then turns through ninety degrees before ending over the side of the running plate; there, by opening the pet cock, the driver could see whether water was spurting out or not, as the engine was running, and so knew if water was going into the boiler. The cock also allowed any air in the pipe delivering water to the clack valve to escape. Engines, of course, had two pumps and there was a similar pet cock on the other side. Thomas Baron is not recorded as working on one of these L&C engines but must have seen them on his trips to Penrith. All in all, a fascinating picture and one which shows that for this type of photography perfection was reached in the early days. But one mystery remains - here the engine is clearly black, as befits a Crewe engine on the duplicate list, but what was the original livery of engines on the Lancaster & Carlisle Railway?

Table 2

Main Down Goods and Mineral Trains North of Preston

	Station	Man Goods (am)	Man Goods (am)	Ore (am)	Goods and Ore Wagons (am)	Goods (am)	Ore Goods (am)	B'ham-W. Mid. Goods (am)	London Goods (am)	B'ham Empty Ore Wagons (pm)	Ore Goods Wagons (pm)	L'pl-Mcr Goods via Parkside (pm)	Salford-L&YR Goods (pm)	Mcr-L'pl Goods (pm)	Mcr-L'pl Express Goods (pm)	Ore Wagons (pm)
	Preston dep	3.45		6.10		7.10		7.40	9.45	1.20	3.0		4.40	5.10	6.0	10.30
21½	Lancaster arr	4.57		7.15		8.25		8.51	11.0	2.28	4.5		5.50	6.56	7.10	11.30
	Lancaster dep	5.7		7.30	7.40	8.35		9.0	11.10	2.38	4.15	5.20	6.5	7.6	7.25	11.40
27	Carnforth arr	5.27			8.0	8.55		9.25	11.10	2.58	4.35	5.40	6.24		7.44	12.0
	Carnforth dep	5.32						9.30	11.55	3.35			6.48		7.46	
40	Kendal Jun arr	6.30		7.30				10.31	12.43	4.35		(2)	7.53	8.20	8.49	
	Kendal Jun dep	6.50		7.40				10.40	12.53	4.40			8.3	8.40	9.4	
	Kendal									4.50						
48½	Low Gill			9.43									9.43			
53	Tebay	7.46		9.57						(1)			9.57			
60½	Shap	8.32														
72½	Penrith arr	9.17		11.16					3.30	5.45			10.18	10.55	11.15	2.29
	Penrith dep	9.22		11.21					3.40	5.55			10.20	11.5	11.23	2.39
90	Carlisle arr	10.17		12.24					4.40	6.40			11.20	12.5	12.20	3.25
	Caledonian Yard	10.27		12.34					4.50	6.50			12.15	12.30		3.30

Notes: (1) 'Stopped at all stations, so in effect a 'pick up goods'.
(2) Left Birmingham at 6.0am.

Date		Name of Engine	Name of Driver	Number of Miles	Remarks
1857					
Aug 17	Mon	*Saddleback*	T. Tyrer	59	to Warrington night mail.
Aug 18	Tues	*Saddleback*	T. Tyrer	59	to Warrington night mail.
Aug 19	Wed	*Saddleback*	T. Tyrer	59	to Warrington night mail.
Aug 20	Thurs	*Saddleback*	T. Tyrer	59	to Warrington night mail.
Aug 21	Fri	*Saddleback*	T. Tyrer	59	to Warrington night mail.
Aug 22	Sat	*Saddleback*	T. Tyrer	59	to Warrington night mail.
Aug 23	Sun	*Saddleback*	T. Tyrer	59	to Warrington Morning Mail 3.44.
Aug 25	Tues	*Saddleback*	T. Tyrer	118	to Warrington 3.44 & 11.15am.
Aug 26	Wed	*Saddleback*	T. Tyrer	133	to Liverpool 6.30, to Warrington 3.30.
Aug 27	Thurs	*Saddleback*	T. Tyrer	74	to Liverpool 8.40am.
Aug 28	Fri	*Saddleback*	T. Tyrer	74	to Liverpool 1.30.
Aug 30	Sun	*Saddleback*	T. Tyrer	74	to Liverpool 3rd Class Sunday.
Aug 31	Mon	*Saddleback*	T. Tyrer	74	to Liverpool 8.30am.
Sept 1	Tues	*Saddleback*	T. Tyrer	74	to Liverpool 12.50.
Sept 2	Wed	*Elk*	J. Wilkinson	59	to Warrington with Special.
Sept 3	Thurs	*Saddleback*	T. Tyrer	118	to Warrington 3.44 & 11.15am.
Sept 4	Fri	*Saddleback*	T. Tyrer	133	to Liverpool 6.30, to Warrington 3.30.
Sept 5	Sat	*Saddleback*	T. Tyrer	74	to Liverpool 8.30am.
Sept 6	Sun	*Saddleback*	T. Tyrer	116	3.44 Mail to Warrington.
Sept 7	Mon	*Saddleback*	T. Tyrer	74	12.50 to Liverpool.
Sept 9	Wed	*Saddleback*	T. Tyrer	116	3.44 Mail and 11.15 to Warrington.
Sept 10	Thurs	*Saddleback*	T. Tyrer	133	6.30 to Liverpool 3.30 to Warrington.
Sept 11	Fri	*Saddleback*	T. Tyrer	74	8.30 to Liverpool.
Sept 12	Sat	*Saddleback*	T. Tyrer	74	12.50 to Liverpool.
Sept 14	Mon	*Saddleback*	T. Tyrer	133	6.30 to Liverpool & 3.30 to Warrington.
Sept 15	Tues	*Saddleback*	T. Tyrer	74	8.30 to Liverpool.
Sept 16	Wed	*Saddleback*	T. Tyrer	74	12.50 to Liverpool.
Sept 18	Fri	*Saddleback*	T. Tyrer	116	3.44 to Liverpool & 11.15 to Warrington.
Sept 19	Sat	*Saddleback*	T. Tyrer	133	6.30 to Liverpool & 3.30 to Warrington.
Sept 21	Mon	*Saddleback*	T. Tyrer	116	3.44 & 11.15 to Warrington.
Sept 22	Tues	*Saddleback*	T. Tyrer	133	6.30 to Liverpool & 3.30 to Warrington.
Sept 23	Wed	*Saddleback*	T. Tyrer	74	8.30 to Liverpool.
Sept 24	Thurs	*Saddleback*	T. Tyrer	148	12.50 & 6.50 to Liverpool.
Sept 26	Sat	*Saddleback*	T. Tyrer	116	3.44 & 11.15 to Warrington.
Sept 27	Sun	*Saddleback*	T. Tyrer	58	10.26 Mail to Warrington.
Sept 28	Mon	*Saddleback*	T. Tyrer	116	12.40 & 10.26 to Warrington.
Sept 29	Tues	*Saddleback*	T. Tyrer	116	12.40 & 10.26 to Warrington.
Sept 30	Fri	*Saddleback*	T. Tyrer	116	12.40 & 10.26 to Warrington.
Oct 1	Thurs	*Saddleback*	T. Tyrer	116	12.40 & 10.26 to Warrington.
Oct 2	Fri	*Saddleback*	T. Tyrer	116	12.40 & 10.26 to Warrington.
Oct 3	Sat	*Saddleback*	T. Tyrer	116	12.40 & 10.26 to Warrington.
Oct 6	Tues	*Saddleback*	T. Tyrer	116	3.44 & 11.15 to Warrington.
Oct 7	Wed	*Saddleback*	T. Tyrer	133	6.30 to Liverpool & 3.30 to Warrington.
Oct 8	Thurs	*Saddleback*	T. Tyrer	74	8.30 to Liverpool & to Manchester.
Oct 9	Fri	*Saddleback*	T. Tyrer	148	12.50 & 6.50 to Liverpool.
Oct 10	Sat	*Delamere*	T. Tyrer	108	from the Works at Crewe.
Oct 11	Sun	*Saddleback*	T. Tyrer	74	8.30 to Liverpool, Sunday.
Oct 12	Mon	*Saddleback*	T. Tyrer	74	8.30 to Liverpool.
Oct 13	Tues	*Saddleback*	T. Tyrer	148	12.50 & 6.50 to Liverpool.
Oct 14	Wed	*Saddleback*	T. Tyrer		(no details entered)
Oct 15	Thurs	*Saddleback*	T. Tyrer	116	3.44 & 11.15 to Warrington.
Oct 16	Fri	*Saddleback*	T. Tyrer	133	6.30 to Liverpool & 3.30 to Warrington.
Oct 17	Sat	*Saddleback*	T. Tyrer	74	8.30 to Liverpool.
Oct 18	Sun	*Saddleback*	T. Tyrer	116	3.44 & 1.00pm to Warrington.
Oct 19	Mon	*Saddleback*	T. Tyrer	148	12.50 & 6.50 to Liverpool.

Plate 16: *Sadly, photographs of 'Crewe Passenger' 2-2-2s, even in Ramsbottom condition, are rare indeed, and this is the earliest known photograph of one of the class,* No. 16 Lynx, *built in 1846, at Broad Green on the Liverpool & Manchester line with an eastbound passenger train. The engine has a Ramsbottom chimney, so the date is probably in the early 1860s.*

Plate 17: *View in Olive Mount cutting looking east probably in the 1880s. On the right, a 'Problem' heads for Liverpool Lime Street with a train that has probably come from Manchester, while the train on the left is about to take the junction for Bootle.*

Michael Bentley collection

Engine classes: *Delamere, Elk* - 'Crewe Goods' 2-4-0s. *Saddleback* - 6ft 'Crewe Passenger' 2-2-2.

Date		Name of Engine	Name of Driver	Number of Miles	Remarks
1857					
Oct 21	Wed	*Saddleback*	T. Tyrer	116	3.44 & 11.15 to Warrington.
Oct 22	Thurs	*Saddleback*	T. Tyrer	133	6.30 to Liverpool & 3.30 to Warrington.
Oct 23	Fri	*Saddleback*	T. Tyrer	74	8.30 to Liverpool.
Oct 24	Sat	*Saddleback*	T. Tyrer	148	12.50 & 6.50 to Liverpool.
Oct 26	Mon	*Saddleback*	T. Tyrer	133	6.30 to Liverpool & 3.30 to Warrington.
Oct 27	Tues	*Saddleback*	T. Tyrer	74	8.30 to Liverpool.
Oct 28	Wed	*Saddleback*	T. Tyrer	148	12.50 & 6.50 to Liverpool.
Oct 30	Fri	*Saddleback*	T. Tyrer	116	3.44 & 11.15 to Warrington.
Oct 31	Sat	*Saddleback*	T. Tyrer	133	6.30 to Liverpool & 3.30 to Warrington.
Nov 2	Mon	*Saddleback*	T. Tyrer	116	3.44 & 11.15 to Warrington.
Nov 3	Tues	*Saddleback*	T. Tyrer	133	6.30 to Liverpool & 3.30 to Warrington.
Nov 4	Wed	*Saddleback*	T. Tyrer	74	8.30 to Liverpool.
Nov 5	Thurs	*Saddleback*	T. Tyrer	74	12.50 to Liverpool.
Nov 7	Sat	*Saddleback*	T. Tyrer	116	3.44 & 11.15 to Warrington.
Nov 8	Sun	*Saddleback*	T. Tyrer	59	10.26 Mail to Warrington, Sunday.
Nov 9	Mon	*Saddleback*	T. Tyrer	116	12.40 & 10.26 to Warrington.
Nov 10	Tues	*Saddleback*	T. Tyrer	116	12.40 & 10.26 to Warrington.
Nov 11	Wed	*Saddleback*	T. Tyrer	116	12.40 & 10.26 to Warrington.
Nov 12	Thurs	*Saddleback*	T. Tyrer	116	12.40 & 10.26 to Warrington.
Nov 13	Fri	*Saddleback*	T. Tyrer	116	12.40 & 10.26 to Warrington.
Nov 14	Sat	*Saddleback*	T. Tyrer	116	12.40 & 10.26 to Warrington.
Nov 17	Tues	*Saddleback*	T. Tyrer	116	3.44 & 11.15 to Warrington.
Nov 18	Wed	*Saddleback*	T. Tyrer	133	6.30 to Liverpool & 3.30 to Warrington.
Nov 19	Thurs	*Saddleback*	T. Tyrer	74	8.30 to Liverpool.
Nov 20	Fri	*Saddleback*	T. Tyrer	74	12.50 to Liverpool.
Nov 22	Sun	*Hardwicke*	T. Tyrer	74	Sunday 8.30 to Liverpool.
Nov 23	Mon	*Saddleback*	T. Tyrer	74	8.30 to Liverpool.
Nov 24	Tues	*Saddleback*	T. Tyrer	74	12.50 to Liverpool.
Nov 26	Thurs	*Saddleback*	T. Tyrer	116	3.44 & 11.15 to Warrington.
Nov 27	Fri	*Saddleback*	T. Tyrer	133	6.30 to Liverpool & 3.30 to Warrington.
Nov 28	Sat	*Saddleback*	T. Tyrer	74	8.30 to Liverpool.
Nov 29	Sun	*Saddleback*	T. Tyrer	116	Sunday, 3.44 & 1.0 to Warrington.
Nov 30	Mon	*Saddleback*	T. Tyrer	74	12.50 to Liverpool.
Dec 1	Tues	*Saddleback*	T. Tyrer	74	8.30 to Liverpool.
Dec 2	Wed	*Saddleback*	T. Tyrer	116	3.44 & 11.15 to Warrington.
Dec 3	Thurs	*Saddleback*	T. Tyrer	133	6.30 to Liverpool & 3.30 to Warrington.
Dec 4	Fri	*Saddleback*	T. Tyrer	74	8.30 to Liverpool.
Dec 5	Sat	*Saddleback*	T. Tyrer	74	12.50 to Liverpool.
Dec 7	Mon	*Saddleback*	J. Lyion	133	6.30 to Liverpool & 3.30 to Warrington.
Dec 8	Tues	*Saddleback*	T. Tyrer	74	8.30 to Liverpool.
Dec 9	Wed	*Saddleback*	T. Tyrer	74	12.50 to Liverpool.
Dec 11	Fri	*Saddleback*	T. Tyrer	116	3.44 & 11.15 to Warrington.
Dec 12	Sat	*Saddleback*	T. Tyrer	133	6.30 to Liverpool & 3.30 to Warrington.
Dec 14	Mon	*Saddleback*	T. Tyrer	116	3.44 & 11.15 to Warrington.
Dec 15	Tues	*Saddleback*	T. Tyrer	133	6.30 to Liverpool & 3.30 to Warrington.
Dec 16	Wed	*Saddleback*	T. Tyrer	74	8.30 to Liverpool.
Dec 17	Thurs	*Saddleback*	T. Tyrer	74	12.50 to Liverpool.
Dec 19	Sat	*Saddleback*	T. Tyrer	116	3.44 & 11.15 to Warrington.
Dec 20	Sun	*Saddleback*	T. Tyrer	58	10.26 Mail to Warrington.
Dec 21	Mon	*Saddleback*	T. Tyrer	116	12.40 & 10.26 Mail to Warrington.
Dec 22	Tues	*Saddleback*	T. Tyrer	116	12.40 & 10.26 Mail to Warrington.
Dec 23	Wed	*Saddleback*	T. Tyrer	116	12.40 & 10.26 Mail to Warrington.
Dec 25	Fri	*Saddleback*	T. Tyrer	58	10.26 Night Mail to Warrington.
Dec 26	Sat	*Saddleback*	T. Tyrer	116	12.40 & 10.26 Mail to Warrington.
Dec 29	Tues	*Saddleback*	T. Tyrer	116	3.44 & 11.15 to Warrington.

Plate 18: *Official view of a small firebox 6ft 2-2-2, built before 1853 and photographed about 1875 in the early Webb period. It has the original boiler fittings except for the Webb chimney, and the wheelbase is 6ft plus 7ft. There is a lamp socket at the top of the smokebox, fitted from about 1872. The rod protruding above the side sheet is the lever of the reverser.*

Plate 19: *No. 1876, originally the last of the small firebox 6ft 'Crewe Singles' No. 291* Prince of Wales, *after being reboilered in 1869 with two safety valves and no dome, as on the original 7ft singles. The photograph was probably taken in 1879 before the engine was transferred to service stock as* Engineer Crewe. *The tender is the original four-wheeled Trevithick type. In both these photographs the pipe supplying water from the tender to the feed pump can be seen through the spokes of the driving wheel near the firebox. Also the same are the clack valve, the pet cock and the rod controlling it from the footplate alongside the boiler handrail.*

Engine classes: *Hardwicke* - 'Crewe Goods' 2-4-0. *Saddleback* - 6ft 'Crewe Passenger' 2-2-2.

Date		Name of Engine	Name of Driver	Number of Miles	Remarks
1857					
Dec 30	Wed	Saddleback	T. Tyrer	133	6.30 to Liverpool & 3.30 to Warrington.
Dec 31	Thurs	Saddleback	T. Tyrer	74	8.30 to Liverpool.
1858					
Jany 1	Fri	Saddleback	T. Tyrer	74	12.50 to Liverpool.
Jany 3	Sun	Marquis	T. Tyrer	74	Sunday, 8.30 to Liverpool.
Jany 4	Mon	Saddleback	T. Tyrer	74	8.30 to Liverpool.
Jany 5	Tues	Saddleback	T. Tyrer	74	12.50 to Liverpool.
Jany 7	Thurs	Saddleback	T. Tyrer	116	3.44 & 11.15 to Warrington.
Jany 8	Fri	Saddleback	T. Tyrer	133	6.30 to Liverpool & 3.30 to Warrington.
Jany 9	Sat	Saddleback	T. Tyrer	74	8.30 to Liverpool.
Jany 10	Sun	Saddleback	T. Tyrer	116	3.44 & 1.00pm to Warrington, Sunday.
Jany 11	Mon	Saddleback	T. Tyrer	74	12.50 to Liverpool.
Jany 13	Wed	Saddleback	T. Tyrer	116	3.44 & 11.15 to Warrington.
Jany 14	Thurs	Saddleback	T. Tyrer	133	6.30 to Liverpool & 3.30 to Warrington.
Jany 15	Fri	Saddleback	T. Tyrer	74	8.30 to Liverpool.
Jany 22	Fri	Saddleback	T. Tyrer	133	6.30 to Liverpool & 3.30 to Warrington.
Jany 29	Fri	Caradoc	R. Anderton	100	Coaling to Springs Branch.
Feby 5	Fri	Marquis	J. Haughton	108	to Crewe with Cattle.
Feby 8	Mon	Menai	J. Haughton	74	to Liverpool, Night Goods.
Feby 9	Tues	Menai	J. Haughton	80	Ballasting to Springs Branch.
Feby 11	Thurs	Caradoc	J. Haughton	74	to Liverpool, Night Goods.
Feby 13	Sat	Menai	R. Anderton	74	to Liverpool, Night Goods.
Feby 20	Sat	Scorpion	R. Mort	116	3.44 & 11.15 to Warrington.
Feby 27	Sat	Vulture	W. Tompson	116	3.44 & 11.15 to Warrington.
Feby 28	Sun	Vulture	W. Tompson	58	10.26 Night Mail to Warrington.
Mch 1	Mon	Vulture	W. Tompson	116	12.40 & 10.26 Mail to Warrington.
Mch 2	Tues	Vulture	W. Tompson	116	12.40 & 10.26 Mail to Warrington.
Mch 3	Wed	Vulture	W. Tompson	116	12.40 & 10.26 Mail to Warrington.
Mch 4	Thurs	Vulture	W. Tompson	116	12.40 & 10.26 Mail to Warrington.
Mch 5	Fri	Vulture	W. Tompson	116	12.40 & 10.26 Mail to Warrington.
Mch 6	Sat	Vulture	W. Tompson	116	12.40 & 10.26 Mail to Warrington.
Mch 8	Mon	Chillington	W. Brown	256	Soldiers to Rugby 5.30pm.
Mch 10	Wed	Vulture	W. Tompson	133	6.30 to Liverpool & 3.30 to Warrington.
Mch 11	Thurs	Vulture	W. Tompson	74	8.30 to Liverpool.
Mch 12	Fri	Vulture	W. Tompson	74	12.50 to Liverpool.
Mch 14	Sun	Vulture	W. Tompson	74	8.30 to Liverpool, Sunday.
Mch 15	Mon	Vulture	W. Tompson	74	8.30 to Liverpool.
Mch 16	Tues	Vulture	W. Tompson	74	12.50 to Liverpool.
Mch 18	Thurs	Vulture	W. Tompson	116	3.44 & 11.15 to Warrington.
Mch 19	Fri	Vulture	W. Tompson	133	6.30 to Liverpool & 3.30 to Warrington.
Mch 20	Sat	Vulture	W. Tompson	74	8.30 to Liverpool.
Mch 21	Sun	Vulture	W. Tompson	116	3.44 & 11.15 to Warrington.
Mch 22	Mon	Vulture	W. Tompson	74	12.50 to Liverpool.
Mch 24	Wed	Vulture	W. Tompson	116	3.44 & 11.15 to Warrington.
Mch 27	Sat	Dalemain	W. Worthington	116	12.40 & 10.26 Mail to Warrington.
Mch 30	Tues	Dalemain	W. Worthington	116	3.44 & 11.15 to Warrington.
Mch 31	Wed	Dalemain	W. Worthington	133	6.30 to Liverpool & 3.30 to Warrington.
Apl 1	Thurs	Dalemain	W. Worthington	74	8.30 to Liverpool.
Apl 2	Fri	Dalemain	W. Worthington	74	12.50 to Liverpool.
Apl 4	Sun	Dalemain	W. Worthington	74	8.30 to Liverpool, Sunday.
Apl 5	Mon	Dalemain	W. Worthington	74	8.30 to Liverpool.
Apl 6	Tues	Dalemain	W. Worthington	74	12.50 to Liverpool, Passengers.
Apl 8	Thurs	Dalemain	W. Worthington	116	3.44 & 11.15 to Warrington.

Plate 20: '*Crewe Single*' *No. 1839 was built in May 1849 as No. 115* Meteor, *with a small firebox but straight frames, and was an engine on which Thomas Baron records having worked only once, with a cattle train from Crewe to Stafford on 9th May 1862. It was rebuilt in January 1858 and renumbered into the duplicate list as 1839 in August 1872. It was scrapped in January 1879, which of course dates this photograph, taken at Banbury by W. H. Dodds, as sometime between the latter two dates. It still has a Trevithick boiler but with Webb chimney, and its six-wheeled tender rather dwarfs the engine.*   LGRP 9847

Plate 21: *Crewe Single No. 1848* Sefton, *which was built at Crewe in 1857, at Prestbury in the mid-1880s with a train from Manchester London Road. It is now in Webb condition, with a Ramsbottom boiler and screw couplings. An additional sandpipe has been rigged at the front of the tender, to help with braking (there are no brakes on the engine, only a hand brake applying wooden blocks on the tender wheels), and visible on the side of the firebox just above the side-sheet are two try-cocks for checking the water level in the boiler. The engine is clean but from the condition of the paintwork,* Sefton *is due for a visit to Crewe Works.*

Date		Name of Engine	Name of Driver	Number of Miles	Remarks
1858					
Apl 9	Fri	*Dalemain*	W. Worthington	133	6.30 to Liverpool & 3.30 to Warrington.
Apl 10	Sat	*Dalemain*	W. Worthington	74	8.30 to Liverpool.
Apl 11	Sun	*Dalemain*	W. Worthington	116	3.44 & 2.00 to Warrington.
Apl 12	Mon	*Liver*	J. Golding	64	Coaling for Smith's & Darlington's.
Apl 14	Wed	*Liver*	J. Golding	80	Coaling for Pearsons to Spring Branch.
Apl 15	Thurs	*Liver*	J. Golding	80	Coaling for Pearsons to Spring Branch.
Apl 16	Fri	*Liver*	J. Golding	80	Coaling for Pearsons to Spring Branch.
Apl 17	Sat	*Liver*	J. Golding	80	Coaling for Pearsons to Spring Branch.
Apl 18	Sun	*Liver*	J. Golding	80	Coaling for Pearsons to Spring Branch.
Apl 19	Mon	*Liver*	J. Golding	80	Coaling for Pearsons to Spring Branch.
Apl 20	Tues	*Liver*	J. Golding	80	Coaling for Pearsons to Spring Branch.
Apl 22	Thurs	*Liver*	J. Golding	80	Coaling for Moss Hall Colliery.
Apl 23	Fri	*Liver*	J. Golding	80	Coaling for Moss Hall Colliery.
Apl 24	Sat	*Liver*	J. Golding	118	Coaling for Moss Hall & Warrington at night.
Apl 26	Mon	*Liver*	J. Golding	80	Coaling for Moss Hall Colliery.
Apl 27	Tues	*Liver*	J. Golding	80	Coaling for Moss Hall Colliery.
Apl 28	Wed	*Liver*	J. Golding	80	Coaling for Moss Hall Colliery.
Apl 30	Fri	*Liver*	J. Golding	90	Coaling for Blundells Colliery.
May 1	Sat	*Liver*	J. Golding	134	Coaling and Liverpool at night.
May 3	Mon	*Liver*	J. Golding	60	Coaling for Smith's & Darlington's.
May 4	Tues	*Liver*	J. Golding	60	Coaling for Smith's & Darlington's.
May 5	Wed	*Liver*	J. Golding	60	Coaling for Smith's & Darlington's.
May 6	Thurs	*Liver*	J. Golding	60	Coaling for Smith's & Darlington's.
May 7	Fri	*Liver*	J. Golding	60	Coaling for Smith's & Darlington's.
May 10	Mon	*Liver*	J. Golding	65	Springs Branch.
May 11	Tues	*Liver*	J. Golding	65	Springs Branch.
May 12	Wed	*Liver*	J.Golding	65	Springs Branch.
May 14	Fri	*Loadstone*	C. Gregory	90	Coaling for Moss Hall.
May 15	Sat	*Loadstone*	C. Gregory	90	Coaling for Moss Hall.
May 18	Tues	*Fly*	J. Haughton	60	Banking to Coppull.
May 20	Thurs	*Baronet*	J. Haughton	40	Banking to Coppull.
May 24	Mon	*Fame*	T. Booth	40	Banking to Coppull.
May 25	Tues	*Elephant*	J. Bate	258	2.45pm Coal to Rugby.
May 27	Thurs	*Elephant*	J. Bate	258	2.45pm Coal to Rugby.
May 29	Sat	*Elephant*	J. Bate	258	2.45pm Coal to Rugby.
June 1	Tues	*Clarendon*	J. Wilkinson	108	Cattle to Crewe.
June 7	Mon	*Herald*	E. Hughes	74	Night Goods to Liverpool.
June 8	Tues	*Herald*	E. Hughes	74	Night Goods to Liverpool.
June 9	Wed	*Herald*	E. Hughes	74	Night Goods to Liverpool.
June 10	Thurs	*Herald*	E. Hughes	74	Night Goods to Liverpool.
June 11	Fri	*Herald*	E.. Hughes	74	Night Goods to Liverpool.
June 12	Sat	*Herald*	E. Hughes	74	Night Goods to Liverpool.
June 15	Tues	*Vulture*	W. Tompson	108	to Crewe for Repairs.
June 21	Mon	*Fly*	T. Booth	100	Ballasting for Pots.
June 22	Tues	*Fly*	T. Booth	100	Ballasting for Pots.
June 23	Wed	*Salopian*	T. Booth	256	to Rugby with Cattle.
June 25	Fri	*Fly*	T. Booth	108	to Crewe for Repairs.
June 26	Sat	*Salopian*	T. Booth	148	two trips to Liverpool, Cattle.
July 11	Sun	*Ingestre*	J. Waterworth	58	Night Mail to Warrington.
July 12	Mon	*Ingestre*	J. Waterworth	116	two Trips to Warrington.
July 16	Fri	*Salopian*	W. Netherland	74	Empty coaches to Manchester.
July 17	Sat	*Salopian*	W. Netherland	74	Cattle to Liverpool.
July 20	Tues	*Ingestre*	J. Waterworth	116	3.44 & 9.55 to Warrington.

Throughout the rest of 1857 and early 1858 Baron works the same sort of turns but then on 29th January 1858 he goes 'coaling to Springs Branch' and later that year he is 'coaling for Smith's & Darlingtons', for 'Pearson's to Springs Branch', for 'Moss Hall Colliery', for 'Blundell's Colliery' and so on. But what exactly does this mean? Was he delivering coal from those places or going to the collieries to collect it? It seems unclear; but quite possibly he was taking empty wagons to the collieries and returning with loaded ones.

On 8th March he goes to Rugby for the first time, 256 miles there and back, with 'soldiers', presumably a special, but later in the year he works there regularly.

On 25th, 27th and 29th May he works 'Coal to Rugby 2.45pm'. The nearest train to this in the 1861 *Working Timetable* is '1.15pm Coal Ince Hall' (Ince Hall presumably being the origin of the coal), which stopped at several places before stopping at Stafford at 7.5-8.20pm, Colwich at 8.30pm, Tamworth at 9.50-10.0pm and Rugby at 11.30pm, where presumably another engine and crew took over, and eventually brought the train into London at 7.45am.

On 21st June he is 'ballasting' - a job which appears occasionally without further details - but in this case he is 'Ballasting for Pots'. Was Pots (or Potts?) a contractor who required an engine to work his ballast wagons and, if so, which line was he working on?

Later he works 'Cattle to Rugby', the cattle presumably being destined for London, and once he does so via Birmingham. Subsequently, he works to Rugby occasionally with coal and cattle, and sometimes on passenger trains.

The coal which is worked southwards by Preston men, either from Preston itself or from points south of Preston such as Ince Hall, all clearly comes from the various pits in the area.

How Baron and his fellow enginemen worked back northwards is only possible to guess, as his diary does not give times of return workings. The timetable, however, gives details of various empty wagon trains, which seem the most likely return workings; but there is not the same number of northbound empty wagon trains as there are southbound loaded trains.

This of course makes sense, because an engine could haul far more wagons empty than loaded. This was recognised in the late nineteenth century and early twentieth centuries all over the LNWR system. Loaded coal trains on the main line south of Rugby and Northampton, for instance, were made up to 60 wagons, whereas down trains of empties from London took 80, every four up trains being balanced by three down; and on the Jellicoe Specials during the Great War loaded trains northbound to Grangemouth were made up to 40 wagons, while southbound trains were made up to 56 empties, so seven down trains were

balanced by five up. But Baron's records show that the practice of running more loaded trains than empty had begun as early as the mid 1850s. This is not surprising, as this method of working only makes good sense, but it is good to have confirmation that it was in use so early.

As Baron does not record details of his northbound workings, it is only possible to look in the *Working Timetable* for trains which might have been the return workings. The 1861 *Working Timetable* shows three possible trains from Rugby to Preston. One is the 11.25pm from London, described in the *Working Timetable* as 'Goods. Scotch', which left Rugby at 4.40am, stopped at Tamworth 6.5-6.15am, Rugeley 6.45am, Stafford 7.25-7.40am, Crewe 8.55am, Warrington 10.0-10.15am, Wigan 11.0am and reached Preston at 12.5pm.

A more likely one perhaps was the 'Preston Empties' (presumably empty coal wagons working back from London), which left Rugby at 6.0pm, stopped at Tamworth 7.30-7.35pm, Stafford 8.50-9.0pm, Crewe 10.10pm and arrived at Preston at 2.15am. A third possibility is 'Goods. Local to Preston. Sundays excepted', which left Rugby at 9pm, stopped at Hartshill Siding at 9.40pm, Atherstone 10.0pm, Tamworth 1025-10.35pm, Lichfield 10.55pm, Rugeley 12.50am, Colwich 1.5am, Stafford 1.25-1.50am, Crewe 3.10-3.30am, Warrington 4.40-4.55am, Wigan 5.55am and was due in Preston at 6.45am.

Another possibility may have been 'Empty Coal Wagons', which arrived at Stafford (origin not stated, but possibly from the Birmingham line) at 10.0am, left at 10.45am, stopped at Crewe at 12.0-12.10pm, Warrington 1.20-1.50pm, Springs Branch 2.30pm, Wigan 3.15pm and Standish 3.30, where it terminated.

The times of the ore trains south of Carnforth as far as Preston are given in Table 3. Times of the main goods, coal and ore trains south of Preston are given in Table 4. Times of the main empty wagon trains working northwards are given in Table 5. Times of the empty ore wagon trains north of Preston are in Table 6.

In almost all cases, the descriptions of the trains at the top of the columns are taken from the May 1861 *Working Timetable* and are not consistent. Northbound, 'Ore' means 'empty ore wagons' but more usually the word 'wagons' is added - 'coal wagons' or 'ore wagons' - to denote 'empty ore wagons', and occasionally the full phrase itself is used. There were, however, also loaded northbound ore trains from Northamptonshire into the Black Country.

Finally, simple calculations of the number of hours required on duty by Thomas Baron and his fellow enginemen when working these trains give results which are enlightening as well as barely believable.

Page 34 Engine classes

Caradoc, Chillington, Marquis, Menai - 'Crewe Goods' 2-4-0s.

Dalemain, Saddleback, Scorpion, Vulture - 'Crewe Passenger' 2-2-2s.

Page 36 (opposite) Engine classes

Baronet, Clarendon, Dalemain, Elephant, Fame, Fly, Herald, Liver, Loadstone, Salopian - 'Crewe Goods' 2-4-0s.

Ingestre, Vulture - 'Crewe Passenger' 2-2-2s.

Table 3
Up Mineral Trains South of Carnforth as far as Preston

Carnforth dep	**1.50**	**8.15**	**9.10**	**11.40**	**5.00**	**6.00**
Lancaster arr	2.15	8.35	9.35	12.00	5.25	6.20
dep	2.25		9.45	12.10	5.35	
Lancaster Jc arr	2.30					
Preston arr	**4.05**		**11.00**	**1.20**	**6.50**	

Table 4
Main Up Goods, Coal and Mineral Trains South of Preston

		Mineral am	Mineral am	Coal am	Goods am	Goods pm	Coal pm	Coal pm	Coal pm	Mineral pm	Goods pm
	Preston dep		4.00		7.30	2.30	1.15			7.30	11.20
	Standish		-.-		7.55	-.-	-.-			-.-	-.-
19¼	Springs Branch		-.-	7.50	-.-	-.-	2.20	4.55	6.00	-.-	-.-
	Wigan		-.-	-.-	8.20	-.-	-.-	-.-	-.-	-.-	-.-
	Warrington arr		5.45	8.35	9.10	4.00	4.55	5.50	6.55	9.20	12.40
	dep		6.00	8.45	9.50	4.45	5.45	6.00	7.00	9.30	1.00
	Preston Brook		-.-	-.-	10.15	-.-	-.-	-.-	-.-	-.-	-.-
	Hartford										1.40
	Winsford		-.-	-.-	-.-	-.-	-.-	6.50	-.-	-.-	
43¾	**Crewe** arr		7.20	10.00	11.20	5.55	6.55	7.05	8.15	10.50	2.20 (1)
	dep		7.35	10.30	12.00	6.30	7.05	7.10	8.20	11.00	3.00
	Whitmore		-.-	-.-	-.-	-.-	-.-	-.-	-.-	11.35 (2)	
62¾	Norton Bridge	6.45 (3)	-.-	-.-	-.-	-.-	-.-	-.-	-.-	-.-	4.00
68½	**Stafford** arr	7.00	8.50	11.45	12.55	7.45	8.20	8.30	9.40	2.45	4.20
	dep	7.10	9.00	11.55	1.15	8.00	8.30	8.40	9.50	3.00	4.30
84½	**Bushbury Jct** arr	8.00	9.40	12.30		8.40		9.20		3.40	5.05
	dep										
84	Wolverhampton dep	8.05	9.45								
86	Ettingshall										
86	Parkfield										
86½	Spring Vale Siding										
87	Deepfields		9.53								
88¼	Bloomfield	8.25	10.00								
89	Tipton		10.06								
90	Dudley Port										
91	Albion		10.13								
92	Oldbury										
93	Spon Lane		10.20								
94	Smethwick		10.55								
95	Soho		11.00								
	Toys' Siding										
96½	Edgbaston		11.05								
97½	**Birmingham New Street**		11.15								
	Birmingham Curzon St		11.20								
3¾	Willenhall					9.00				4.20	5.20
5¼	Darlaston					9.10				4.45	5.30
	Bescot Goods Siding										5.40
6½	**Bescot** arr					9.20				**5.00**	5.45
	dep					9.30					5.50
16	**Birmingham Curzon St arr**					10.00					6.15
	Rugeley					1.30					
	Tamworth arr					2.25	9.50				
	dep					2.50	9.55				
	Atherstone					3.15					
	Nuneaton					3.30		11.50			
	Rugby					4.36	11.45	12.35			
201¾	**London**					11.55pm	7.00am				

Notes
1) Shunts at Crewe for 'Irish Mail'.

2) Shunts at Whitmore for 10.45pm and 11.14pm from Preston, and 11.05pm Goods from Manchester.

3) NSR Mineral, NSR engine. Presumably, this train conveys iron ore from North Staffordshire to the iron works at Bloomfield and possibly to others nearby..

Table 5
Empty Wagon Trains Northbound

			Mineral Wagons	Mineral	Coal Wagons	Goods & Red Ore Empty	Iron Ore	Coal Wagons
			am	am	am	am	pm	pm
	Birmingham Curzon St	dep				11.25	4.25	
	Birmingham New St	dep				11.35	4.30	
1	Edgbaston					11.40	4.35	
1¼	Toys' Siding							
2½	Soho					11.50	(2)	
3½	Smethwick					12.00		
4½	Spon Lane					12.10		
5	Spon Lane Basin					12.18		
5½	Oldbury							
6	Albion					12.26		
7	Dudley Port				(1)	12.37		
8	Tipton					12.58		
8¾	Bloomfield				9.20			
10	Deepfields					1.15		
	Spring Vale Siding							
11	Parkfield				9.28			
11	Ettingshall							
13	Wolverhampton	arr			9.35	1.25		
	Wolverhampton	dep			9.40	1.30		
9½	**Bescot**	**dep**	6.00					
14½	**Bushbury Jct**	arr						
		dep	6.20		**2.40**	1.55		(3)
29	**Stafford**	arr	7.35	10.15	3.20	2.30		7.45
		dep	7.45		3.30	3.15		8.40
34½	Norton Bridge	arr	8.00	10.35				
42¾	Whitmore		8.35			4.00		
45¾	Madeley				4.25			
53¾	Crewe	arr	9.15		4.50	4.30		9.55
		dep	9.35		5.00	4.45		10.10
65¼	Hartford					5.10		
77¾	Warrington	arr	10.50		6.10	5.55		11.20
		dep	11.05		6.20	6.15		11.30
83½	Preston Junction	arr	11.30					
	Park Lane Siding	arr	12.20					
88½	Springs Branch	arr			**7.00am**	6.50		12.25
90½	Wigan					7.05		1.35
105½	**Preston**	arr	**1.25pm**			**8.15pm**		**2.35am**

1) North Staffordshire Railway train.
2) From Northampton (loaded ore train).
3) Coal Wagons from Rugby to Ince Hall: Rugby dep 5.15pm; Nuneaton 5.55; Tamworth 6.25; Lichfield 6.50.

Table 6
Empty Wagon Trains Northbound

			Ore Wagons	Ore Wagons S & M Exc	Ore	Birmingham Empty Ore Wagons	Ore
			am	am	am	am	pm
	Preston	**dep**		**9.30**		**3.00**	
21½	Lancaster	arr		10.35		4.05	
		dep	7.40	10.45	11.00	4.15	5.20
27	**Carnforth**	**arr**	**8.00**	**11.05**	**11.20**	**4.35**	**5.40**

Date		Name of Engine	Name of Driver	Number of Miles	Remarks
1858					
July 21	Wed	*Ingestre*	J. Waterworth	133	6.30 to Liverpool & 3.30 to Warrington.
July 22	Thurs	*Ingestre*	J. Waterworth	72	8.45 to Liverpool.
July 23	Fri	*Ingestre*	J. Waterworth	72	12.10 to Liverpool.
Aug		*Fame*	T. Booth	100	Banking to Coppull.
Aug 7	Sat	*Admiral*	J. Wilkinson	108	from the Works at Crewe.
Aug 9	Mon	*Hardwicke*	J. Waterworth	256	to Rugby with Excursion.
Aug 11	Wed	*Colossus*	J. Waterworth	72	to Liverpool, Excursion.
Aug 12	Thurs	*Colossus*	J. Waterworth	72	Ballasting.
Aug 13	Fri	*Colossus*	J. Waterworth	80	Ballasting.
Aug 14	Sat	*Colossus*	J. Waterworth	30	Ballasting.
Aug 18	Wed	*Ellesmere*	W. Dent	108	to Crewe, Empty Coaches.
Aug 19	Thurs	*Hardwicke*	J. Waterworth	72	Excursion to Knowsley Hall.
Aug 21	Sat	*Hardwicke*	J. Kirbey	72	Cattle to Liverpool.
Aug 22	Sun	*Albion*	W. Morris	57	to Warrington for Mail.
Aug 23	Mon	*Fame*	T. Booth	57	Ballasting.
Aug 28	Sat	*Loadstone*	J. Kirbey	256	Cattle to Rugby.
Aug 31	Tues	*Marquis*	J. Kirbey	72	Night Goods to Liverpool.
Sept 8	Wed	*Salopian*	W. Netherland	72	Night Goods to Liverpool.
Sept 9	Thurs	*Salopian*	W. Netherland	40	Ballasting.
Sept 10	Fri	*Salopian*	J. Haughton	40	Ballasting.
Sept 11	Sat	*Marquis*	J. Haughton	72	Cattle to Liverpool.
Sept 13	Mon	*Baronet*	J. Haughton	100	Ballasting.
Sept 14	Tues	*Fame*	J. Fiddler	57	Cattle to Warrington.
Sept 15	Wed	*Fame*	J. Haughton	76	to Preston Brook.
Sept 16	Thurs	*Marquis*	W. Netherland	100	to Liverpool & Manchester.
Sept 17	Fri	*Liver*	J. Golding	100	Coaling for Moss Hall.
Sept 18	Sat	*Salopian*	J. Golding	72	to Liverpool.
Sept 24	Fri	*Colossus*	W. Netherland	72	Cattle to Liverpool.
Sept 24	Fri	*Colossus*	W. Netherland	108	to Crewe, London Goods.
Sept 25	Sat	*Scorpion*	T. Booth	114	12.00 & 10.26 to Warrington.
Sept 26	Sun	*Scorpion*	T. Booth	57	Empty Coaches to Warrington.
Sept 27	Mon	*Scorpion*	J. Haughton	90	Excursion to Warrington & Banking.
Sept 27	Mon	*Marquis*	J. Wilkinson	72	Night Goods to Liverpool.
Sept 28	Tues	*Marquis*	J. Wilkinson	72	Cattle to Liverpool.
Sept 28	Tues	*Tiger*	J. Wilkinson	32	Banking Express to Wigan.
Sept 30	Thurs	*Marquis*	J. Wilkinson	72	Night Goods to Liverpool.
Oct 1	Fri	*Tiger*	J. Wilkinson	48	Assisting Express to Newton.
Oct 2	Sat	*Tiger*	J. Wilkinson	48	Assisting Express to Newton.
Oct 3	Sun	*Mersey*	R. Mort	72	8.30 to Liverpool, Sunday.
Oct 4	Mon	*Marquis*	W. Netherland	72	Night Goods to Liverpool.
Oct 7	Thurs	*Hardwicke*	J. Golding	36	One trip of Coal from Wigan.
Oct 9	Sat	*Albion*	W. Morris	72	12.10 to Liverpool.
Oct 12	Tues	*Chillington*	C. Gregory	80	Coaling for Smith's & Darlington's.
Oct 13	Wed	*Chillington*	C. Gregory	80	Coaling for Smith's & Darlington's.
Oct 14	Thurs	*Hardwicke*	W. Netherland	256	to Rugby with Cattle via Birmingham.
Oct 21	Thurs	*Ingestre*	J. Waterworth	116	3.44 & 10.00 to Warrington.
Oct 22	Fri	*Tiger*	W. Netherland	40	Banking to Coppull.
Oct 23	Sat	*Salopian*	W. Netherland	72	to Liverpool, 8.05 Goods.
Oct 30	Sun	*Salopian*	W. Netherland	72	to Liverpool, 8.05 Goods.
Nov 1	Mon	*Fly*	R. Howard	256	to Rugby.
Nov 4	Thurs	*Herald*	T. Booth	256	Cattle to Rugby.
Nov 12	Fri	*Admiral*	W. Netherland	108	from the Works, Crewe.
Nov 13	Sat	*Ant*	G. Fisher	108	to Crewe for Repairs.

As well as coal, goods and cattle, soon Baron is working 'Iron Ore' southwards also. This comes on to the LNWR at Carnforth and is described in the Carnforth-Preston timetable simply as 'Ore', in the Preston-Birmingham table as 'Mineral', and sometimes the term is explained vertically in the columns as 'Red Ore Train'. Baron himself refers to it either as 'Mineral' or as 'Iron Ore'. More scientifically perhaps, it was haematite from Ulverston. It seems from the timetable that these trains did not work through south of Preston but were re-marshalled there into trains for the south.

The main long-distance workings were to the West Midlands, the 'Black Country' as it was known then. Two such trains are shown in the 1861 *Working Timetable*, one leaving Preston at 4am and the other at 7.30pm. The 4am from Preston went to Wolverhampton and then by the Stour Valley line, stopping at numerous points *en route*, clearly to drop off wagons of ore at the many ironworks served by the Stour Valley line, and eventually terminated at Curzon Street. In the 1861 *Working Timetable* it is shown as 'Red Ore', stopped at Crewe at 7.35am, Stafford 8.50-9.0am, Bushbury 9.40am, Wolverhampton 9.45am, Deepfields 9.53am, Bloomfield 10am, Tipton 10.6am, Albion 10.13am, Spon Lane 10.20am, Smethwick 10.55am, Soho 11.0am, Edgbaston 11.5am, Birmingham New Street 11.15am and Curzon Street at 11.20am.

The 7.30pm from Preston took the Grand Junction line at Bushbury and dropped off wagons at Willenhall and Darlaston before stopping at Bescot, presumably for its wagons to be taken on by the South Staffordshire Railway to iron works on its lines. Goods trains from Preston, such as the 2.30pm and 11.20pm, which also took this route, the original Grand Junction line, did not stop at Bescot but ran through to Curzon Street.

In the early months of 1859 Baron frequently works the 7.30pm to Bushbury and Bescot, which is shown as 'Mineral' in the 1861 *Working Timetable*. It stopped at Crewe at 11.0pm, Stafford 2.45-3.0am, Bushbury 3.40, Willenhall 4.20am, Darlaston 4.45am and arrived at Bescot Junction at 5.0am.

From the diary entries, however, it seems that Baron did not work this 4.0am 'Red Ore' train at this time, though he did later as far as Crewe only, but he worked both the 11.15pm Goods and the 11.15am Passenger to Birmingham. South of Stafford the 11.15pm Goods, 11.20pm in the 1861 *Working Timetable*, ran via Bescot, stopping at Bushbury at 5.5am, then Willenhall 5.20am, Darlaston 5.30am, Bescot 5.40am and Bescot Junction 5.45-5.50am, and arrived at Curzon Street at 6.15am.

No 11.15am or 11.15pm Passenger is shown in the 1861 *Working Timetable*. The nearest train is the

10.45pm Passenger on Sundays, which south of Stafford stopped at Bushbury at 1.58am, where it had connections both from and to Wolverhampton, and then ran non-stop via Bescot to Curzon Street.

In none of these cases does Baron give details of the trains on which he worked back to Preston. So it is only possible to look in the *Working Timetable* for trains which might have been the return workings. The 1861 *Working Timetable* shows three possible trains from Rugby to Preston. One is the 11.25pm from London, described in the *Working Timetable* as 'Goods. Scotch', which left Rugby at 4.40am, stopped at Tamworth 6.5-6.15am, Rugeley 6.45am, Stafford 7.25-7.40am, Crewe 8.55am, Warrington 10.0-10.15am, Wigan 11.0am and reached Preston at 12.5pm. A more likely one perhaps was the 'Preston Empties' (presumably empty coal wagons working back from London), which left Rugby at 6.0pm, stopped at Tamworth 7.30-7.35pm, Stafford 8.50-9.0pm, Crewe 10.10pm and arrived at Preston at 2.15am. A third possibility is 'Goods. Local to Preston. Sundays excepted', which left Rugby at 9pm, stopped at Hartshill Siding at 9.40pm, Atherstone 10.0pm, Tamworth 1025-10.35pm, Lichfield 10.55pm, Rugeley 12.50am, Colwich 1.5am, Stafford 1.25-1.50am, Crewe 3.10-3.30am, Warrington 4.40-4.55am, Wigan 5.55am and was due in Preston at 6.45am.

Another possibility may have been 'Empty Coal Wagons', which arrived at Stafford (origin not stated, but possibly from the Birmingham line) at 10.0am, left at 10.45am, stopped at Crewe at 12.0-12.10pm, Warrington 1.20-1.50pm, Springs Branch 2.30pm, Wigan 3.15pm and Standish 3.30, where it terminated.

In the down direction the 'Irish Mail' left Euston at 8.25pm (according to the Trent Valley Line tables) but at 8.30pm (in the Main Line tables). It stopped at Rugby at 10.25-10.28pm, Stafford at 11.40-11.43pm, passed Crewe at 12.19am, stopped at Chester at 12.48am and arrived at Holyhead at 3.5am.

In the up direction the 'Irish Mail' left Holyhead at 12.0 mid-night, Chester at 2.15am, passed Crewe at 2.45am, stopped at Stafford 3.20-3.23am, Rugby 4.36-4.39am, and arrived at Euston at 6.45am.

The down 'Limited Mail' followed the 'Irish Mail', leaving Euston at 8.35pm, stopped at Rugby 10.40-10.44pm, Tamworth 11.20-11.24pm, Crewe at 12.32am, Preston 1.59-2.5am, Kendal Junction 3.5-3.8am, and reached Carlisle at 4.31am.

The up 'Limited Mail' left Carlisle at 8.44pm, stopped at Kendal Junction at 10.3-10.6pm, Preston at 11.10-11.14pm, Crewe 12.44am, Stafford 1.19-1.23am, Tamworth 1.56am, Rugby 2.36-2.40am, Bletchley 3.28am, Camden for Dock Line 4.33am, London 4.37am.

Engine classes

Admiral, Ant, Baronet, Chillington, Colossus, Ellesmere, Fame, Fly, Hardwicke, Herald, Liver, Loadstone, Marquis, Salopian - 'Crewe Goods' 2-4-0s.
Albion, Ingestre, Mersey, Scorpion, Tiger - 6ft 'Crewe Passenger' 2-2-2s.

19th August. The nearest station to Knowsley Hall, the home of Lord Derby, with a vast park around it, was Rainhill, so presumably the excursionists were conveyed to the hall by horse-drawn vehicles, horse-buses or whatever. But what was the occasion which caused an excursion to be run that day?

Plate 22: 6ft 'Crewe Single' 2-2-2 No. 179 Nun posed alongside the paint shop at Crewe Works before withdrawal in November 1886. It has been painted in photographic grey for its final photographs. In general, the engine seems rather dwarfed by the six-wheel tender, which is fitted with struts for the communication cord on the right-hand side and a stanchion for the Webb chain brake on the left-hand side. On the side sheet of the footplate is the wheel to operate the brake. The nameplate has single-row subsidiary inscriptions, photographs of which are quite rare. *Crewe OS52*

The 'Limited Mail': The LNWR public timetable for January 1865 had the following note in the column for the down 'Limited Scotch Mail', also described elsewhere in the timetable as the 'Limited Express Mail' and the 'Limited Mail: 'By special arrangement with the Postmaster-General, a limited number of passengers to Edinburgh, Glasgow and the North of Scotland will be allowed to travel by the "Limited Mail Train" leaving Euston at 8.40pm; and to avoid disappointment, passengers are recommended to secure places beforehand.' This train was, incidentally, preceded from Euston by the 'Express Irish Mail' at 8.25pm - 'Passengers by this train are only booked from London and intermediate stations to Holyhead and Ireland, and from London to Chester' - and was followed at 9pm by a train with the note: 'Horses and Carriages from London to Scotland only are conveyed by this train.' It arrived in Edinburgh at 9.40am and Glasgow at 10.5am.

The times of departure and arrival of the 'Limited Express Mail' are shown in Table 7 below:

Table 7 Timings of 'Limited Express Mail' January 1865				
Station	*Down*	*Time*	*Up*	*Time*
Euston	dep	8.40pm	arr	4.37am
Rugby	arr	10.40pm	dep	2.36am
	dep	10.44pm	arr	2.32am
Tamworth	arr	11.20pm	arr	1.50am
Stafford	arr	11.55pm	dep	1.18am
	dep	11.59pm	arr	1.13am
Crewe Junction	arr	12.32pm	dep	12.38am
	dep	12.40pm	arr	12.30am
Newton Bridge	arr	1.20am	arr	11.46pm
Preston	arr	1.56am	arr	11.9pm
Carlisle	arr	4.28am	dep	8.44pm
	dep	4.36am	arr	
Edinburgh (Lothian Road)	arr	7.10am	dep	6.5pm
Glasgow (Buchanan Street)	arr	7.22am	dep	5.53pm

The *Railway Gazette* for 15th January 1937 published a 'Letter to the Editor' raising the question as to when the term 'Limited' was first used in relation to trains and quoting the 8.40pm LNWR Euston to Scotland and the 9pm GWR Paddington to Bristol. The editor replied: 'The West Coast Limited Mail to Scotland was a development of the 8.30pm first-class train that ran in 1839 when the railway was completed only as far as Preston. In 1846 it had become the 8.45pm ex Euston and was described as the 'night mail'. Subsequently it was limited only so far as concerned passengers on what became a mail train owing to the increasing demands of the Post Office.'

G. P. Neele refers to the 'Limited Mail' on page 105 of his *Railway Reminiscences,* which he wrote in about 1900 after he had retired: 'The train service to and from Scotland, judged by present lights, was of a very indifferent character, so far as speed was concerned. There was no 10 o'clock day express till June 1862; the morning train from Euston left at 9am, 1st and 2nd class only, and did not reach Edinburgh till 8.45pm nor Glasgow till 9.10pm. The night train for general Scotch traffic left Euston at 9pm and took upwards of 12½ hours to reach Edinburgh and 13 hours to Glasgow. The "Limited Mail", 1st and 2nd class, then leaving Euston at 8.40am, was limited to three carriages only, so far as passengers were concerned; one running to Perth, one to Edinburgh and one to Glasgow. The train had no competitive service from King's Cross and was timed to reach Edinburgh at 7.10am and Glasgow at 7.22am. The restrictions on the train at the hands of the Post Office authorities were very close and the concession of an extra vehicle to accommodate royalty entailed a visit to the Post Office to ask concurrence, and an undertaking that the punctual arrival should be maintained. The manager, Mr Cawkwell, refused to allow the Directors' Passes to be available by the train, and even when I had occasion to travel in attendance on any special parties, I had to take a ticket for my journey.'

In several places in this book tragic events are recorded such as accidents in which railway men lost their lives. The Railway Inspectorate has an archive which contains, among other things, statistics of railway servants killed at work. The numbers for 'train accidents' are those killed in collisions, derailments, boiler explosions and such like that were investigated by the Railway Inspectorate. The 'other causes' are shunting accidents, falls, 'struck by train' and such like that were investigated by the companies. These figures are probably 'light', since much under-reporting seems to have taken place, especially by the smaller companies.

	Train accidents	*Other causes*
1851	64	53
1852	57	63
1853	62	97
1854	39	73
1855	28	97
1856	30	112
1857	18	75
1858	17	114
1859	14	103
1860	17	104
1861	22	105
1862	20	89
1863	11	87
1864	15	88
1865	28	94
1866	17	83
1867	15	90
1868	19	64
1869	22	129

Date		Name of Engine	Name of Driver	Number of Miles	Remarks
1858					
Nov 16	Tues	*Colossus*	T. Booth	356	Ballasting and to Rugby.
Nov 18	Thurs	*Colossus*	T. Booth	296	Coaling & to Rugby, Cattle.
Nov 20	Sat	*Colossus*	T. Booth	72	to Liverpool with Cattle.
Nov 22	Mon	*Colossus*	T. Booth	256	to Rugby, London Coal.
Nov 24	Wed	*Loadstone*	T. Booth	170	to Liverpool & Manchester & Sutton.
Nov 26	Fri	*Colossus*	W. Netherland	346	Coaling & to Rugby, London Coal.
Nov 29	Mon	*Clarendon*	W. Netherland	60	to Springs Branch.
Nov 30	Tues	*Clarendon*	W. Netherland	60	to Springs Branch.
Dec 1	Wed	*Clarendon*	W. Netherland	60	to Springs Branch.
Dec 2	Thurs	*Chillington*	W. Netherland	60	to Springs Branch.
Dec 3	Fri	*Clarendon*	W. Netherland	60	to Springs Branch.
Dec 4	Sat	*Chillington*	W. Netherland	60	to Springs Branch, working up branch.
Dec 6	Mon	*Chillington*	W. Netherland	60	to Springs Branch, working up branch.
Dec 7	Tues	*Chillington*	W. Netherland	60	to Springs Branch, working up branch.
Dec 8	Wed	*Clarendon*	W. Netherland	60	to Springs Branch, working up branch.
Dec 9	Thurs	*Clarendon*	W. Netherland	60	to Springs Branch, working up branch.
Dec 10	Fri	*Clarendon*	W. Netherland	60	to Springs Branch, working up branch.
Dec 11	Sat	*Clarendon*	W. Netherland	60	to Springs Branch, working up branch.
Dec 13	Mon	*Clarendon*	W. Netherland	60	to Springs Branch, working up branch.
Dec 14	Tues	*Clarendon*	W. Netherland	60	to Springs Branch, working up branch.
Dec 15	Wed	*Clarendon*	W. Netherland	60	to Springs Branch, working up branch.
Dec 16	Thurs	*Clarendon*	W. Netherland	60	to Springs Branch, working up branch.
Dec 17	Fri	*Clarendon*	W. Netherland	60	to Springs Branch, working up branch.
Dec 18	Sat	*Clarendon*	W. Netherland	60	to Springs Branch, working up branch.
Dec 21	Tues	*Adjutant*	G. Scott	256	to Rugby, London Coal.
Dec 23	Thurs	*Adjutant*	G. Scott	256	to Rugby, London Coal.
Dec 28	Tues	*Adjutant*	G. Scott	256	8.05 Goods to Rugby.
Dec 30	Thurs	*Adjutant*	G. Scott	256	8.05 Goods to Rugby.
1859					
Jany 1	Sat	*Adjutant*	G. Scott	256	8.05 Goods to Rugby.
Jany 4	Tues	*Adjutant*	G. Scott	206	to Bushbury & Bescot, Iron Ore.
Jany 6	Thurs	*Adjutant*	G. Scott	206	to Bushbury & Bescot, Iron Ore.
Jany 8	Sat	*Adjutant*	G. Scott	206	to Bushbury & Bescot, Iron Ore.
Jany 10	Mon	*Adjutant*	G. Scott	206	to Bushbury & Bescot, Iron Ore.
Jany 12	Wed	*Adjutant*	G. Scott	206	to Bushbury & Bescot, Iron Ore.
Jany 14	Fri	*Adjutant*	G. Scott	212	to Bushbury & Bescot, Iron Ore.
Jany 17	Mon	*Adjutant*	G. Scott	215	11.15pm Goods to Birmingham.
Jany 19	Wed	*Adjutant*	G. Scott	215	11.15pm Goods to Birmingham.
Jany 21	Fri	*Adjutant*	G. Scott	215	11.15pm Goods to Birmingham.
Jany 24	Mon	*Adjutant*	G. Scott	256	to Rugby, London Coal.
Jany 26	Wed	*Adjutant*	G. Scott	256	to Rugby, London Coal.
Jany 28	Fri	*Adjutant*	G. Scott	256	to Rugby, London Coal.
Jany 31	Mon	*Adjutant*	G. Scott	256	to Rugby, 8.05 Goods.
Feby 2	Wed	*Adjutant*	G. Scott	256	to Rugby, 8.05 Goods.
Feby 4	Fri	*Adjutant*	G. Scott	256	to Rugby, 8.05 Goods.
Feby 8	Tues	*Adjutant*	G. Scott	256	to Rugby, London Coal.
Feby 10	Thurs	*Adjutant*	G. Scott	256	to Rugby, London Coal.
Feby 12	Sat	*Adjutant*	G. Scott	256	to Rugby, London Coal.
Feby 15	Tues	*Adjutant*	G. Scott	256	to Rugby, 8.05 Goods.
Feby 17	Thurs	*Adjutant*	G. Scott	256	to Rugby, 8.05 Goods.
Feby 19	Sat	*Adjutant*	G. Scott	256	to Rugby, 8.05 Goods.
Feby 22	Tues	*Adjutant*	G. Scott	212	to Bushbury & Bescot, Iron Ore.

Engine classes: *Adjutant, Chillington, Clarendon, Colossus, Loadstone* - all 'Crewe Goods' 2-4-0s.

Iron Ore Traffic. Before the coming of railways, iron ore from Cumbria - from Whitehaven, Barrow and Ulverston - was transported to iron works in other parts of the country by sea. Two routes were used to transport ore to the iron works of the Black Country: one was to Ellesmere Port on the Mersey, where the ore was transferred to canal boats on the Shropshire Union Canal for transport to its destination, and the other was by sea to Runcorn and then by the Trent & Mersey Canal. A third possible route opened up by sea to Saltney, Chester, Connah's Quay or perhaps Birkenhead, and onwards by rail, when the Great Western Railway line was completed between those ports and the Black Country about 1850. This route then served iron works connected to the Oxford, Worcester and Wolverhampton Railway.

When the so called 'Ulverstone & Lancaster Railway' (Ulverston being spelt, for some reason, with a final 'e' in the title of the company but not generally otherwise) was opened on 10th August 1857, connecting Ulverston and the Cumbrian mines with the LNWR at Carnforth, this iron-ore traffic began to be moved by rail throughout. The Working Timetables show that some of it went off the Lancaster & Carlisle at Lancaster and presumably then went over the Midland Railway to destinations in West Yorkshire such as Low Moor and Bradford, while rather more was taken south over the London & North Western Railway to destinations in the Black Country. One train daily ran via Wolverhampton High Level and the Stour Valley line through New Street to Curzon Street, presumably dropping off wagons of ore at the various iron works on the way, while another train ran to Bescot, where presumably its traffic was handed over to the South Staffordshire Railway, which delivered it to iron works at various points on its line to Dudley. It was perhaps no coincidence that John Robinson Maclean was a major shareholder in both the iron-ore mines of Ulverston and the South Staffordshire Railway, as well as being engineer of the Ulverston Railway.

Details of how these trains of ore were made up and worked are scant indeed. But records of two accidents give some indication. On 21st January 1861 an accident occurred at Coppull, 7½ miles south of Preston, to the 7.30am from Preston to Bescot Junction. The train consisted of an engine and tender, nineteen wagons of Ulverston iron, six loaded goods wagons, nine empties and a brake van, with a banking engine in the rear. The other accident was that which occurred at Stafford on 12th March 1859, in which it is clear from the report in the *Staffordshire Advertiser* that the train consisted of 40 wagons of iron ore hauled by two engines. One of them is shown as 'Crewe Goods' 2-4-0 *Adjutant* in Baron's diary and it seems highly likely that the other was a 'Crewe Goods' too. From this, and from Baron's diary in general, the engines used for these trains seem to have been 'Crewe Goods' 2-4-0s, while the wagons used for the ore seem likely to have been side-tipping, at first with wooden bodies but later of iron.

It is clear from the LNWR Working Timetables that there was also regular traffic in iron ore from the Northamptonshire ironstone fields to the Black Country, and quite possibly from North Staffordshire too; a train coming from the North Staffordshire Railway on to the LNWR main line at Norton Bridge is described as 'Mineral', which could have been iron ore or limestone but seems more likely to have been the former. Its destination was Bloomfield, where there was an interchange basin with the Birmingham Canal, from which the 'mineral' was conveyed by canal boat to iron works in the area, including to Bloomfield Iron Works itself; the latter was connected to the rail system only when the Princes End branch was opened in September 1863.

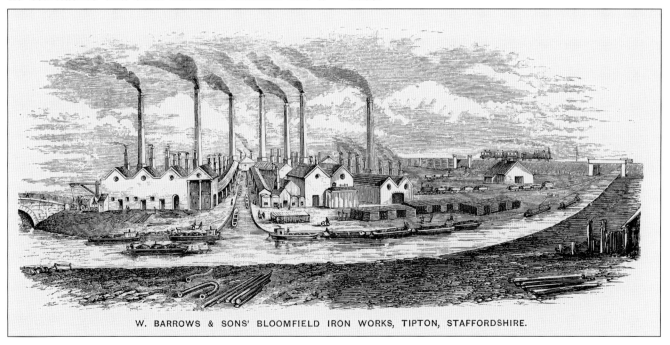

W. BARROWS & SONS' BLOOMFIELD IRON WORKS, TIPTON, STAFFORDSHIRE.

Date	Name of Engine	Name of Driver	Number of Miles	Remarks
1859				
Feby 25 Fri	*Elk*	G. Scott	74	to Liverpool, Extra.
Feby 26 Sat	*Adjutant*	G. Scott	212	to Bushbury & Bescot, 7.30pm.
Feby 28 Mon	*Adjutant*	G. Scott	212	to Bushbury & Bescot, 7.30pm.
Mch 2 Wed	*Adjutant*	G. Scott	212	to Bushbury & Bescot, 7.30pm.
Mch 4 Fri	*Adjutant*	G. Scott	212	to Bushbury & Bescot, 7.30pm. My Mate killed at Stafford. I worked the train Back.
Mch 8 Tues	*Snowdon*	J. Waterworth	72	Goods to Liverpool.
Mch 9 Wed	*Adjutant*	W. Leech	215	to My Mate's Funeral at Bolton & Work.
Mch 11 Fri	*Adjutant*	W. Leech	215	11.15 Birmingham.
Mch 14 Mon	*Adjutant*	W. Leech	256	to Rugby, London Coal.
Mch 16 Wed	*Adjutant*	W. Leech	256	to Rugby, London Coal.
Mch 18 Fri	*Adjutant*	W. Leech	256	to Rugby, London Coal.
Mch 21 Mon	*Adjutant*	W. Leech	256	to Rugby, 8.05 Goods.
Mch 23 Wed	*Adjutant*	W. Leech	256	to Rugby, 8.05 Goods.
Mch 25 Fri	*Adjutant*	W. Leech	256	to Rugby, 8.05 Goods.
Mch 29 Tues	*Adjutant*	W. Leech	256	to Rugby, London Coal.
Mch 31 Thurs	*Adjutant*	W. Leech	256	to Rugby, London Coal.
Apl 2 Sat	*Adjutant*	W. Leech	256	to Rugby, London Coal.
Apl 5 Tues	*Adjutant*	W. Leech	256	to Rugby, 8.05 Goods.
Apl 7 Thurs	*Vampire*	W. Leech	256	to Rugby, 8.05 Goods.
Apl 9 Sat	*Vampire*	W. Leech	256	to Rugby, 8.05 Goods.
Apl 11 Mon	*Vampire*	W. Leech	72	Extra to Liverpool.
Apl 12 Tues	*Vampire*	W. Leech	212	to Bescot Junction, Iron Ore.
Apl 14 Thurs	*Vampire*	W. Leech	212	to Bescot Junction, Iron Ore.
Apl 16 Sat	*Vampire*	W. Leech	292	Liverpool, Cattle, & Bescot Junction.
Apl 18 Mon	*Vampire*	W. Leech	212	to Bescot Junction, Iron Ore.
Apl 20 Wed	*Stentor*	W. Leech	212	to Bescot Junction, Iron Ore.
Apl 23 Sat	*Hardwicke*	W. Leech	108	to Crewe Works, Repairs.
Apl 25 Mon	*Stentor*	W. Leech	215	11.15 Goods to Birmingham.
Apl 27 Wed	*Stentor*	W. Leech	215	11.15 Goods to Birmingham.
Apl 29 Fri	*Stentor*	W. Leech	215	11.15 Goods to Birmingham.
May 2 Mon	*Stentor*	W. Leech	256	2.15pm to Rugby, London Coal.
May 4 Wed	*Stentor*	W. Leech	256	2.15pm to Rugby, London Coal.
May 6 Fri	*Stentor*	W. Leech	256	2.15pm to Rugby, London Coal.
May 9 Mon	*Stentor*	W. Leech	256	8.05am Goods to Rugby.
May 11 Wed	*Stentor*	W. Leech	256	8.05am Goods to Rugby.
May 13 Fri	*Stentor*	W. Leech	256	8.05am Goods to Rugby.
May 17 Tues	*Stentor*	W. Leech	256	2.15pm to Rugby, London Coal.
May 19 Thurs	*Stentor*	W. Leech	256	2.15pm to Rugby, London Coal.
May 21 Sat	*Stentor*	W. Leech	256	2.15pm to Rugby, London Coal.
May 24 Tues	*Stentor*	W. Leech	256	8.0am Goods to Rugby.
May 26 Thurs	*Stentor*	W. Leech	256	8.05am Goods to Rugby.
May 28 Sat	*Stentor*	W. Leech	256	8.05am Goods to Rugby.
May 31 Tues	*Stentor*	W. Leech	212	7.30 Iron Ore to Bescot Junction.
June 2 Thurs	*Stentor*	W. Leech	212	7.30 Iron Ore to Bescot Junction.
June 4 Sat	*Stentor*	W. Leech	212	7.30 Iron Ore to Bescot Junction.
June 6 Mon	*Stentor*	W. Leech	212	7.30 Iron Ore to Bescot Junction.
June 8 Wed	*Stentor*	W. Leech	212	7.30 Iron Ore to Bescot Junction.
June 10 Fri	*Stentor*	W. Leech	212	7.30 Iron Ore to Bescot Junction.
June 13 Mon	*Stentor*	W. Leech	215	11.15pm Goods to Birmingham.
June 15 Wed	*Stentor*	W. Leech	215	11.15pm Goods to Birmingham.
June 17 Fri	*Stentor*	W. Leech	215	11.15pm Goods to Birmingham.
June 20 Mon	*Stentor*	W. Leech	256	to Rugby, London Coal.

In the early months of 1859 Baron frequently works the 7.30pm to Bushbury and Bescot, which is shown as 'Mineral' in the 1861 *Working Timetable*. It stopped at Crewe at 11.00pm, Stafford 2.45-3.00am, Bushbury 3.40am, Willenhall 4.20am, Darlaston 4.45am and arrived at Bescot Junction at 5.00am. A further explanation in the same column states 'Red Ore Train', traffic which came on to the LNWR at Carnforth and originated in the iron-ore quarries at Ulverston.

It was after working this train on 4th March 1859 that he records: 'My Mate killed at Stafford. I worked the train Back'. Baron gives no explanation either as to how his mate was killed or of the return journey to Preston, on which he drove the engine, and the only other reference in the diary to this tragic event comes five days later when he records that he went to his mate's funeral and afterwards continued to work. It may seem strange that the entry is so brief, but the diary was written presumably for Baron's own satisfaction and as he was hardly likely to forget what happened, he perhaps felt he needed no further account of it.

Fortunately, however, the events were recorded in *The Staffordshire Advertiser* for 12th March 1859 as follows:

Stafford - Horrible Death at the Railway Station

Early on Saturday morning last, a fearful accident occurred at the Railway Station, in this town, by which an engine driver was almost instantly deprived of his life. It appears from information derived at the time, and also from evidence given at the inquest, which was held on Monday last, before Mr W. W. Ward, that the deceased, George Scott, of Preston, was an engine driver, the duties of which he had discharged for seven years. On the evening of Friday, accompanied by Thomas Barron, his stoker, he brought a mineral train from Preston for Bushbury and Bescot. On arriving at Stafford, about half-past twelve o'clock at night, he got off his engine to enquire of the inspector on duty whether he should proceed with his train before or after the mail. Finding that the mail train was to leave first, Barron shunted the mineral train to the Shropshire Union line, and after the former had passed and gone forwards, Barron brought the train to the station, when the deceased attempted to get on his engine, but in doing so he missed his footing and fell underneath the train, the wheels of the tender and three following carriages passing over his body. There were two engines to the train, which consisted of 40 carriages, and it was almost immediately stopped; but on the body of the unfortunate man being got from between the rails and placed on the platform, it was discovered that both legs were frightfully mangled, and from the abdomen, which had been cut open slantingly, the bowels protruded. The poor fellow gasped three times after he was removed to the platform, but gave no other indication of life. It transpired at the inquest that the deceased was acting contrary to instructions in getting off his engine, but there was no evidence to show that he was in any way inebriated at the time of the sad occurrence. He was unmarried. The jury returned a verdict of "accidental death" and the body was subsequently conveyed to Preston for interment.

The 7.30pm from Preston must have run well that night to have arrived at Stafford about 12.30am According to the timetable (see Table 4), it was due to arrive at Whitmore at 11.35pm and to shunt there (reverse into a siding) to allow the 10.45pm and 11.14pm from Preston, and the 11.05pm Goods from Manchester, to pass. The 11.14pm from Preston was the 'Limited Mail', about which Driver Scott enquired on arriving at Stafford, so obviously he had been allowed to precede it from Whitmore. The 'Mail' was due to arrive at Stafford at 1.19am and depart at 1.23am along the Trent Valley line.

An important piece of information in the newspaper report, which is not mentioned anywhere in Baron's diary, is that the train was double-headed, presumably by two 'Crewe Goods' 2-4-0s, with a load of forty wagons of ore. It seems reasonable to assume that many, possibly all, of the long-distance coal and ore trains south from Preston were double-headed. The 'Crewe Goods' were actually very small engines, as one glance at the preserved 'Crewe Passenger' *Columbine*, now numbered 1868 in the Science Museum, South Kensington, can confirm, and their replacement by Ramsbottom's 'DX' class 0-6-0s must have been a great advance, almost revolutionary.

It is now only possible to guess why Driver Scott left his engine when it was necessary to back the train up the Shrewsbury line but obviously he knew Baron was competent to do so by himself. Whatever the reason, Scott had already spent five hours on an exposed footplate on a March night that might well have been freezing cold or pouring with rain. He may have been tired and cold, and may even have been unwell and have gone somewhere warm to rest for half an hour or so. He was not 'inebriated' but if he had gone somewhere for a warming drink in the circumstances, it would be at least understandable.

Although it was against the regulations for him to leave Baron to back the train up the Shrewsbury line, Baron was clearly well capable of handling the engine, as the train was quickly stopped when Scott fell under it. Why he fell is perhaps more easily explained – with only oil lamps by which to see the steps and handrails, a momentary lapse of concentration on a dark night might result in a slip which would be enough to put him under the engine.

Baron records that he 'worked the train back' but gives no more details. Presumably, the two engines continued to Bescot, where they were due at 5.0am; presumably at some stage, as Baron was driving, a substitute fireman was appointed to work for him; and presumably again, they returned with the 6.0am Mineral Wagons, due at Preston at 1.25pm, 17 hours and 55 minutes after departure the previous evening, a long and eventful day for Fireman Baron at the age of only twenty three.

His diary shows that the usual procedure was that the crew returned to the shed the following day in time to prepare their engine to take the 7.30pm train again. So in effect they had just over a day in which to rest before doing the return trip to Bescot once more.

Engine classes: *Adjutant, Elk, Hardwicke, Snowdon, Stentor, Vampire* - 'Crewe Goods' 2-4-0s.

Plate 23: *This broadside view of 'Crewe Goods' No. 155* Ousel *shows clearly how exposed the enginemen were on the footplate. There was no cab, just a small spectacle plate, seen end on in this photograph, behind which to shelter when running forwards into any kind of weather, the side-sheets on the engine were low and there were none at all on the tender; thus, the gap between engine and tender was wide, offering no protection from side winds. The picture also shows the footsteps giving access from the ground to the footplate: put the right foot on the step by the axle-box, reach up, grab the handrail and step up; put the left foot on the step under the beam across the front of the tender and with a firm grip on the handrail step up; then, gripping the top of the tender or the engine side-sheet, step up on to the footplate. It seems simple, but a slight loss of concentration or a slip, especially on a dark night, perhaps in rain or snow, could easily result in a fall, especially on an engine that was moving, however slowly, with tragic consequences, as befell Baron's mate, Driver G. Scott. The arrangement of footsteps on these engines changed from time to time, and it is well worthwhile comparing the various pictures in this book.*

The engine seems to be largely as built at Crewe in November 1854, with the original boiler fittings and green livery, but with a Ramsbottom chimney. There is no injector, which would be visible above the side-sheet, and the clack valve allowing water from the pump to enter the boiler can be seen just to the rear of the smokebox with the usual rod coming down from the boiler handrail to actuate the pet cock. Slots in the driving splasher appear to have been filled with sheet metal and are a darker colour, presumably black. So the date is probably about 1860. The tender is the later Trevithick six-wheel type rather than the four-wheel type that would have been fitted from new. The connecting rod is polished and the coupling rod painted or blackened in some way. To stop, the engine would generally be put into reverse gear, the only form of braking being on the tender, which has wooden brake blocks applied by a hand brake.

Plate 24: *'Crewe Goods' No. 159* Adjutant *some fifteen years after the tragic incident at Stafford but still essentially the same except that it has here a Webb chimney and is painted black; at the time of the accident it would have had either its original chimney or one with a Ramsbottom castellated cap, and been painted green with black lining. From 21st December 1858 to 5th April 1859* Adjutant *ran 11,313 miles on coal and goods trains to Rugby, iron ore trains to Bushbury and Bescot, and goods trains to Birmingham.*

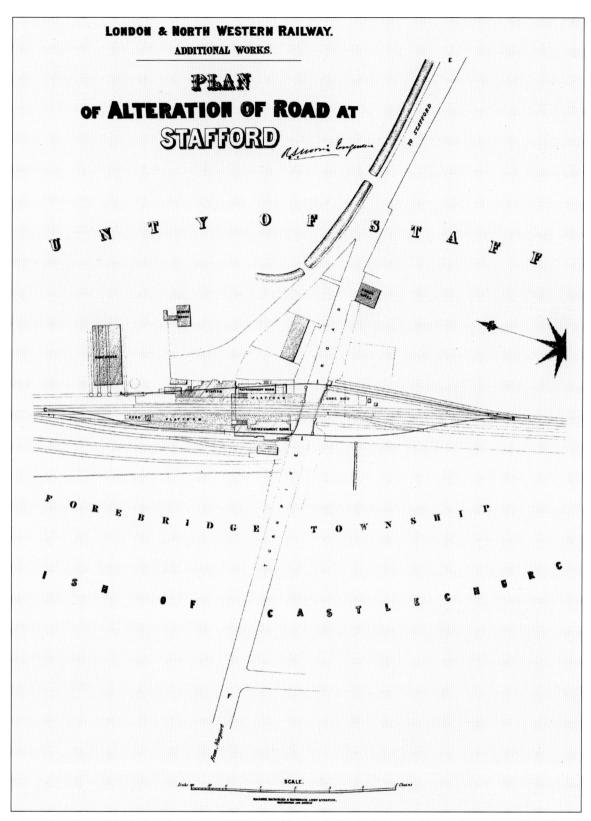

Figure 6: *Plan of Stafford station about 1860, signed by R. S. Norris, Engineer. This is the station which Thomas Baron worked through regularly and must have known well, and where his mate was killed in March 1859. Unfortunately, the plan does not show the junction with the line to Shrewsbury or the engine shed on the down side north of the station, as it was prepared to show alterations to the roads to the south of the station, the Newport Road, which crosses the station at the south end, and Station Road, the approach road to the station off the Newport Road, in readiness for the new much larger station built in 1864. In the rebuilding of the mid 1960s, which created the present-day station, Station Road, which curves gently away from Newport Road in this plan, was altered to run parallel to the station and form a T-junction with Newport Road, and the cottages by the bridge were demolished*

47

Plate 25: *Stafford railway station in the 1850s, the entrance and buildings on the up side facing the town. Newport Road bridge is on the left.*

Plate 26: *Stafford railway station in the 1850s; the buildings on the down platform as seen from Newport Road bridge. The two tracks passed between the two buildings..*

Plate 27: *Scene at Curzon Street station, Birmingham, about 1859, at the time when Thomas Baron was working into Birmingham regularly. The engine is a Jones & Potts 4-2-0, ordered for the Chester & Holyhead Railway in 1847 but delivered new to the LNWR Southern Division in 1848 as No. 189. The London & Birmingham part of the station is on the left of the picture, with the Derby and Gloucester bays on the right and the former Grand Junction station beyond. Passenger facilities at Curzon Street had been transferred to New Street in 1854. Driver Bowker is on the footplate.*

Plate 28, opposite: *View of Sutton Coldfield in 1863, with a suburban train to Birmingham standing in the platform. The engine is McConnell 'M' class 0-4-2 tank No. 734, which was built at Wolverton in May 1862, shortly after the abolition of separate divisional responsibility for locomotive matters. It therefore never received a Southern Division number, which would have been 134, since 600 was added to the SD numbers in the unified numbering scheme. It is in original condition and is painted in the green livery with black lining which became standard for the whole company in 1862. This is the only known rear view of one of these engines and indeed the only known good view of a tank engine in this livery, and so is evidence that painted numbers were displayed on the rear of tank engines. On the engine's weatherboard is a shedplate '10' (Monument Lane, later Aston); this system of shed plates began in January 1863. The lamp is placed in a socket attached to a bracket which seems to have been added as an afterthought, using the upper two bolts of the buffer. Another socket of the same type, tapering inwards towards the bottom, like those used on stage coaches, is fitted in the middle of the rear of the coal bunker, above the toolboxes running the full width of the engine. The first six four-wheel carriages are close-coupled into a permanent set. The four middle carriages of the set are 1st/2nd compos, with louvre ventilators over each door. They have waist panels and are possibly the first carriages built with the 'traditional' style of LNWR panelling. At either end are brake thirds, which are unusual in having only one window between two doors, and so must have had half partitions. All the carriages have continuous lower footboards with short upper steps under each door, normal for the period, and all have destination boards positioned centrally just above window level. At the rear of the set is another four-wheeler of much older design.*

The signal was supplied by Stevens & Sons and is probably painted white, the base being red oxide. The arm has no stripe and works in a slot in the post. It is hand-operated by the quadrant, which has three holes allowing the arm to be pegged in one of three positions, at 90°, 45° and 0° degrees (vertical inside the slot) to the post. The spectacle has two glasses, one red and one green, to denote stop (90°) and caution (45°) respectively. In the third position (arm vertical inside the post) the spectacle moves clear of the lamp to show a white light, indicating 'all right'. The three-position signals were found all over the LNWR system in 'time-interval' signalling days. White glass for 'all right' was replaced by green from 1894, though green had already been in use for some years at junctions.

The wooden station seat on the right with curved ironwork is similar to the standard LNWR type developed later and still found on some BR stations in 1980. Both the enginemen are in light-coloured clothing, perhaps white, but the guard, standing near the engine, already has a uniform with the typical LNWR wide belt and the familiar cap. The signalman's uniform is also familiar, except perhaps for the bow tie, while the platelayer has the waistcoat, neckerchief and broad-brimmed round-topped hat commonly worn by his trade at the time. Among the 'civilians', the top hat seems commonplace. All in all a fascinating glimpse of a railway scene in the 1860s.

Plate 29: *One of Wolverton's last new engines, a 'Mixed Traffic class N' built in September 1862. It is standing outside Monument Lane shed, which is off to the right under St Vincent Street bridge, with the Stour Valley line behind the engine. The date is 1863-9 and No. 601 is in as built condition, with injectors (the driver's left hand is on the wheel controlling the water supply, the injector itself being visible below the side-sheet on the side of the firebox) and other Ramsbottom modifications - castellated chimney top, smokebox front handrail, lamp sockets and cylinder lubricator. The engine was later rebuilt as a saddle tank and worked as a banker on Camden incline; it was scrapped in 1886.*

Date		Name of Engine	Name of Driver	Number of Miles	Remarks
1859					
June 22	Wed	*Stentor*	W. Leech	256	to Rugby, London Coal.
June 24	Fri	*Stentor*	W. Leech	256	to Rugby, London Coal.
June 26	Sun	*Stentor*	W. Leech	256	8.05am Goods to Rugby.
June 28	Tues	*Stentor*	W. Leech	256	8.05am Goods to Rugby.
June 30	Thurs	*Stentor*	W. Leech	256	8.05am Goods to Rugby.
July 1	Fri	*Cerberus*	T. Brindle	108	3.42 Express to Crewe.
July 4	Mon	*Ant*	J. Ireland	212	11.15pm Goods to Birmingham.
July 6	Wed	*Ant*	J. Ireland	212	11.15pm Goods to Birmingham.
July 11	Mon	*Mersey*	R. Mort	144	6.30 & 12.20 to Liverpool passengers.
July 20	Wed	*Wasp*	J. Haughton	50	to Springs Branch.
July 28	Thurs	*Saddleback*	J. Helm	74	12.20 to Liverpool passengers.
Aug 1	Mon	*Cerberus*	T. Brindle	108	3.42 Express to Crewe.
Aug 2	Tues	*Cerberus*	T. Brindle	72	to Liverpool to attend Board.
Aug 7	Sun	*Admiral*	J. Evans	72	7.45am Goods to Liverpool.
Aug 13	Sat	*Herald*	T. Tyrer	120	to Manchester, Ballasting.
Aug 20	Sat	*Colossus*	T. Wittel	72	11.15 Goods to Liverpool.
Aug 31	Wed	*Cerberus*	W. Dent	108	3.42 Express to Crewe.
Sept 1	Thurs	*Cerberus*	W. Dent	108	3.42 Express to Crewe.
Sept 2	Fri	*Cerberus*	W. Dent	108	3.42 Express to Crewe.
Sept 3	Sat	*Cerberus*	W. Dent	108	3.42 Express to Crewe.
Sept 4	Sun	*Cerberus*	W. Dent	108	3.42 Express to Crewe.
Sept 5	Mon	*Vulture*	W. Tompson	144	6.30 & 12.20 to Liverpool passengers.
Sept 7	Wed	*Hardwicke*	J. Octleston	108	from Repairs at Crewe.
Sept 8	Thurs	*Fly*	R. Kirkham	72	7.45am Goods to Liverpool.
Sept 8	Thurs	*Fly*	R. Kirkham	72	7.40pm Goods to Liverpool.
Sept 10	Sat	*Vulture*	W. Tompson	144	6.30 & 12.20 to Liverpool passengers.
Sept 13	Tues	*Admiral*	J. Jackson	72	7.45am Goods to Liverpool.
Sept 13	Tues	*Clarendon*	J. Jackson	72	7.40pm Goods to Liverpool.
Sept 14	Wed	*Clarendon*	J. Jackson	72	7.40pm Goods to Liverpool.
Sept 15	Thurs	*Adjutant*	W. Melling	212	7.30pm to Bescot Junction.
Sept 19	Mon	*Ingestre*	J. Waterworth	148	6.30 & 12.20 to Liverpool passengers.
Sept 20	Tues	*Ingestre*	J. Waterworth	116	
Sept 21	Wed	*Mersey*	R. Mort	148	to Warrington & Liverpool passengers.
Sept 22	Thurs	*Mersey*	R. Mort	72	8.00am to Liverpool, passengers.
Sept 23	Fri	*Mersey*	R. Mort	148	9.00 & 3.15 to Liverpool, passengers.
Sept 25	Sun	*Mersey*	R. Mort	72	8.00am to Liverpool, Sunday, passengers.
Sept 26	Mon	*Mersey*	R. Mort	72	8.00am to Liverpool, passengers.
Sept 27	Tues	*Mersey*	R. Mort	148	9.00 & 3.15 to Liverpool, passengers.
Sept 29	Thurs	*Mersey*	R. Mort	116	3.44 & 9.55 to Warrington, passengers.
Sept 30	Fri	*Mersey*	R. Mort	148	6.30 & 12.20 to Liverpool passengers.
Oct 1	Sat	*Mersey*	R. Mort	120	8.00am to Liverpool and Newton.
Oct 2	Sun	*Mersey*	R. Mort	116	3.44 & 2.00pm to Warrington, passengers.
Oct 3	Mon	*Mersey*	R. Mort	148	9.00 & 3.15 to Liverpool, passengers.
Oct 5	Wed	*Mersey*	R. Mort	116	3.44 & 9.55 to Warrington, passengers.
Oct 6	Thurs	*Mersey*	R. Mort	148	6.30 & 3.15 to Liverpool passengers.
Oct 7	Fri	*Mersey*	R. Mort	86	to Liverpool & Euxton.
Oct 8	Sat	*Mersey*	R. Mort	148	two trips to Liverpool, passengers.
Oct 10	Mon	*Mersey*	R. Mort	148	two trips to Liverpool, passengers.
Oct 11	Tues	*Mersey*	R. Mort	74	one trip to Liverpool, passengers.
Oct 12	Wed	*Mersey*	R. Mort	148	two trips to Liverpool, passengers.
Oct 14	Fri	*Mersey*	R. Mort	116	two trips to Warrington.
Oct 15	Sat	*Mersey*	R. Mort	120	one trip to Liverpool. Standing pilot for the Queen.
Oct 17	Mon	*Mersey*	R. Mort	116	two trips to Warrington.

15th Oct 1859. After completing a trip from Preston to Liverpool, Baron was 'standing pilot for the Queen', that is, acting as standby pilot engine for the Royal Train. The pilot engine ran 15 minutes in front of the Royal Train to ensure the line was safe for it to pass.

The Royal Train left Edinburgh on Saturday, 15th October at 9.00am amid vast crowds. According to *The Scotsman*, its route was Carlisle - Lancaster - Preston - Chester (arr 4.00pm), with arrival punctually 'as planned' at Bangor at 5.40pm, amid vast crowds. The party included Queen Victoria, Prince Albert, and four princes and princesses. On page 460 of *Railway Reminiscences*, G. P. Neele confirms the arrival and departure times, and adds the arrival time at Carlisle, 11.45am, and a half-hour stop at Lancaster for lunch.

Neele is wrong, however, in giving the date of the journey as 22nd October 1859. He is a week late.

Engine classes

Adjutant, Admiral, Ant, Clarendon, Colossus, Fly, Hardwicke, Herald, Salopian - all 'Crewe Goods' 2-4-0s. *Cerberus* - 7ft 'Crewe Passenger' 2-2-2. *Ingestre, Mersey, Saddleback, Vulture* - 6ft 'Crewe Passenger' 2-2-2s.

Engine mileage

In January *Adjutant* ran 3167 miles in 14 trips, in February 3108 miles in 11 trips and in March 2902 miles in 12 days. It was still running to Bescot, the turn it was on when Baron's mate was killed, in September. In May *Stentor* ran 3284 miles in 13 days and in June 3241 miles in 14 days. In October *Mersey* ran 2844 miles in 24 days.

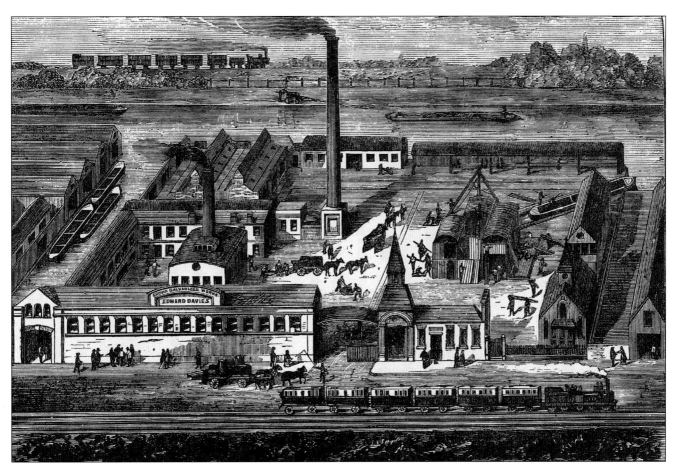

Plate 30: *Edward Davies's Crown Galvanising Works was situated north of Wolverhampton High Level station. This view is from the west, with the Great Western line in the foreground, and the Wolverhampton lock flight of the Birmingham Canal Navigation and the LNWR Stour Valley line beyond the galvanising works.* From Griffiths Guide to the Iron Trade

Date		Name of Engine	Name of Driver	Number of Miles	Remarks
1859					
Oct 18	Tues	*Mersey*	R. Mort	148	two trips to Liverpool.
Oct 19	Wed	*Mersey*	R. Mort	74	one trip to Liverpool.
Oct 20	Thurs	*Mersey*	R. Mort	148	two trips to Liverpool.
Oct 22	Sat	*Mersey*	R. Mort	116	two trips to Warrington.
Oct 23	Sun	*Mersey*	R. Mort	58	10.30 Night Mail to Warrington.
Oct 24	Mon	*Mersey*	R. Mort	116	two trips to Warrington.
Oct 25	Tues	*Mersey*	R. Mort	116	two trips to Warrington.
Oct 26	Wed	*Mersey*	R. Mort	116	two trips to Warrington.
Oct 27	Thurs	*Mersey*	R. Mort	116	two trips to Warrington.
Oct 28	Fri	*Mersey*	R. Mort	116	two trips to Warrington.
Oct 29	Sat	*Mersey*	R. Mort	116	two trips to Warrington, Saturday.
Nov 1	Tues	*Mersey*	R. Mort	116	two trips to Warrington.
Nov 2	Wed	*Mersey*	R. Mort	148	two trips to Liverpool.
Nov 3	Thurs	*Mersey*	R. Mort	144	to Whitmore and Manchester.
Nov 4	Fri	*Mersey*	R. Mort	148	two trips to Liverpool.
Nov 5	Sat	*Cerberus*	W. Dent	108	one trip to Crewe, Mail.
Nov 6	Sun	*Mersey*	R. Mort	74	one trip to Liverpool, Sunday.
Nov 7	Mon	*Loadstone*	E. Wane	80	Wigan Bank on Days.
Nov 8	Tues	*Loadstone*	E. Wane	80	Wigan Bank on Days.
Nov 9	Wed	*Loadstone*	E. Wane	80	Wigan Bank on Days.
Nov 10	Thurs	*Loadstone*	C. Gregory	80	Wigan Bank on Days.
Nov 11	Fri	*Loadstone*	C. Gregory	80	Wigan Bank on Days.
Nov 12	Sat	*Loadstone*	C. Gregory	80	Wigan Bank on Days.
Nov 14	Mon	*Loadstone*	C. Gregory	80	Wigan Bank on Nights.
Nov 15	Tues	*Loadstone*	C. Gregory	80	Wigan Bank on Nights.
Nov 16	Wed	*Loadstone*	C. Gregory	80	Wigan Bank on Nights.
Nov 17	Thurs	*Loadstone*	S. Leakin	80	Wigan Bank on Nights.
Nov 18	Fri	*Loadstone*	J. Elm	80	Wigan Bank on Nights.
Nov 19	Sat	*Loadstone*	J. Elm	80	Wigan Bank on Nights.
Nov 21	Mon	*Loadstone*	J. Elm	80	Wigan Bank on Days, Monday.
Nov 22	Tues	*Admiral*	J. Elm	80	Wigan Bank on Days.
Nov 23	Wed	*Admiral*	J. Elm	80	Wigan Bank on Days.
Nov 24	Thurs	*Admiral*	C. Gregory	80	Wigan Bank on Days.
Nov 25	Fri	*Admiral*	C. Gregory	80	Wigan Bank on Days.
Nov 26	Sat	*Admiral*	C. Gregory	80	Wigan Bank on Days.
Nov 29	Tues	*Loadstone*	C. Gregory	80	Wigan Bank on Nights, Monday. [28-29 November]
Nov 30	Wed	*Loadstone*	C. Gregory	80	Wigan Bank on Nights. [29-30 November]
Nov 31		*Loadstone*	C. Gregory	80	Wigan Bank on Nights. [31 November - no such date!]
Dec 1	Thurs	*Loadstone*	C. Gregory	80	Wigan Bank on Nights.
Dec 2	Fri	*Loadstone*	C. Gregory	80	Banking at Wigan, night Friday.
Dec 3	Sat	*Loadstone*	C. Gregory	80	Banking at Wigan, night.
Dec 5	Mon	*Loadstone*	C. Gregory	80	Banking at Wigan, days, Monday.
Dec 6	Tues	*Loadstone*	C. Gregory	80	Banking at Wigan, day.
Dec 7	Wed	*Loadstone*	C. Gregory	80	Banking at Wigan, day.
Dec 8	Thurs	*Loadstone*	C. Gregory	80	Banking at Wigan, day.
Dec 9	Fri	*Loadstone*	C. Gregory	80	Banking at Wigan, day.
Dec 10	Sat	*Loadstone*	C. Gregory	80	Banking at Wigan, day.
Dec 12	Mon	*Loadstone*	C. Gregory	80	Banking at Wigan, night.
Dec 13	Tues	*Loadstone*	C. Gregory	80	Banking at Wigan, night.
Dec 14	Wed	*Loadstone*	C. Gregory	80	Banking at Wigan, night.
Dec 15	Thurs	*Commodore*	C. Gregory	80	Banking at Wigan, night.
Dec 17	Sat	*Fly*	J. Waterworth	40	to Wigan & Warrington.

Engine classes: *Admiral, Fly, Loadstone* - all 'Crewe Goods' 2-4-0s. *Cerberus* - 7ft 'Crewe Passenger' 2-2-2. *Mersey* - 6ft 'Crewe Passenger' 2-2-2.

Plate 31: *LNWR Southern Division No. 35 at Market Harborough with an up train to Rugby or Northampton in 1857-60. The engine is a 'Sharpie' or 'Sharp Single' 2-2-2, built by Sharp Brothers in 1847. There appears to be a flag attached to the engine's safety valve which might suggest that the date is February 1859 when passenger trains first ran from Market Harborough to Northampton.*

Plate 32: *LNWR Sharp 2-2-2 saddle tank No. 316 at Hinckley on the Nuneaton-Leicester line about 1868. It was built originally as a 2-2-2 tender engine in the 1850s and obtained by the Birkenhead, Lancashire & Cheshire Junction Railway, on which it was No. 21; it was acquired by the LNWR in November 1860, worked on the Cromford & High Peak line for a short time only and was eventually rebuilt as a tank engine in April 1868; as it is in ex works condition, that might well be the date of the photograph. According to Alfred Rosling Bennett in* The Chronicles of Boulton's Siding, *the passenger service on the branch was worked wholly by Sharp 2-2-2 saddle tanks for 'a good portion of the 1870s'.*

Date		Name of Engine	Name of Driver	Number of Miles	Remarks
1859					
Dec 19	Mon	*Commodore*	J. Waterworth	80	Coaling for Moss Hall.
Dec 21	Wed	*Commodore*	J. Waterworth	80	Coaling for Moss Hall.
Dec 22	Thurs	*Mercury*	T. Brindle	108	to Crewe, Express.
Dec 23	Fri	*Cerberus*	T. Brindle	108	to Crewe, Express.
Dec 24	Sat	*Cerberus*	T. Brindle	108	to Crewe, Express .
Dec 25	Sun	*Cerberus*	T. Brindle	108	to Crewe, Express .
Dec 26	Mon	*Cerberus*	T. Brindle	108	to Crewe, Express, Monday.
Dec 27	Tues	*Ixion*	W. Netherland	80	Banking & to Wigan.
Dec 28	Wed	*Ixion*	W. Netherland	72	to Liverpool.
Dec 29	Thurs	*Commodore*	J. Waterworth	110	Coaling to Wigan.
Dec 30	Fri	*Clarendon*	J. Waterworth	256	to Rugby, Cattle.
1860					
Jany 2	Mon	*Commodore*	J. Waterworth	70	Coaling for Smith's, Wigan.
Jany 3	Tues	*Commodore*	J. Waterworth	70	Coaling for Smith's, Wigan.
Jany 4	Wed	*Commodore*	J. Waterworth	70	Coaling for Smith's, Wigan.
Jany 5	Thurs	*Commodore*	J. Waterworth	70	Coaling for Smith's, Wigan.
Jany 6	Fri	*Commodore*	J. Waterworth	70	Coaling for Smith's, Wigan.
Jany 7	Sat	*Cadmus*	J. Evans	123	to Liverpool & Manchester.
Jany 9	Mon	*Commodore*	J. Waterworth	80	Coaling for Pearson's.
Jany 10	Tues	*Commodore*	J. Waterworth	80	Coaling for Pearson's.
Jany 11	Wed	*Commodore*	J. Waterworth	80	Coaling for Pearson's.
Jany 18	Wed	*Commodore*	J. Waterworth	72	to Liverpool.
Jany 19	Thurs	*Commodore*	J. Waterworth	80	Coaling for Moss Hall.
Jany 20	Fri	*Commodore*	J. Waterworth	80	Coaling for Moss Hall, Friday.
Jany 21	Sat	*Commodore*	J. Waterworth	80	Coaling for Moss Hall.
Jany 23	Mon	*Commodore*	J. Waterworth	112	Coaling for Moss Hall.
Jany 24	Tues	*Commodore*	J. Waterworth	80	Coaling for Moss Hall.
Jany 25	Wed	*Commodore*	J. Waterworth	112	Coaling for Moss Hall.
Jany 27	Fri	*Commodore*	J. Waterworth	110	Coaling for Brin Hall.
Jany 28	Sat	*Commodore*	J. Waterworth	110	Coaling for Brin Hall.
Jany 30	Mon	*Commodore*	J. Waterworth	110	Coaling for Brin Hall.
Jany 31	Tues	*Commodore*	J. Waterworth	110	Coaling for Brin Hall.
Feby 1	Wed	*Commodore*	J. Waterworth	110	Coaling for Brin Hall.
Feby 2	Thurs	*Commodore*	J. Waterworth	110	Coaling for Brin Hall.
Feby 4	Sat	*Commodore*	J. Waterworth	70	Coaling for Smith's.
Feby 6	Mon	*Commodore*	J. Waterworth	70	Coaling for Smith's.
Feby 7	Tues	*Commodore*	J. Waterworth	70	Coaling for Smith's, Wigan.
Feby 8	Wed	*Commodore*	J. Waterworth	70	Coaling for Smith's, Wigan.
Feby 9	Thurs	*Commodore*	J. Waterworth	70	Coaling for Smith's, Wigan.
Feby 10	Fri	*Commodore*	J. Waterworth	70	Coaling for Smith's, Saturday. [a mistake by Baron?
Feby 10	Fri	*Commodore*	J. Waterworth	72	to Liverpool. Saturday was 11th.]
Feby 13	Mon	*Commodore*	J. Waterworth	72	to Liverpool.
Feby 14	Tues	*Commodore*	J. Waterworth	80	Coaling for Pearson's, Wigan.
Feby 15	Wed	*Commodore*	J. Waterworth	80	Coaling for Pearson's, Wigan.
Feby 16	Thurs	*Commodore*	J. Waterworth	80	Coaling for Pearson's, Wigan.
Feby 17	Fri	*Commodore*	J. Waterworth	80	Coaling for Pearson's, Wigan.
Feby 18	Sat	*Commodore*	J. Waterworth	80	Coaling for Pearson's, Wigan.
Feby 20	Mon	*Commodore*	J. Waterworth	80	Coaling for Pearson's, Wigan.
Feby 22	Wed	*Commodore*	J. Waterworth	72	to Liverpool, Goods.
Feby 23	Thurs	*Commodore*	J. Waterworth	80	Coaling for Moss Hall, Wigan.
Feby 24	Fri	*Commodore*	J. Waterworth	130	Coaling for Moss Hall, Wigan.
Feby 25	Sat	*Commodore*	J. Waterworth	80	Coaling for Moss Hall, Wigan.

Engine classes: *Cadmus, Clarendon, Commodore, Ixion* - 'Crewe Goods' 2-4-0s. *Cerberus, Mercury* - 7ft 'Crewe Passenger' 2-2-2s   **Engine mileage:** *Commodore* ran 1860 miles in January and 1898 miles in February 1860.

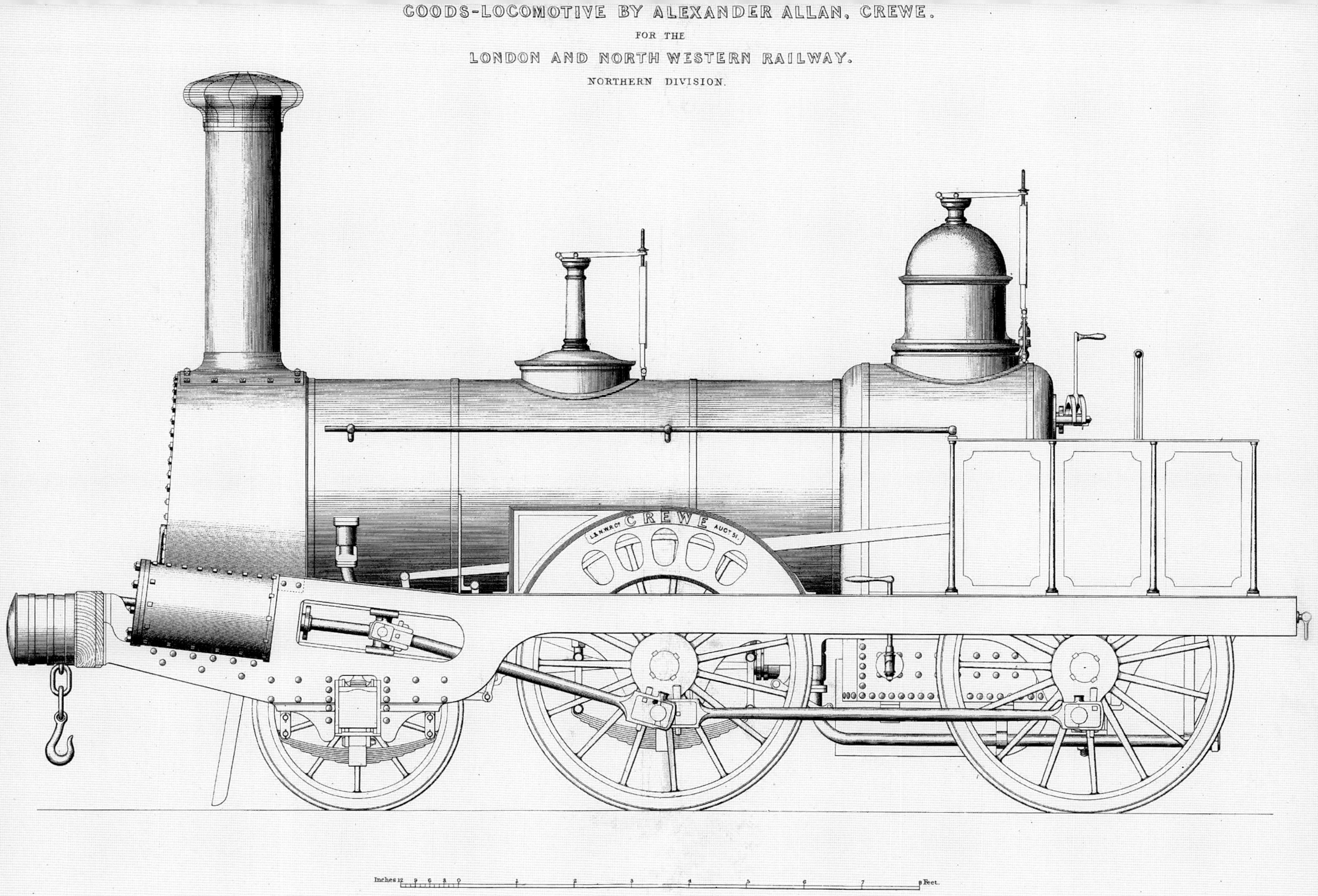

GOODS-LOCOMOTIVE BY ALEXANDER ALLAN, CREWE.

FOR THE

LONDON AND NORTH WESTERN RAILWAY.

NORTHERN DIVISION.

CREWE
AUG 51

Figure 7: *Drawing of 'Goods-Locomotive by Alexander Allan, Crewe, for the London & North Western Railway, Northern Division'. The drawing shows a 'Small Firebox Crewe Goods'; whereas Crewe was actually a 'Large Firebox' engine. See The Crewe Type in the Profile series, page 59. From Railway Machinery by D. K. Clark*

Date	Name of Engine	Name of Driver	Number of Miles	Remarks
1860				
Feby 27 Mon	Commodore	J. Waterworth	112	Coaling for Moss Hall, Wigan.
Feby 28 Tues	Commodore	J. Waterworth	80	Coaling for Moss Hall, Wigan.
Feby 29 Wed	Commodore	J. Waterworth	80	Coaling for Moss Hall, Wigan.
Mch 2 Fri	Commodore	J. Waterworth	100	Coaling for Brin Hall, Wigan.
Mch 3 Sat	Commodore	J. Waterworth	110	Coaling for Brin Hall, Wigan.
Mch 5 Mon	Commodore	J. Waterworth	110	Coaling for Brin Hall, Wigan.
Mch 6 Tues	Commodore	J. Waterworth	110	Coaling from Wigan.
Mch 7 Wed	Commodore	J. Waterworth	110	Coaling from Wigan.
Mch 8 Thurs	Commodore	J. Waterworth	110	Coaling from Wigan.
Mch 9 Fri	Vampire	T. Wittle	110	Coaling from Wigan.
Mch 10 Sat	Commodore	J. Waterworth	80	Coaling from Wigan.
Mch 12 Mon	Cadmus	J. Tortington	178	to Wigan & Stafford.
Mch 15 Thurs	Chillington	J. Tortington	181	to Bushbury.
Mch 16 Fri	Chillington	J. Tortington	190	to Stafford.
Mch 19 Mon	Chillington	J. Tortington	35	to Wigan.
Mch 20 Tues	Chillington	J. Tortington	70	Coaling from Wigan.
Mch 21 Wed	Chillington	J. Tortington	70	Coaling from Wigan, Wednesday.
Mch 22 Thurs	Chillington	J. Tortington	70	Coaling from Wigan.
Mch 23 Fri	Chillington	J. Tortington	70	Coaling from Wigan.
Mch 24 Sat	Chillington	J. Tortington	70	Coaling from Wigan.
Mch 26 Mon	Chillington	J. Helm	70	Coaling from Wigan.
Mch 27 Tues	Chillington	J. Helm	228	Coaling from Wigan & Stafford.
Mch 29 Thurs	Chillington	J. Tortington	70	Coaling from Wigan.
Mch 31 Sat	Caradoc	J. Tortington	148	two trips to Liverpool.
Apl 2 Mon	Fly	E. Wane	80	Wigan Bank, Night.
Apl 3 Tues	Fly	E. Wane	80	Wigan Bank, Night.
Apl 4 Wed	Fly	E. Wane	80	Wigan Bank, Night.
Apl 5 Thurs	Fly	E. Wane	80	Wigan Bank, Night.
Apl 6 Fri	Caradoc	E. Wane	80	Wigan Bank, Night.
Apl 7 Sat	Caradoc	E. Wane	80	Wigan Bank, Night.
Apl 9 Mon	Liver	E. Wane	80	Wigan Bank, Day.
Apl 10 Tues	Liver	E. Wane	80	Wigan Bank, Day.
Apl 11 Wed	Ixion	E. Wane	80	Wigan Bank, Day.
Apl 12 Thurs	Ixion	E. Wane	80	Wigan Bank, Day.
Apl 13 Fri	Ixion	E. Wane	80	Wigan Bank, Day.
Apl 14 Sat	Ixion	E. Wane	80	Wigan Bank, Day.
Apl 16 Mon	Loadstone	E. Wane	80	Wigan Bank, Night.
Apl 17 Tues	Loadstone	E. Wane	80	Wigan Bank, Night.
Apl 18 Wed	Loadstone	E. Wane	80	Wigan Bank, Night.
Apl 19 Thurs	Loadstone	E. Wane	80	Wigan Bank, Night.
Apl 20 Fri	Loadstone	E. Wane	80	Wigan Bank, Night.
Apl 21 Sat	Loadstone	E. Wane	80	Wigan Bank, Night.
Apl 23 Mon	Loadstone	E. Wane	80	Wigan Bank, Day.
Apl 24 Tues	Loadstone	E. Wane	80	Wigan Bank, Day.
Apl 25 Wed	Loadstone	E. Wane	80	Wigan Bank, Day.
Apl 26 Thurs	Loadstone	E. Wane	80	Wigan Bank, Day.
Apl 27 Fri	Loadstone	E. Wane	80	Wigan Bank, Day.
Apl 28 Sat	Loadstone	E. Wane	80	Wigan Bank, Day.
Apl 30 Mon	Loadstone	E. Wane	80	Wigan Bank, Night.
May 1 Tues	Loadstone	E. Wane	80	Wigan Bank, Night.
May 2 Wed	Loadstone	E. Wane	80	Wigan Bank, Night.
May 3 Thurs	Loadstone	E. Wane	80	Wigan Bank, Night.

Engine classes: Cadmus, Caradoc, Chillington, Commodore, Fly, Ixion, Liver, Loadstone, Vampire - all 'Crewe Goods' 2-4-0s.

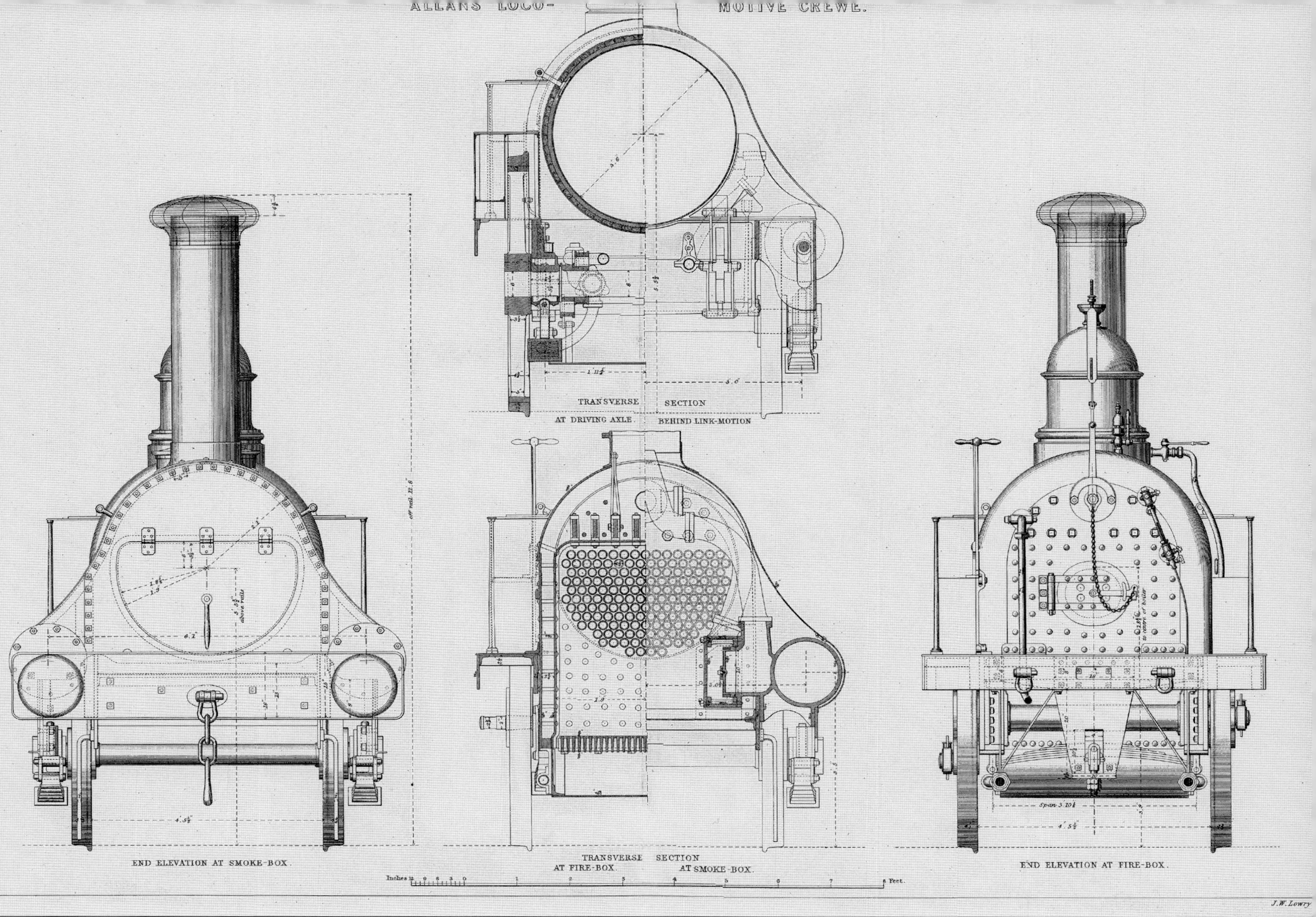
ALLANS LOCO-
MOTIVE CREWE.
TRANSVERSE SECTION
AT DRIVING AXLE.
BEHIND LINK-MOTION
END ELEVATION AT SMOKE-BOX.
TRANSVERSE SECTION
AT FIRE-BOX.
AT SMOKE-BOX.
END ELEVATION AT FIRE-BOX.
Inches
Feet.
J.W. Lowry

Figure 8: *Transverse sections of 'Goods-Locomotive'* Crewe. From *Railway Machinery* by D. K. Clark

Date		Name of Engine	Name of Driver	Number of Miles	Remarks
1860					
May 4	Fri	Loadstone	E. Wane	80	Wigan Bank, Night.
May 5	Sat	Loadstone	E. Wane	80	Wigan Bank, Night, Saturday.
May 7	Mon	Herald	E. Wane	80	Wigan Bank, Day.
May 8	Tues	Herald	E. Wane	80	Wigan Bank, Day.
May 9	Wed	Herald	E. Wane	80	Wigan Bank, Day.
May 10	Thurs	Herald	E. Wane	80	Wigan Bank, Day.
May 11	Fri	Herald	E. Wane	80	Wigan Bank, Day.
May 12	Sat	Herald	E. Wane	80	Wigan Bank, Day.
May 14	Mon	Loadstone	J. Waterworth	80	Wigan Bank, Night.
May 15	Tues	Loadstone	J. Waterworth	80	Wigan Bank, Night.
May 16	Wed	Loadstone	J. Waterworth	80	Wigan Bank, Night.
May 17	Thurs	Loadstone	J. Waterworth	80	Wigan Bank, Night.
May 18	Fri	Loadstone	J. Waterworth	80	Wigan Bank, Night.
May 19	Sat	Loadstone	J. Waterworth	80	Wigan Bank, Night.
May 21	Mon	Loadstone	J. Waterworth	80	Wigan Bank, Day.
May 22	Tues	Loadstone	J. Waterworth	80	Wigan Bank, Day.
May 23	Wed	Loadstone	J. Waterworth	80	Wigan Bank, Day.
May 24	Thurs	Loadstone	J. Waterworth	80	Wigan Bank, Day.
May 25	Fri	Loadstone	J. Waterworth	80	Wigan Bank, Day.
May 26	Sat	Loadstone	J. Waterworth	80	Wigan Bank, Day.
May 28	Mon	Loadstone	J. Waterworth	80	Wigan Bank, Night.
May 29	Tues	Loadstone	J. Waterworth	80	Wigan Bank, Night.
May 30	Wed	Loadstone	J. Waterworth	80	Wigan Bank, Night.
May 31	Thurs	Loadstone	J. Waterworth	80	Wigan Bank, Night.
June 1	Fri	Loadstone	J. Waterworth	80	Wigan Bank, Night.
June 2	Sat	Loadstone	J. Waterworth	80	Wigan Bank, Night.
June 4	Mon	Loadstone	J. Waterworth	80	Wigan Bank, Day, Monday.
June 5	Tues	Loadstone	J. Waterworth	80	Wigan Bank, Day.
June 6	Wed	Loadstone	J. Waterworth	80	Wigan Bank, Day.
June 7	Thurs	Loadstone	J. Waterworth	80	Wigan Bank, Day.
June 8	Fri	Loadstone	J. Waterworth	80	Wigan Bank, Day.
June 9	Sat	Loadstone	J. Waterworth	80	Wigan Bank, Day.
June 11	Mon	Loadstone	J. Waterworth	80	Wigan Bank, Night, Monday.
June 12	Tues	Loadstone	J. Waterworth	80	Wigan Bank, Night.
June 13	Wed	Loadstone	J. Waterworth	80	Wigan Bank, Night.
June 14	Thurs	Loadstone	J. Waterworth	80	Wigan Bank, Night.
June 15	Fri	Loadstone	J. Waterworth	80	Wigan Bank, Night.
June 16	Sat	Loadstone	J. Waterworth	80	Wigan Bank, Night.
June 18	Mon	Loadstone	J. Waterworth	80	Wigan Bank, Day, Monday.
June 19	Tues	Loadstone	J. Waterworth	80	Wigan Bank, Day.
June 20	Wed	Loadstone	J. Waterworth	80	Wigan Bank, Day.
June 21	Thurs	Loadstone	J. Waterworth	80	Wigan Bank, Day.
June 22	Fri	Loadstone	J. Waterworth	80	Wigan Bank, Day.
June 23	Sat	Loadstone	J. Waterworth	80	Wigan Bank, Day.
June 25	Mon	Loadstone	J. Waterworth	80	Wigan Bank, Night, Monday.
June 26	Tues	Loadstone	J. Waterworth	80	Wigan Bank, Night.
June 27	Wed	Loadstone	J. Waterworth	80	Wigan Bank, Night.
June 28	Thurs	Loadstone	J. Waterworth	80	Wigan Bank, Night.
June 29	Fri	Loadstone	J. Waterworth	80	Wigan Bank, Night.
June 30	Sat	Loadstone	J. Waterworth	80	Wigan Bank, Night.
July 2	Mon	Loadstone	J. Waterworth	80	Wigan Bank, Day, Monday.
July 3	Tues	Loadstone	J. Waterworth	80	Wigan Bank, Day.

Engine classes: Herald, Loadstone - 'Crewe Goods' 2-4-0. **Engine mileage:** Although not running a large mileage in total, because of the nature of the work, Loadstone was in use almost daily during June and July.

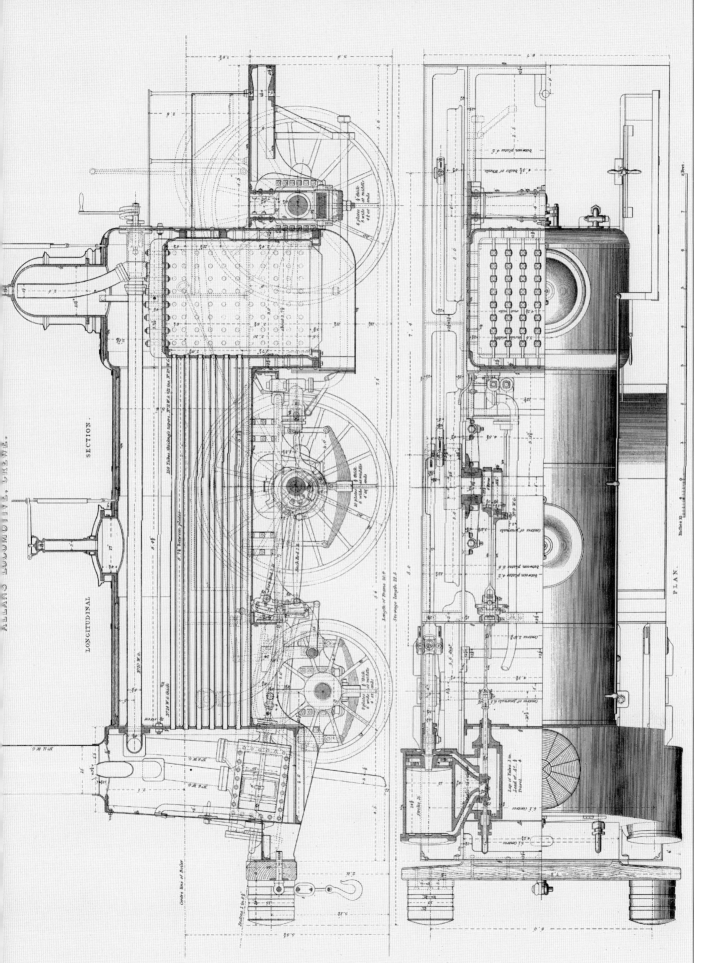

Figure 9: *Longitudinal section of 'Goods-Locomotive' Crewe.* From *Railway Machinery* by D. K. Clark

Date		Name of Engine	Name of Driver	Number of Miles	Remarks
1860					
July 4	Wed	*Loadstone*	J. Waterworth	80	Wigan Bank, Day.
July 5	Thurs	*Loadstone*	J. Waterworth	80	Wigan Bank, Day.
July 6	Fri	*Loadstone*	J. Waterworth	80	Wigan Bank, Day.
July 7	Sat	*Loadstone*	J. Waterworth	80	Wigan Bank, Day.
July 9	Mon	*Loadstone*	J. Waterworth	80	Wigan Bank, Night, Monday.
July 10	Tues	*Loadstone*	J. Waterworth	80	Wigan Bank, Night.
July 11	Wed	*Loadstone*	J. Waterworth	80	Wigan Bank, Night.
July 12	Thurs	*Loadstone*	J. Waterworth	80	Wigan Bank, Night.
July 13	Fri	*Loadstone*	J. Waterworth	80	Wigan Bank, Night.
July 14	Sat	*Loadstone*	J. Waterworth	80	Wigan Bank, Night.
July 16	Mon	*Loadstone*	J. Waterworth	80	Wigan Bank, Day, Monday.
July 17	Tues	*Loadstone*	J. Waterworth	80	Wigan Bank, Day.
July 18	Wed	*Loadstone*	J. Waterworth	80	Wigan Bank, Day.
July 19	Thurs	*Loadstone*	J. Waterworth	80	Wigan Bank, Day.
July 20	Fri	*Loadstone*	J. Waterworth	80	Wigan Bank, Day.
July 21	Sat	*Loadstone*	J. Waterworth	80	Wigan Bank, Day.
July 23	Mon	*Loadstone*	J. Waterworth	80	Wigan Bank, Night, Monday.
July 24	Tues	*Loadstone*	J. Waterworth	80	Wigan Bank, Night.
July 25	Wed	*Loadstone*	J. Waterworth	80	Wigan Bank, Night, Wednesday.
July 26	Thurs	*Loadstone*	J. Waterworth	80	Wigan Bank, Night.
July 27	Fri	*Loadstone*	J. Waterworth	80	Wigan Bank, Night.
July 28	Sat	*Loadstone*	J. Waterworth	80	Wigan Bank, Night.
July 30	Mon	*Loadstone*	J. Waterworth	80	Wigan Bank, Day, Monday.
July 31	Tues	*Loadstone*	J. Waterworth	80	Wigan Bank, Day.
Aug 1	Wed	*Loadstone*	J. Waterworth	80	Wigan Bank, Day.
Aug 2	Thurs	*Loadstone*	J. Waterworth	80	Wigan Bank, Day.
Aug 3	Fri	*Loadstone*	J. Waterworth	80	Wigan Bank, Day.
Aug 4	Sat	*Loadstone*	J. Waterworth	80	Wigan Bank, Day.
Aug 6	Mon	*Ingestre*	J. Waterworth	44	Express to Windermere all night.
Aug 7	Tues	*Ingestre*	J. Waterworth	102	to Warrington from Windermere.
Aug 8	Wed	*Ingestre*	J. Waterworth	148	two trips to Liverpool.
Aug 9	Thurs	*Ingestre*	J. Waterworth	148	two trips to Liverpool.
Aug 10	Fri	*Ingestre*	J. Waterworth	44	to Kendal all night.
Aug 11	Sat	*Ingestre*	J. Waterworth	102	to Warrington & home.
Aug 12	Sun	*Ingestre*	J. Waterworth	74	8.30am to Liverpool, Sunday.
Aug 13	Mon	*Ingestre*	J. Waterworth	148	two trips to Liverpool.
Aug 14	Tues	*Ingestre*	J. Waterworth	44	to Kendal all night, passenger.
Aug 15	Wed	*Ingestre*	J. Waterworth	102	to Warrington & home.
Aug 16	Thurs	*Ingestre*	J. Waterworth	148	two trips to Liverpool.
Aug 17	Fri	*Ingestre*	J. Waterworth	148	two trips to Liverpool.
Aug 18	Sat	*Dromedary*	J. Waterworth	44	to Kendal all night, Saturday.
Aug 19	Sun	*Dromedary*	J. Waterworth		at Kendal all night Sunday.
Aug 20	Mon	*Dromedary*	J. Waterworth	102	to Warrington & home, Monday.
Aug 21	Tues	*Dromedary*	J. Waterworth	148	two trips to Liverpool.
Aug 22	Wed	*Dromedary*	J. Waterworth	148	two trips to Liverpool.
Aug 23	Thurs	*Dromedary*	J. Waterworth	44	Shed & Kendal all night.
Aug 24	Fri	*Dromedary*	J. Waterworth	102	to Warrington & home.
Aug 25	Sat	*Dromedary*	J. Waterworth	148	two trips to Liverpool.
Aug 27	Mon	*Dromedary*	J. Waterworth	164	to Warrington & Windermere.
Aug 28	Tues	*Dromedary*	J. Waterworth	164	to Warrington & Windermere.
Aug 29	Wed	*Dromedary*	J. Waterworth	164	to Warrington & Windermere.
Aug 30	Thurs	*Dromedary*	J. Waterworth	164	to Warrington & Windermere.
Aug 31	Fri	*Dromedary*	J. Waterworth	164	to Warrington & Windermere.

Engine classes: *Loadstone* - 'Crewe Goods' 2-4-0. *Dromedary, Ingestre* - 6ft 'Crewe Passenger' 2-2-2s.

Plate 33: *Accident at Leek Wootton, near Kenilworth, Warwickshire, on Tuesday 11th June 1861. LNWR Southern Division 0-6-0 No. 282 was running tender-first on a train of empty coal wagons from Leamington to Victoria Colliery, Coventry, and reached the bridge over Leek Wootton crossroads about 7am. The transverse beams of the bridge had not been properly repaired and gave way under the 33-ton engine, which dropped 16ft to the road beneath, pulling the tender down with it. The footplatemen were buried under tons of falling coal and pinned against the firebox, where they burned to death. Both lived in lodgings in Warwick. The driver, George Rowley, came from Brockhall, near Weedon; the fireman, John Wade, was from Preston and about the same age as Thomas Baron, so they probably knew each other.*

Date		Name of Engine	Name of Driver	Number of Miles	Remarks
1860					
Sept 1	Sat	*Dromedary*	J. Waterworth	164	to Warrington & Windermere, Saturday.
Sept 3	Mon	*Dromedary*	J. Waterworth	148	two trips to Liverpool.
Sept 4	Tues	*Dromedary*	J. Waterworth	148	two trips to Liverpool.
Sept 5	Wed	*Ingestre*	J. Waterworth	44	Shed & Kendal all night.
Sept 6	Thurs	*Ingestre*	J. Waterworth	102	to Warrington & home.
Sept 7	Fri	*Ingestre*	J. Waterworth	148	two trips to Liverpool.
Sept 8	Sat	*Ingestre*	J. Waterworth	214	to Liverpool & Stafford.
Sept 9	Sun	*Ingestre*	J. Waterworth		at Wigan, Sunday.
Sept 10	Mon	*Ingestre*	J. Waterworth	44	Shed & Kendal all night.
Sept 11	Tues	*Ingestre*	J. Waterworth	102	to Warrington & home.
Sept 12	Wed	*Ingestre*	J. Waterworth	148	two trips to Liverpool.
Sept 13	Thurs	*Ingestre*	J. Waterworth	148	two trips to Liverpool.
Sept 14	Fri	*Ingestre*	J. Waterworth	44	Shed & Kendal all night.
Sept 15	Sat	*Ingestre*	J. Waterworth	102	to Warrington & home.
Sept 16	Sun	*Ingestre*	J. Waterworth	74	Sunday 8.30 to Liverpool.
Sept 17	Mon	*Ingestre*	J. Waterworth	148	two trips to Liverpool.
Sept 18	Tues	*Ingestre*	J. Waterworth	44	Shed & Kendal all night.
Sept 19	Wed	*Ingestre*	J. Waterworth	102	to Warrington & home.
Sept 20	Thurs	*Ingestre*	J. Waterworth	148	two trips to Liverpool.
Sept 21	Fri	*Ingestre*	J. Waterworth	148	two trips to Liverpool.
Sept 22	Sat	*Ingestre*	J. Waterworth	44	Shed & to Kendal.
Sept 23	Sun	*Ingestre*	J. Waterworth		to Kendal passenger Sunday.
Sept 24	Mon	*Ingestre*	J. Waterworth	102	to Warrington & home.
Sept 25	Tues	*Ingestre*	J. Waterworth	148	two trips to Liverpool.
Sept 26	Wed	*Ingestre*	J. Waterworth		at Morecambe & Lancaster, Pleasure.
Sept 27	Thurs	*Ingestre*	J. Waterworth	44	Shed & Kendal all night.
Sept 28	Fri	*Ingestre*	J. Waterworth	102	to Warrington & home.
Sept 29	Sat	*Ingestre*	J. Waterworth	148	two trips to Liverpool.
Oct 1	Mon	*Ingestre*	J. Waterworth	100	to Warrington & Lancaster.
Oct 2	Tues	*Ingestre*	J. Waterworth	100	to Warrington & Lancaster.
Oct 3	Wed	*Ingestre*	J. Waterworth	100	to Warrington & Lancaster.
Oct 4	Thurs	*Ingestre*	J. Waterworth	100	to Warrington & Lancaster.
Oct 5	Fri	*Ingestre*	J. Waterworth	100	to Warrington & Lancaster.
Oct 6	Sat	*Ingestre*	J. Waterworth	58	to Warrington.
Oct 8	Mon	*Ingestre*	J. Waterworth	148	two trips to Liverpool, Monday.
Oct 9	Tues	*Ingestre*	J. Waterworth	148	two trips to Liverpool.
Oct 10	Wed	*Ingestre*	J. Waterworth	44	Shed & Kendal all night.
Oct 11	Thurs	*Ingestre*	J. Waterworth	102	to Warrington & home.
Oct 12	Fri	*Ingestre*	J. Waterworth	148	two trips to Liverpool.
Oct 13	Sat	*Ingestre*	J. Waterworth	148	two trips to Liverpool.
Oct 15	Mon	*Ingestre*	J. Waterworth	44	Shed & Kendal all night.
Oct 16	Tues	*Ingestre*	J. Waterworth	102	to Warrington & home.
Oct 17	Wed	*Ingestre*	J. Waterworth	148	two trips to Liverpool.
Oct 18	Thurs	*Ingestre*	J. Waterworth	148	two trips to Liverpool.
Oct 19	Fri	*Ingestre*	J. Waterworth	44	Shed & Kendal all night.
Oct 20	Sat	*Ingestre*	J. Waterworth	102	to Warrington & home.
Oct 21	Sun	*Ingestre*	J. Waterworth	74	Sunday 8.30 to Liverpool.
Oct 22	Mon	*Ingestre*	J. Waterworth	148	two trips to Liverpool.
Oct 23	Tues	*Ingestre*	J. Waterworth	44	Shed & Kendal all night.
Oct 24	Wed	*Ingestre*	J. Waterworth	102	to Warrington & home.
Oct 25	Thurs	*Ingestre*	J. Waterworth	148	two trips to Liverpool.
Oct 26	Fri	*Ingestre*	J. Waterworth	148	two trips to Liverpool.
Oct 27	Sat	*Ingestre*	J. Waterworth	88	Shed & Kendal & home.
Oct 28	Sun	*Ingestre*	J. Waterworth	44	Sunday to Kendal.

Engine classes: *Dromedary, Ingestre* - 6ft 'Crewe Passenger' 2-2-2s.

Engine mileage: *Ingestre* ran the following mileages: October - 3078 in 29 days; November - 2613 in 20 days.

Plate 34: *Leek Wootton accident from the east. Engine No. 282 was built by William Fairbairn & Sons of Manchester, one of a batch ordered in January 1852 but not delivered until November 1854. The delay was mostly caused by the difficulty of making McConnell's patent firebox, which contained three longitudinal midfeathers and a combustion chamber, which was so long that the rear tubeplate of the boiler was under the centre of the dome. The engine was renumbered 882 in the unified LNWR series in April 1862, was rebuilt at Crewe in 1864 and was scrapped in 1879.*

Date		Name of Engine	Name of Driver	Number of Miles	Remarks
1860					
Oct 29	Mon	Ingestre	J. Waterworth	102	to Warrington & home.
Oct 30	Tues	Ingestre	J. Waterworth	148	two trips to Liverpool.
Oct 31	Wed	Ingestre	J. Waterworth	148	two trips to Liverpool.
Nov 1	Thurs				in shed all day.
Nov 2	Fri	Ingestre	J. Waterworth	148	two trips to Liverpool.
Nov 3	Sat	Ingestre	J. Waterworth	146	to Warrington & Kendal.
Nov 5	Mon	Ingestre	J. Waterworth	79	to Liverpool & Lancaster all night.
Nov 6	Tues	Ingestre	J. Waterworth	169	to Liverpool & home from Lancaster.
Nov 8	Thurs	Ingestre	J. Waterworth	148	two trips to Liverpool.
Nov 9	Fri	Ingestre	J. Waterworth	146	to Warrington & Kendal.
Nov 10	Sat	Ingestre	J. Waterworth	58	to Warrington.
Nov 12	Mon	Ingestre	J. Waterworth	188	two trips to Liverpool.
Nov 14	Wed	Ingestre	J. Waterworth	148	two trips to Liverpool, Wednesday.
Nov 15	Thurs	Ingestre	J. Waterworth	146	to Warrington & Kendal.
Nov 16	Fri	Ingestre	J. Waterworth	79	to Warrington & Lancaster.
Nov 17	Sat	Ingestre	J. Waterworth	169	to Liverpool & home.
Nov 20	Tues	Ingestre	J. Waterworth	148	two trips to Liverpool.
Nov 21	Wed	Ingestre	J. Waterworth	146	to Warrington & Kendal.
Nov 22	Thurs	Ingestre	J. Waterworth	79	to Warrington & Lancaster.
Nov 23	Fri	Banshee	J. Waterworth	169	to Liverpool & home.
Nov 25	Sun	Ingestre	J. Waterworth	74	Sunday 8.30 to Liverpool.
Nov 26	Mon	Ingestre	J. Waterworth	148	two trips to Liverpool.
Nov 27	Tues	Ingestre	J. Waterworth	146	to Warrington & Kendal.
Nov 28	Wed	Ingestre	J. Waterworth	79	to Warrington & Lancaster.
Nov 29	Thurs	Ingestre	J. Waterworth	169	to Liverpool & home.
Dec 1	Sat	Ingestre	J. Waterworth	148	two trips to Liverpool.
Dec 3	Mon	Ingestre	J. Waterworth	146	to Warrington & Kendal.
Dec 4	Tues	Ingestre	J. Waterworth	79	to Warrington & Lancaster.
Dec 5	Wed	Ingestre	J. Waterworth	169	to Liverpool & home.
Dec 7	Fri	Ingestre	J. Waterworth	148	two trips to Liverpool.
Dec 8	Sat	Ingestre	J. Waterworth	146	to Warrington & Kendal.
Dec 10	Mon	Ingestre	J. Waterworth	79	to Warrington & Lancaster, all night.
Dec 11	Tues	Ingestre	J. Waterworth	21	to Preston only.
Dec 12	Wed	Ingestre	J. Waterworth		Shed & burying child.
Dec 13	Thurs	Ingestre	J. Waterworth	148	two trips to Liverpool.
Dec 14	Fri	Ingestre	J. Waterworth	146	to Warrington & Kendal.
Dec 15	Sat	Ingestre	J. Waterworth	58	to Warrington only.
Dec 17	Mon	Ingestre	J. Waterworth	189	to Lancaster & Liverpool.
Dec 19	Wed	Bela	J. Waterworth	120	to Liverpool & Warrington Jct.
Dec 20	Thurs	Ingestre	J. Waterworth	146	to Warrington & Kendal.
Dec 21	Fri	Ingestre	J. Waterworth	79	to Warrington & Lancaster.
Dec 22	Sat	Ingestre	J. Waterworth	169	to Liverpool & Lancaster.
Dec 23	Sun	Ingestre	J. Waterworth		Sunday Standing Pilot.
Dec 24	Mon	Goldfinch	J. Ratliff	140	to Crewe Pilot.
Dec 26	Wed	Ingestre	J. Waterworth	146	to Warrington & Kendal.
Dec 27	Thurs	Ingestre	J. Waterworth	79	to Warrington & Lancaster.
Dec 28	Fri	Ingestre	J. Waterworth	169	to Liverpool.
Dec 29	Sat	Canning	J. Bell	180	to Stafford & Liverpool.
Dec 31	Mon	Ingestre	J. Waterworth	148	two trips to Liverpool.

Engine classes: Bela - 'Crewe Goods' 2-4-0; Canning, Ingestre - 6ft 'Crewe Passenger' 2-2-2; Goldfinch - 7ft 'Crewe Passenger' 2-2-2; Banshee, 'DX' class 0-6-0, the first to be recorded by Baron.

Plate 35: *LNWR Southern Division 0-6-0 No. 1850 at Bushbury in 1877 with Low Hill Hall in the distance, photographed by Richard Bleasdale. It was built as No. 275 by Fairbairn in July 1853, became 875 in April 1862, when 600 was added to the Southern Division numbers to create the LNWR unified list, and was rebuilt in 1864. It was put on the duplicate list as 1850 in June 1877 and was withdrawn a year later in June 1878; despite its imminent withdrawal, however, it seems in immaculate condition here. The four railwaymen in the picture seem to each have their own unique headgear; the driver in a homburg and the fireman a military cap. The man with his foot on the tender footstep is thought likely to be Wilson Worsdell, who was shed foreman at Bushbury from 1876 to October 1877. The same man appears in several of Bleasdale's 1877 pictures at Bushbury. The engine details are noteworthy: the clack valve is supplied by a pipe that is connected to a drive off the near-side cylinder piston rod.*

Date			Name of Engine	Name of Driver	Number of Miles	Remarks
1861						
Jany 1	Tue		Ingestre	J. Waterworth	146	to Warrington & Kendal, Tuesday.
Jany 2	Wed		Ingestre	J. Waterworth	79	to Warrington & Lancaster.
Jany 3	Thurs		Ingestre	J. Waterworth	169	to Liverpool & Lancaster.
Jany 5	Sat		Ingestre	J. Waterworth	148	two trips to Liverpool.
Jany 7	Mon		Ingestre	J. Waterworth	146	to Warrington & Kendal.
Jany 8	Tues		Ingestre	J. Waterworth	79	to Warrington & Lancaster.
Jany 9	Wed		Ingestre	J. Waterworth	169	to Liverpool & Lancaster.
Jany 11	Fri		Ingestre	J. Waterworth	148	two trips to Liverpool.
Jany 12	Sat		Ingestre	J. Waterworth	146	to Warrington & Kendal.
Jany 14	Mon		Ingestre	J. Waterworth	100	to Warrington & Lancaster, all night.
Jany 15	Tues		Ingestre	J. Waterworth	169	to Liverpool & Lancaster.
Jany 16	Wed		Colossus	T. Baron		Shunting Goods Yard.
Jany 17	Thurs		Ingestre	J. Waterworth	148	two trips to Liverpool.
Jany 18	Fri		Ingestre	J. Waterworth	146	to Warrington & Kendal.
Jany 19	Sat		Ingestre	J. Waterworth	58	to Warrington only.
Jany 21	Mon		Ingestre	J. Waterworth	189	to Lancaster & Liverpool.
Jany 23	Wed		Ingestre	J. Waterworth	148	two trips to Liverpool.
Jany 24	Thurs		Ingestre	J. Waterworth	146	to Warrington & Kendal.
Jany 25	Fri		Ingestre	R. Kirkham	100	to Warrington & Lancaster.
Jany 26	Sat		Ingestre	R. Kirkham	169	to Liverpool & Lancaster.
Jany 29	Tues		Ingestre	J. Waterworth	148	two trips to Liverpool.
Jany 30	Wed		Ingestre	J. Waterworth	146	to Warrington & Kendal.
Jany 31	Thurs		Ingestre	J. Waterworth	100	to Warrington & Lancaster.
Feby 1	Fri		Ingestre	J. Waterworth	169	from Lancaster, two trips to Liverpool.
Feby 2	Sat		Colossus	T. Baron		Shunting Goods Yard.
Feby 3	Sun		Saddleback	J. Waterworth	74	Sunday 8.30 to Liverpool.
Feby 4	Mon		Saddleback	J. Waterworth	148	two trips to Liverpool.
Feby 5	Tues		Saddleback	J. Waterworth	146	to Warrington & Kendal.
Feby 6	Wed		Saddleback	J. Waterworth	100	to Warrington & Lancaster all night.
Feby 7	Thurs		Saddleback	J. Waterworth	169	to Liverpool & home.
Feby 8	Fri		Colossus	T. Baron		Shunting Goods Yard.
Feby 9	Sat		Wennington	T. Baron		Shunting Goods Yard.
Feby 10	Sun		Clarendon	T. Baron	20	Shunting & Banking.
Feby 11	Mon		Saddleback	J. Waterworth	146	to Warrington & Kendal.
Feby 12	Tues		Saddleback	J. Waterworth	100	to Warrington & Lancaster.
Feby 13	Wed		Saddleback	J. Waterworth	169	from Lancaster, two trips to Liverpool.
1861						
Feby 14	Thurs		Clarendon	T. Baron	20	Turning & up Bank.
Feby 14			Clarendon	T. Baron		Turning all night.
Feby 16	Sat		Saddleback	J. Waterworth	146	to Warrington & Kendal.
Feby 18	Mon		Saddleback	J. Waterworth	100	to Warrington & Lancaster all night.
Feby 19	Tues		Saddleback	J. Waterworth	169	from Lancaster, two trips to Liverpool.
Feby 21	Thurs		Saddleback	J. Waterworth	148	two trips to Liverpool.
Feby 22	Fri		Newby	R. Clark	108	to Crewe, 4.0am Mineral.
Feby 23	Sat		Newby	R. Clark	108	to Crewe, 4.0am Mineral.
Feby 26	Tues		No. 450	W. Brown	158	to Stafford, London Goods.
Feby 27	Wed		No. 450	W. Brown	158	to Stafford, London Goods.
Feby 28	Thurs		Clarendon	W. Brown		Shunting, Thursday.
Mch 1	Fri		No. 450	W. Brown	158	to Stafford, London Goods.
Mch 2	Sat		No. 450	W. Brown	158	to Stafford, London Goods.

14th February. 'Turning all night'. Baron worked all night, turning engines, preparing them for the following day's work and arranging them in the best way for them to leave the shed in the correct order.

Engine classes: *Clarendon, Colossus* - 'Crewe Goods' 2-4-0s; *Saddleback, Tantalus* - 6ft 'Crewe Passenger' 2-2-2s; 450, 548 - 'DX' 0-6-0s. *Newby* - Rothwell 2-4-0 for the Lancaster & Carlisle Railway. *Wennington* - Passenger 2-2-2 by Fairbairn for Lancaster & Carlisle Railway.

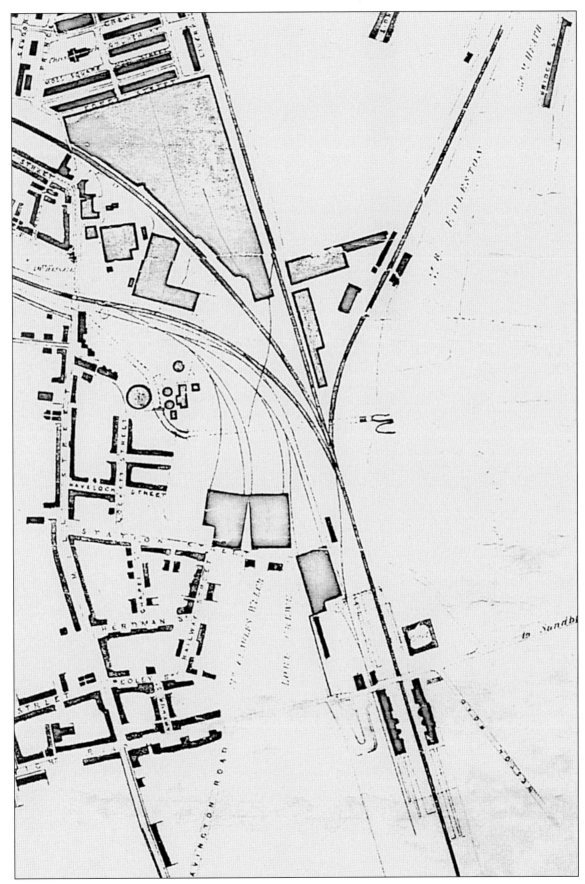

Figure 10: *Plan of Crewe North Junction with south at the bottom, of course, and north at the top. It is dated August 1868 and shows the new Chester line as completed.*

Plate 36: *View of Crewe North Junction looking south, taken from the roof of No. 1 Erecting Shop (known as No. 2 until May 1865) in 1866-7. The Manchester line curves away in the middle distance on the left, behind the signal box, the main line to Liverpool and the North, still only double track, of course, runs on the near side of the signal box and seems to be perfectly straight through the station, while the Chester line curves away just behind the engines in the right foreground. Work is going on to clear the ground for the construction of the Deviation, the new Chester line which was built to avoid Crewe Works, and was opened in 1868. So many workshops had been built on either side of the original Chester line, that Works traffic across the line between the various shops was so busy that it hindered the passage of trains along it. In the left distance the familiar outline of the Crewe Arms Hotel can be discerned, though the later extension at the front of the hotel on Nantwich Road was not added till 1880. The station is the second one to be built, while to the right of it are extensive engine sheds. Those immediately to the right must have been demolished as the station was expanded on the west side and finally made way for the goods lines and tunnels of the early 1900s. Old stone sleepers are piled up in the right foreground, doubtless removed in the ground-clearing work.*

There seems to be a hand-crane in the centre of the picture and more than enough assorted carriages to tantalise carriage enthusiasts to the left of it; similarly with the wagons on the right. The engines in the foreground are of two types only, 'Crewe' or 'Old Crewe' type 2-2-2s and 2-4-0s, with 'square' weather boards, and Ramsbottom 'DX' 0-6-0s with curved weather boards. The Trevithick 2-4-0 in the right foreground seems to be No. 327 Maberley, which was rebuilt at Crewe in October 1867 and perhaps dates the picture at Autumn 1867. In front of it is the only engine identifiable by its number, 'DX' No. 1068, which was built in 1863 and after four years would be ready for overhaul. Quite a lot of Crewe Goods 2-4-0s were rebuilt in September and December 1867, so this lovely collection of 'Old Crewe Types' could well be those engines.

On his trips between Stafford and Holyhead Thomas Baron would have seen this view from the footplate many times, and must have thought going south that there were only just another 24 miles to go, while in the other direction there were still 105¾ miles left. Nowadays the old concrete Crewe North Junction signal box, part of the Heritage Centre, stands somewhere beyond the engines in the foreground, in the vee of the main line to the north and the Chester line.

Date		Name of Engine	Name of Driver	Number of Miles	Remarks
1861					
Mch 5	Tues	*Newby*	W. Brown	108	to Crewe 4.0am Mineral.
Mch 6	Wed	*Newby*	W. Brown	108	to Crewe 4.0am Mineral.
Mch 7	Thurs	*Newby*	W. Brown	108	to Crewe 4.0am Mineral.
Mch 8	Fri	*Newby*	W. Brown	108	to Crewe 4.0am Mineral.
Mch 9	Sat	*Newby*	W. Brown	108	to Crewe 4.0am Mineral, Saturday.
Mch 11	Mon	No. 548	W. Brown	20	New engine to Coppull, trying her injectors.
Mch 12	Tues	No. 548	W. Brown	158	to Stafford, London Goods.
Mch 13	Wed	No. 548	W. Brown	158	to Stafford, London Goods.
Mch 14	Thurs	No. 548	W. Brown	158	to Stafford, London Goods.
Mch 15	Fri	No. 548	W. Brown	158	to Stafford, London Goods.
Mch 16	Sat	No. 548	W. Brown	158	to Stafford, London Goods.
Mch 18	Mon	No. 548	W. Brown	106	Shed & to Crewe, 7.30 Mineral.
Mch 20	Wed	No. 548	W. Brown	106	Shed & to Crewe, 7.30 Mineral.
Mch 21	Thurs	No. 548	W. Brown	106	Shed & to Crewe, 7.30 Mineral.
Mch 22	Fri	No. 548	W. Brown	106	Shed & to Crewe, 7.30 Mineral.
Mch 23	Sat	No. 548	W. Brown	158	to Stafford, London Goods.
Mch 26	Tues	No. 548	W. Brown	106	to Crewe, 4.0am Mineral.
Mch 27	Wed	No. 548	W. Brown	106	to Crewe, 4.0am Mineral.
Mch 28	Thurs	No. 548	W. Brown	106	to Crewe, 4.0am Mineral.
Mch 29	Fri	No. 548	W. Brown	106	to Crewe, 4.0am Mineral.
Mch 30	Sat				to Wigan me & Wife seeing friends.
Apl 2	Tues	No. 548	W. Brown	158	to Stafford, 2.0pm London Goods.
Apl 3	Wed	No. 548	W. Brown	158	to Stafford, 2.0pm London Goods, Wednesday.
Apl 4	Thurs	No. 548	W. Brown	158	to Stafford, 2.0pm London Goods.
Apl 5	Fri	No. 548	W. Brown	158	to Stafford, 2.0pm London Goods.
Apl 6	Sat	No. 548	W. Brown	158	to Stafford, 2.0pm London Goods.
Apl 8	Mon	No. 548	W. Brown	106	to Crewe, 7.30pm Mineral.
Apl 10	Wed	No. 548	W. Brown	106	to Crewe, 7.30pm Mineral.
Apl 11	Thurs	No. 548	W. Brown	106	to Crewe, 7.30pm Mineral.
Apl 12	Fri	No. 548	W. Brown	106	to Crewe, 7.30pm Mineral.
Apl 13	Sat	*Tantalus*	W. Brown		on Shed.
Apl 16	Tues	No. 548	W. Brown	106	to Crewe, 4.0am Mineral.
Apl 17	Wed	No. 548	W. Brown	106	to Crewe, 4.0am Mineral.
Apl 18	Thurs	No. 548	W. Brown	106	to Crewe, 4.0am Mineral.
Apl 19	Fri	No. 548	W. Brown	106	to Crewe, 4.0am Mineral.
Apl 20	Sat	No. 548	W. Brown	106	to Crewe, 4.0am Mineral.
Apl 23	Thurs	No. 548	W. Brown	158	to Stafford, 2.0pm London Goods.
Apl 24	Fri	No. 548	W. Brown	158	to Stafford, 2.0pm London Goods.
Apl 25	Sat	No. 548	W. Brown	158	to Stafford, 2.0pm London Goods.
Apl 26	Sun	No. 548	W. Brown	158	to Stafford, 2.0pm London Goods.
Apl 27	Mon	No. 548	W. Brown	158	to Stafford, 2.0pm London Goods.
Apl 29	Wed	No. 548	W. Brown	160	Shed & to Crewe, 7.30pm Mineral.
May 1	Wed	No. 548	W. Brown	106	to Crewe 7.30pm Mineral.
May 2	Thurs	No. 548	W. Brown	106	to Crewe 7.30pm Mineral.
May 3	Fri	No. 548	W. Brown	106	to Crewe 7.30pm Mineral.
May 4	Sat	No. 548	W. Brown	106	to Crewe 7.30pm Mineral.
May 7	Tues	No. 548	W. Brown	106	to Crewe 4.0am Mineral.
May 8	Wed	No. 548	W. Brown	106	to Crewe 4.0am Mineral.
May 9	Thurs	No. 548	W. Brown	106	to Crewe 4.0am Mineral.
May 10	Fri	No. 548	W. Brown	106	to Crewe 4.0am Mineral.
May 11	Sat	No. 548	W. Brown	106	to Crewe 4.0am Mineral, Saturday.
May 14	Tues	No. 548	W. Brown	156	to Stafford, London Goods.
May 15	Wed	No. 548	W. Brown	156	to Stafford, London Goods.
May 16	Thurs	No. 548	W. Brown	156	to Stafford, London Goods.
May 17	Fri	No. 548	W. Brown	156	to Stafford, London Goods.

Plate 38: *North London Railway No 15A at Hammersmith station about 1877-80. It was built originally as a Bury-type 2-2-0 by Rothwell & Co in 1837 for the London & Birmingham Railway, on which it was No 25, and it continued with that number on the LNWR Southern Division from 1846. Rebuilt in 1851-2 as a 2-2-2 well tank, it was hired to the North London Railway in 1854 and sold to that company in October 1855. It became NLR No 15, was put on the duplicate list as 15A in 1869 and was scrapped sometime after 1880. Standing by the front of the engine is Driver Alf Warner and on the footplate is Fireman Billy Clarke; they were the regular crew on the Acton – Hammersmith service until 1910.*

Plate 38: *This 2-2-2 saddle tank, in Boulton's siding probably not long before it was scrapped, was built originally by Sharp Roberts in November 1842 as a 2-2-2 for the Manchester & Birmingham Railway which numbered it 19. It became 419A in the Northern Division duplicate list in 1860 and 1125 on the duplicate list of the unified system in April 1862. In March 1866 it was sold to Boulton & Watt, which rebuilt it as a 2-2-2 saddle tank and hired it in the same year to the Northampton & Banbury Junction Railway.*

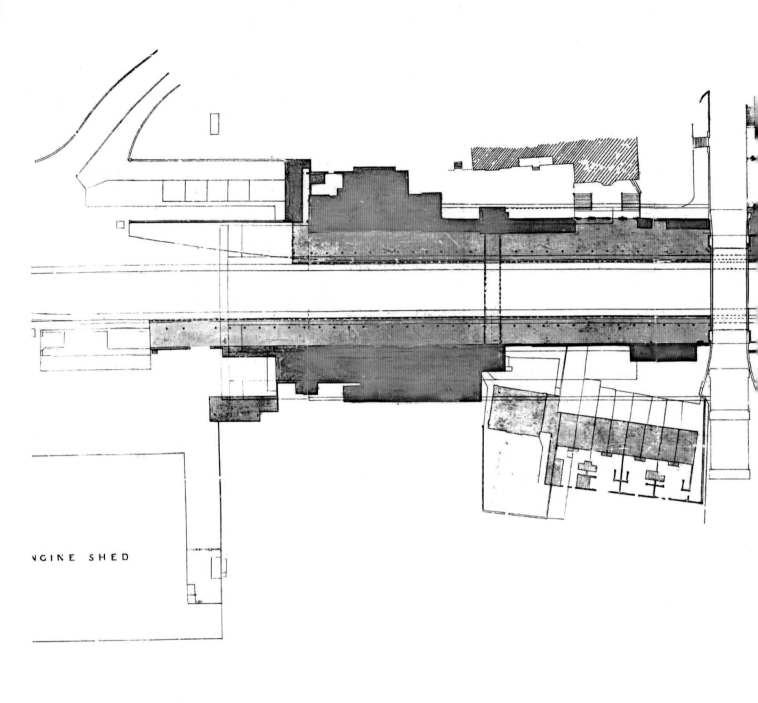

ENGINE SHED

Scal

Note: The new Station Buildings are etched in red.
Block No. 1, tinted Neutral, shews the Buildings to be taken down *after* the creation of the new Station Buildings.
Block No. 2, tinted Green, shews the Buildings to be taken down *during* the creation of the new Station Buildings.
Block No. 3, tinted Blue, shews the Buildings to be taken down *preparatory* to the creation of the new Station Buildings.

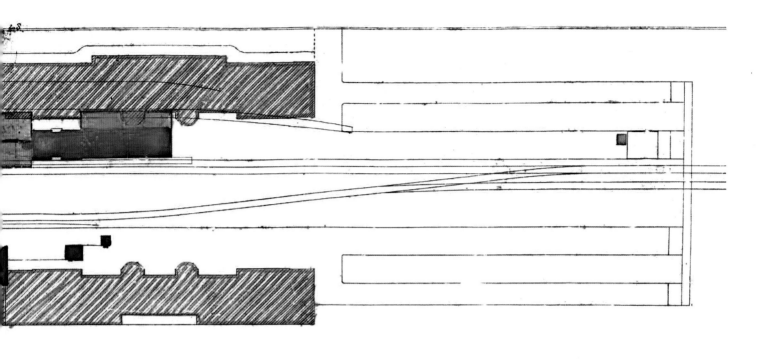

Figure 11: *This drawing was signed by William Baker, LNWR Engineer, on 4th May 1865, and also by J. Parnell, of Rugby, who had the contract for the erection of the new buildings. Parnell was also responsible for building the new station at Stafford completed the previous year. It is not so much an architectural drawing of the buildings, though it seems accurate enough so far as it goes, but rather is a 'Plan Shewing Buildings to be Pulled Down' and shows the order in which the older buildings were to be pulled down and the new ones erected. Crewe North Junction is to the left, Crewe South Junction to the right.*

Public acess to the platforms seems to have been from ground level on both sides of the buildings and not by means of steps down from the road bridge crossing the site. Steps give access to the station from the Crewe Arms Hotel and also from the Sandbach Road into the hotel. This part of the hotel must have been altered when the up through line was installed later to the east of Platform 5.

The buildings in red still stand today on platforms 5 and 6 but the station was later enlarged on the west side of the site which must have necessitated the demolition of the cottages just north of the Sandbach Road bridge and also the engine shed.

Date	Name of Engine	Name of Driver	Number of Miles	Remarks
1861				
May 18 Sat	No. 548	W. Brown	156	to Stafford, London Goods.
May 20 Mon	No. 548	W. Brown		Whit Monday, mist running.
May 22 Wed	No. 548	W. Brown	106	Shed & to Crewe, 7.30pm Mineral.
May 23 Thurs	No. 548	W. Brown	106	Shed & to Crewe, 7.30pm Mineral.
May 24 Fri	No. 548	W. Brown	106	Shed & to Crewe, 7.30pm Mineral.
May 25 Sat	No. 548	W. Brown	156	to Stafford.
May 27 Mon	No. 548	W. Brown		Shed
May 28 Tues	No. 548	W. Brown	106	to Crewe 4.0am Mineral.
May 29 Wed	No. 548	W. Brown	106	to Crewe 4.0am Mineral.
May 30 Thurs	No. 548	W. Brown	106	to Crewe 4.0am Mineral.
May 31 Fri	No. 548	W. Brown	106	to Crewe 4.0am Mineral.
June 1 Sat	No. 548	W. Brown	106	to Crewe 4.0am Mineral.
June 3 Mon	No. 548	W. Brown	110	two trips to Carnforth.
June 4 Tues	No. 548	W. Brown	110	two trips to Carnforth.
June 5 Wed	No. 548	W. Brown	110	two trips to Carnforth.
June 7 Fri	No. 548	W. Brown	156	to Stafford, London Goods.
June 8 Sat	No. 548	W. Brown	156	to Stafford, London Goods.
June 10 Mon	No. 548	W. Brown	156	to Stafford, London Goods.
June 11 Tues	No. 548	W. Brown	156	to Stafford, London Goods.
June 12 Wed	No. 548	W. Brown	156	to Stafford, London Goods.
June 13 Thurs	No. 548	W. Brown	156	to Stafford, London Goods.
June 14 Fri	No. 548	W. Brown	110	two trips to Carnforth.
June 15 Sat	No. 548	W. Brown	110	two trips to Carnforth.
June 17 Mon	No. 548	W. Brown	106	Shed & to Crewe, 7.30pm Mineral.
June 19 Wed	No. 548	W. Brown	106	Shed & to Crewe, 7.30pm Mineral.
June 20 Thurs	No. 548	W. Brown	106	Shed & to Crewe, 7.30pm Mineral.
June 21 Fri	No. 548	W. Brown	106	Shed & to Crewe, 7.30pm Mineral.
June 22 Sat	No. 548	W. Brown	156	to Stafford.
June 24 Mon	No. 548	W. Brown		in Shed.
June 25 Tues	No. 548	W. Brown	106	to Crewe 4.0am Mineral.
June 26 Wed	No. 548	W. Brown	106	to Crewe 4.0am Mineral.
June 27 Thurs	No. 548	W. Brown	106	to Crewe 4.0am Mineral.
June 28 Fri	No. 548	W. Brown	106	to Crewe 4.0am Mineral.
June 29 Sat	No. 548	W. Brown	106	to Crewe 4.0am Mineral.
July 1 Mon	No. 548	W. Brown	78	Excursion to Belle Vue.
July 2 Tues	No. 548	W. Brown	110	two trips to Carnforth.
July 3 Wed	No. 548	W. Brown	110	two trips to Carnforth.
July 4 Thurs	No. 548	W. Brown		in Shed.
July 5 Fri	No. 548	W. Brown	156	to Stafford London Goods.
July 6 Sat	No. 548	W. Brown	156	to Stafford London Goods.
July 8 Mon	No. 548	W. Brown		in Shed.
July 9 Tues	No. 548	W. Brown	156	to Stafford London Goods.
July 10 Wed	No. 548	W. Brown	156	to Stafford London Goods.
July 11 Thurs	No. 548	W. Brown	156	to Stafford London Goods.
July 12 Fri	No. 548	W. Brown	110	two trips to Carnforth.
July 13 Sat	No. 548	W. Brown	110	two trips to Carnforth.
July 15 Mon	No. 548	W. Brown	106	to Crewe 7.30pm Mineral.
July 17 Wed	No. 548	W. Brown	106	to Crewe 7.30pm Mineral.
July 18 Thurs	No. 548	W. Brown	106	to Crewe 7.30pm Mineral.
July 19 Fri	No. 548	W. Brown	106	to Crewe 7.30pm Mineral.
July 20 Sat	No. 548	W. Brown	156	to Stafford London Goods.
July 22 Mon	No. 548	W. Brown		in Shed.
July 23 Tues	No. 548	W. Brown	106	to Crewe 4.0am Mineral.
July 24 Wed	No. 548	W. Brown	106	to Crewe 4.0am Mineral.
July 25 Thurs	No. 548	W. Brown	106	to Crewe 4.0am Mineral.

Engine classes: *Tantalus* - 6ft 'Crewe Passenger' 2-2-2; 548 - 'DX' 0-6-0. *Newby* - Rothwell 2-4-0 for the Lancaster & Carlisle Railway.

Engine mileages: On 11th March Baron and his mate have new 'DX' 0-6-0 No. 548, which is fitted with an injector, and run light engine to Coppull to try the new device out. Obviously, the trip was successful, as the following day they used No. 548 to take the London Goods to Stafford. Baron and his mate then had the same engine almost every day until early October, and No. 548 achieved the following mileages: March - 1816; April - 2694; May - 2632; June - 2702; July - 2738; August - 2752; September - 2465.

20th May. 'Mist running' means 'missed running'; that is, he did not go to work, not that he regretted not going to work.

1st July. The excursion to Belle Vue, Manchester, ran to Longsight station, which was near the rear entrance to Belle Vue gardens, zoo and so forth.

The following details are based on an advertisement which appeared in *The Preston Guardian* of Wednesday 26th June under the heading 'Cheap Trip to Belle Vue Gardens on Monday 1st July':

The excursion left Carlisle at 5am, made various stops to pick up passengers and stopped to change engines at Preston, where Driver Brown and Fireman Baron took over with 'DX' No. 548 and left at 9am. Modern thinking as to their route would take them through Bolton to Manchester. But in LNWR days, and surely in 1861, they went up the main line to Parkside East Junction on to the Liverpool & Manchester main line, turned right at Ordsall Lane on to the Manchester South Junction & Altrincham Railway past London Road to the excursion platforms at Longsight, reached probably about 10am.

They left Longsight at 10.30pm 'after the fireworks'. Presumably, as they had nothing else to do, Baron and his mate also visited Belle Vue - a long day for both passengers and crew, especially those who had started at Carlisle at 5am!

Plate 39: *Evocative platform scene at the west end of Manchester Victoria about 1868, as 'DX' 0-6-0 No. 1080, which was built in July 1863 and still has all the early fittings of the day, including Giffard injector and numberplate in the style of a nameplate on the driving splasher, awaits departure. The station was extended in 1865 and was further extended in 1882 (details can be found in John Marshall's* History of the Lancashire & Yorkshire Railway Volume Two, *published by David & Charles in 1970). The LNWR Exchange station was opened in 1884.*

Date		Name of Engine	Name of Driver	Number of Miles	Remarks
1861					
July 26	Fri	No. 548	W. Brown	106	to Crewe 4.0am Mineral.
July 27	Sat	No. 548	W. Brown	106	to Crewe 4.0am Mineral.
July 29	Mon	No. 548	W. Brown	110	Shed & to Carnforth.
July 30	Tues	No. 548	W. Brown	110	two trips to Carnforth.
July 31	Wed	No. 548	W. Brown	110	two trips to Carnforth.
Aug 2	Fri	No. 548	W. Brown	156	to Stafford London Goods.
Aug 3	Sat	No. 548	W. Brown	156	to Stafford London Goods.
Aug 5	Mon	No. 548	W. Brown		in Shed.
Aug 6	Tues	No. 548	W. Brown	156	to Stafford London Goods.
Aug 7	Wed	No. 548	W. Brown	156	to Stafford London Goods.
Aug 8	Thurs	No. 548	W. Brown	156	to Stafford London Goods.
Aug 9	Fri	No. 548	W. Brown	110	two trips to Carnforth.
Aug 10	Sat	No. 548	W. Brown	110	two trips to Carnforth.
Aug 12	Mon	No. 548	W. Brown	106	to Crewe 7.30pm Mineral.
Aug 14	Wed	No. 548	W. Brown	106	to Crewe 7.30pm Mineral.
Aug 15	Thurs	No. 548	W. Brown	106	to Crewe 7.30pm Mineral.
Aug 16	Fri	No. 548	W. Brown	106	to Crewe 7.30pm Mineral.
Aug 17	Sat	No. 548	W. Brown	156	to Stafford London Goods.
Aug 19	Mon	No. 548	W. Brown		in Shed.
Aug 20	Tues	No. 548	W. Brown	106	to Crewe 4.0am Mineral.
Aug 21	Wed	No. 548	W. Brown	106	to Crewe 4.0am Mineral.
Aug 22	Thurs	No. 548	W. Brown	106	to Crewe 4.0am Mineral.
Aug 23	Fri	No. 548	W. Brown	106	to Crewe 4.0am Mineral.
Aug 24	Sat	No. 548	W. Brown	106	to Crewe 4.0am Mineral.
Aug 26	Mon	No. 548	W. Brown	110	two trips to Carnforth.
Aug 27	Tues	No. 548	W. Brown	110	two trips to Carnforth.
Aug 28	Wed	No. 548	W. Brown	110	two trips to Carnforth.
Aug 29	Thurs	No. 548	W. Brown	156	to Stafford 8.50pm Cattle.
Aug 30	Fri	No. 548	W. Brown	156	to Stafford 10.0pm Cattle.
Sept 2	Mon	No. 548	W. Brown	75	Excursion to Manchester.
Sept 3	Tues	No. 548	W. Brown	156	to Stafford London Goods.
Sept 4	Wed	No. 548	W. Brown	156	to Stafford London Goods.
Sept 5	Thurs	No. 548	W. Brown	156	to Stafford London Goods.
Sept 6	Fri	No. 548	W. Brown	60	to Carnforth.
Sept 7	Sat	No. 548	W. Brown	110	two trips to Carnforth.
Sept 9	Mon	No. 548	W. Brown	106	Shed & to Crewe 7.30pm.
Sept 11	Wed	No. 548	W. Brown	106	Shed & to Crewe 7.30pm.
Sept 12	Thurs	No. 548	W. Brown	106	Shed & to Crewe 7.30pm.
Sept 13	Fri	No. 548	W. Brown	106	Shed & to Crewe 7.30pm.
Sept 14	Sat	No. 548	W. Brown	156	to Stafford London Goods.
Sept 16	Mon	No. 548	W. Brown		in Shed.
Sept 17	Tues	No. 548	W. Brown	106	to Crewe 4.0am Mineral.
Sept 18	Wed	No. 548	W. Brown	106	to Crewe 4.0am Mineral.
Sept 19	Thurs	No. 548	W. Brown	106	to Crewe 4.0am Mineral.
Sept 20	Fri	No. 548	W. Brown	106	to Crewe 4.0am Mineral.
Sept 21	Sat	No. 548	W. Brown	106	to Crewe 4.0am Mineral.
Sept 23	Mon	No. 548	W. Brown	110	two trips to Carnforth.
Sept 24	Tues	No. 548	W. Brown	110	two trips to Carnforth.
Sept 25	Wed	No. 548	W. Brown	110	two trips to Carnforth.
Sept 27	Fri	No. 548	W. Brown	156	to Stafford London Goods.
Sept 28	Sat	No. 548	W. Brown	156	to Stafford London Goods.
Oct 1	Tues	No. 548	W. Brown	156	to Stafford London Goods.
Oct 2	Wed	No. 548	W. Brown	156	to Stafford London Goods.
Oct 3	Thurs	No. 548	W. Brown	156	to Stafford London Goods.

Plate 40: *Local train just east of Patricroft station on the Liverpool & Manchester line hauled by 2-2-2 saddle tank No. 402 about 1870. The engine was originally a Sharp single built for the Manchester & Birmingham Railway in 1840, was rebuilt at Longsight in 1856 and rebuilt again as a saddle tank in 1868. It was renumbered 1856 on the duplicate list in 1874 and was scrapped in February 1879. The first five carriages are believed to date from 1863.*

The two tracks curving north-east under the train are the start of the three and a half mile branch to Molyneux Junction on the LYR/East Lancashire Railway line from Manchester to Bury. This LNWR branch opened in February 1850 but passenger traffic lasted for only three months, after which the line, though little used, survived for a further 103 years. Its end was dramatic, when part of Clifton Hall tunnel ('the Black 'Arry') collapsed in April 1953, bringing down two houses above and killing their five sleeping occupants.

Plate 41: *In 1857 the last two Trevithick 5ft 2-4-0 Goods engines to be built with large fireboxes, straight frames and direct action were turned out as side-tank engines and by 1871 over 100 of the small firebox engines had been converted to side-tank engines also, their curved nameplates being transferred from their driving splashers to their side tanks. Here one of the converted engines, unidentifiable unfortunately but in green livery with Ramsbottom castellated chimney, stands at the recently opened (1866) station at Cheadle on the line from Warrington to Stockport awaiting departure with a local passenger train to Oldham. This passenger service ran through Stockport to Cheadle, where the engine ran round, presumably to avoid occupying a platform at the much busier station at Stockport. Its route was: Cheadle-Stockport-Denton-Ashton-Oldham.*

Date		Name of Engine	Name of Driver	Number of Miles	Remarks
1861					
Oct 4	Fri	Newby	W. Brown	55	to Carnforth.
Oct 5	Sat	Hardwicke	G. Fisher	53	7.30am to Crewe to Live.
			My Work now commences from Crewe.		
Oct 8	Tues	No. 571	J. Worthington	106	3.10 to Preston.
Oct 9	Wed	No. 571	J. Worthington	143	8.50am to Carlisle.
Oct 10	Thurs	No. 571	J. Worthington	143	Carlisle to Crewe.
Oct 11	Fri	No. 571	J. Worthington	143	3.30am to Carlisle.
Oct 12	Sat	No. 571	J. Worthington	143	4.15am Carlisle to Crewe.
Oct 12	Sat				Passenger to Preston.
Oct 14	Mon	No. 571	J. Worthington	106	3.10am to Preston.
Oct 15	Tues	No. 571	J. Worthington	143	8.50am to Carlisle.
Oct 16	Wed	No. 571	J. Worthington	143	Carlisle to Crewe.
Oct 17	Thurs	No. 571	J. Worthington	143	3.30am to Carlisle.
Oct 18	Fri	No. 571	J. Worthington	143	12.30am Carlisle to Crewe.
Oct 19	Sat				Passenger to Preston.
Oct 19	Sat	No. 571	J. Worthington	106	3.10am to Preston.
Oct 23	Wed	No. 571	J. Worthington	143	3.30am to Carlisle.
Oct 24	Thurs	No. 571	J. Worthington	143	12.30am Carlisle to Crewe.
Oct 25	Fri	No. 571	J. Worthington	106	3.10 to Preston.
Oct 26	Sat	No. 571	J. Worthington	143	8.50 to Carlisle.
Oct 27	Sun	No. 571	J. Worthington	92	Carlisle to Preston.
Oct 28	Mon	No. 571	J. Worthington	92	Preston to Carlisle.
Oct 29	Tues	No. 571	J. Worthington	143	4.15 Carlisle to Crewe.
Oct 30	Wed	No. 571	J. Worthington	143	3.30 Crewe to Carlisle.
Oct 31	Thurs	No. 571	J. Worthington	143	Carlisle to Crewe.
Nov 1	Fri	No. 571	J. Worthington	143	to Carlisle.
Nov 2	Sat	No. 571	J. Worthington	143	Carlisle to Crewe.
Nov 2	Sat				Passenger to Preston.
Nov 4	Mon				Passenger to Crewe.
Nov 4	Mon	No. 571	J. Worthington	143	10.10pm Crewe to Carlisle.
Nov 5	Tues	No. 571	J. Worthington	143	Carlisle to Crewe.
Nov 7	Thurs	No. 571	J. Worthington	143	Crewe to Carlisle.
Nov 8	Fri	No. 571	J. Worthington	143	Carlisle to Crewe.
Nov 9	Sat	No. 571	J. Worthington	106	3.10 to Preston.
Nov 10	Sun	- Sick.			
Nov 11	Mon	- Sick			
Nov 12	Tues	- Sick			
Nov 13	Wed	No. 571	J. Worthington	143	Crewe to Carlisle.
Nov 14	Thurs	No. 571	J. Worthington	143	Carlisle to Crewe.
Nov 16	Sat	No. 571	J. Worthington	143	8.30 Crewe to Carlisle.
Nov 17	Sun	No. 571	J. Worthington	143	Carlisle to Crewe.
Nov 19	Tues	No. 571	J. Worthington	143	to Carlisle.
Nov 20	Wed	No. 571	J. Worthington	143	Carlisle to Crewe.
Nov 22	Fri	No. 571	J. Worthington	143	3.30am to Carlisle.
Nov 23	Sat	No. 571	J. Worthington	143	12.50am Carlisle to Crewe.
Nov 24	Sun	No. 561	T. Jones	131	11.40 Stafford to Holyhead Irish Mail.
Nov 25	Mon	No. 561	T. Jones	156	11.40 Holyhead to Stafford & Crewe.
Nov 26	Tues	No. 561	T. Jones	156	to Stafford & Holyhead Mail.
Nov 29	Fri	No. 561	T. Jones	156	to Stafford & Holyhead Mail.
Nov 30	Sat	No. 561	T. Jones	156	Holyhead to Stafford & Crewe.
Dec 2	Mon	No. 561	T. Jones	156	to Stafford & Holyhead, Irish Mail.
Dec 3	Tues	No. 561	T. Jones	156	Holyhead to Stafford & Crewe.

5th October. '7.30am to Crewe to Live'. The larger than normal writing of the last two words seems to indicate that Baron is delighted with the move to Crewe.

October 1861. Baron's work schedule at Crewe is interesting. On 8th October he works to Preston and back; the next day to Carlisle; the next day back to Crewe; the next day to Carlisle again; and the next day back to Crewe, after which he returns to Preston for a day at home. On 14th October he starts the same cycle again, with an earlier train back to Crewe on the last day, which probably gave him more time at home. On 27th October he works back from Carlisle as far as Preston only, and returns to Carlisle on 28th October, so presumably was able to spend the night of 27th at home.

24th November 1861. 'The Irish Mail'

After less than two months at Crewe, Baron has his first trip as fireman on the 'Irish Mail', probably the most prestigious train in the country and certainly the LNWR's 'crack express' at the time. This train had only two stops between Euston and Holyhead, at Stafford, which was very nearly half-way between the two, to change engines, and at Chester. It is clear from Baron's diary that between Stafford and Holyhead, the train was worked by a Crewe engine which ran to Stafford to pick up the train, and on the return journey did the same thing in reverse.

Whether the engine ran light between Crewe and Stafford, or worked a train, or double-headed another engine, is unknown, and nowhere in Baron's diary is there any clue. However, the need to do this must have added probably an hour and a half to the enginemen's work on each run.

4th January 1862. 'Saw Madox hung at Stafford'.

In January 1862 *The Staffordshire Advertiser* reported that three men, Maddocks, Jones and Brandrick, burgled a house in Bilston belonging to a Mr Bagott. At first Bagott slept while the three were in his house but eventually he awoke as the trio disturbed him in trying to find money. A fight ensued in which after a struggle Bagott was killed. All three were tried for murder, found guilty and condemned to death, but Maddocks and Jones were reprieved by the Home Secretary, and only Brandrick was hanged.

So it seems that Baron was mistaken in thinking he 'saw Madox hung', as the man who was hanged was Brandrick.

Engine classes. *Newby* - 'Crewe Goods' 2-4-0 by Rothwell for the Lancaster & Carlisle Railway. Hardwicke - 'Crewe Goods' 2-4-0. No. 571 - 'DX' 0-6-0. No 561 - 'Problem' 2-2-2. No. 561 was completed only in May 1861 and was later named *Prince Oscar.*.

Boiler explosion on the 'Irish Mail'. On 4th July 1861, some three months before Baron moved to Crewe to work, the boiler of the 'Bloomer' on the down 'Irish Mail' exploded north of Rugby. The following account is taken from the report by Capt H. W. Tyler published by the Board of Trade on 30th July 1861:

'The fast train known as the "Irish Mail" train, leaving London at 8.25pm, and Rugby at 10.28pm, started from Rugby punctually on that evening, composed of an engine and tender, two post-office vehicles, two composite carriages, two first-class carriages, and two break vans. It had proceeded for a little more than four miles, and was approaching a bridge over the railway, called the Easenhall Bridge, when the boiler of the engine suddenly exploded. It had not, at this time, reached its full speed, but is stated to have been running at the rate of thirty-five or thirty-six miles an hour, after travelling over gradients, sometimes rising, sometimes falling, but nowhere more severe than 1 in 330, between Rugby and the bridge in question.'

Insert in the November 1859 LNWR Passenger Timetable.

Date		Name of Engine	Name of Driver	Number of Miles	Remarks
1861					
Dec 5	Thurs	No. 561	T. Jones	156	to Stafford & Holyhead.
Dec 6	Fri	No. 561	T. Jones	156	Holyhead to Stafford & Crewe.
Dec 7	Sat	No. 561	T. Jones	156	to Stafford & Holyhead, Mail.
Dec 8	Sun	No. 561	T. Jones	106	Holyhead to Crewe.
Dec 11	Wed	No. 561	T. Jones	212	9.30 to Holyhead and back.
Dec 12	Thurs	No. 561	T. Jones	143	to Stafford & Holyhead.
Dec 13	Fri	No. 561	T. Jones	143	Holyhead to Stafford & Crewe.
Dec 14	Sat	No. 561	T. Jones	212	9.30 to Holyhead and back.
Dec 17	Tues	No. 561	T. Jones	212	Holyhead 9.30am. ????
Dec 18	Wed	No. 561	T. Jones	156	Holyhead to Stafford and Crewe.
Dec 19	Thurs	No. 561	T. Jones	156	Holyhead to Stafford and Crewe.
Dec 20	Fri	No. 561	T. Jones	156	to Stafford & Holyhead, Mail.
Dec 21	Sat	No. 561	T. Jones	156	Holyhead to Stafford & Crewe, Mail.
Dec 23	Mon	No. 561	J. Newton	156	to Stafford & Holyhead.
Dec 24	Tues	No. 561	J. Newton	156	to Stafford & Crewe.
Dec 25	Wed	No. 561	J. Newton	156	Crewe to Stafford & Holyhead.
Dec 26	Thurs	No. 561	J. Newton	156	Holyhead to Stafford & Crewe.
Dec 27	Fri	No. 561	T. Jones	212	9.30 to Holyhead & Back.
Dec 29	Sun	No. 561	T. Jones	106	Crewe to Holyhead.
Dec 30	Mon	No. 561	T. Jones	156	Holyhead to Stafford & Crewe.
Dec 31	Tues	No. 561	T. Jones	156	Crewe to Holyhead & Stafford.
1862					
Jany 1	Wed	No. 561	T. Jones	156	Holyhead to Stafford & Crewe.
Jany 4	Sat	No. 561	T. Jones	156	to Holyhead. Saw Madox hung at Stafford.
Jany 5	Sun	No. 561	T. Jones	156	Back.
Jany 5	Sun	No. 561	T. Jones	156	to Stafford & Holyhead Mail.
Jany 6	Mon	No. 561	T. Jones	156	Back.
Jany 7	Tues	No. 1	T. Jones	156	to Stafford & Holyhead.
Jany 8	Wed	No. 1	T. Jones	156	Back, Irish Mail.
Jany 10	Fri	No. 1	T. Jones	156	to Stafford & Holyhead.
Jany 11	Sat	No. 1	T. Jones	156	Back.
Jany 11	Sat	No. 1	T. Baron		Relieving
Jany 13	Mon	No. 1	T. Jones	156	to Stafford & Holyhead.
Jany 14	Tues	No. 1	T. Jones	156	Back.
Jany 16	Thurs	No. 1	T. Jones	156	to Stafford & Holyhead.
Jany 17	Fri	No. 1	T. Jones	156	Back.
Jany 18	Sat	No. 1	T. Jones	156	to Stafford & Holyhead.
Jany 19	Sun	No. 1	T. Jones	106	Back to Crewe.
Jany 20	Mon	No. 1	T. Jones	212	to Holyhead & Back.
Jany 22	Wed	No. 1	T. Jones	212	to Holyhead & Back.
Jany 23	Thurs	No. 1	T. Jones	156	to Stafford & Holyhead.
Jany 24	Fri	No. 1	T. Jones	156	Back Irish Mail.
Jany 25	Sat	No. 1	T. Jones	212	9.30 to Holyhead & Back.
Jany 27	Mon	*Star*	J. Tesdale	135	6.30 to Liverpool, 10.30 to Stafford.
Jany 28	Tues	*Star*	J. Tesdale	135	6.30 to Liverpool, 10.30 to Stafford.
Jany 29	Wed	*Star*	J. Tesdale	135	6.30 to Liverpool, 10.30 to Stafford.
Jany 30	Thurs	*Star*	J. Tesdale	135	6.30 to Liverpool, 10.30 to Stafford.
Jany 31	Fri	*Star*	J. Tesdale	135	6.30 to Liverpool, 10.30 to Stafford.
Feby 1	Sat	*Star*	J. Tesdale	135	6.30 to Liverpool, 10.30 to Stafford.
Feby 2	Sun	*Star*	J. Tesdale	156	3.30 to Preston & Stafford, L. Mail.
Feby 3	Mon	*Star*	J. Tesdale	156	to Stafford & Preston.
Feby 4	Tues	*Star*	J. Tesdale	156	to Preston & Stafford.
Feby 5	Wed	*Star*	J. Tesdale	156	to Stafford & Preston, Mail.

Engine classes. *Star*, No 1 and 561 - 'Problem' 2-2-2s. No. 1 and 561 were completed only in November and May 1861 respectively and were later named *Saracen* and *Prince Oscar*.

Table 8

Timings of the 'Irish Mail' - Working Timetable May 1862

Miles	Stations		Down Trains			Up Trains	
	Euston	**dep**	**7.30am**	**8.30pm**	**arr**	**6.45am**	**6.25pm**
	Camden						
3	Kilburn		7.36	8.36		6.39	6.18
6¼	Willesden		7.41	8.41		6.35	6.14
8¼	Sudbury		7.44	8.44		6.31	6.11
11	Harrow		7.49	8.49		6.27	6.6
13	Pinner		7.52	8.52		6.24	6.4
16¼	Bushey		7.56	8.57		6.20	6.0
17	Watford		7.58	8.59		6.17	5.57
21	King's Langley		8.3	9.3		6.13	5.53
24	Boxmoor		8.8	9.8		6.6	5.46
28	Berkhamstead		8.13	9.13		6.1	5.41
31¾	Tring		8.18	9.18		5.55	5.35
36¼	Cheddington		8.24	9.24		5.48	5.28
40	Leighton		8.29	9.29		5.41	5.21
46¾	Bletchley		8.37	9.37		5.32	5.12
52¼	Wolverton		8.44	9.44		5.24	5.4
60	Roade		8.55	9.55		5.13	4.53
63	Blisworth		8.59	9.59		5.8	4.48
69¾	Weedon		9.8	10.8		4.59	4.39
76¼	Crick		9.17	10.17		4.50	4.30
82¾	**Rugby**	**arr**	**9.25**	**10.25**	**dep**	**4.39**	**4.19**
		dep	**9.28**	**10.27**	**arr**	**4.36**	**4.16**
88¼	Stretton		9.37	10.38		4.28	4.8
91½	Shilton		9.41	10.42		4.24	4.3
93½	Bulkington		9.44	10.45		4.21	4.0
97¼	Nuneaton		9.50	10.50		4.15	3.55
102½	Atherstone		9.57	10.57		4.8	3.48
106½	Polesworth		10.3	11.3		4.2	3.42
110	Tamworth		10.8	11.8		3.57	3.37
116½	Lichfield		10.17	11.17		3.48	3.28
121	Armitage		10.23	11.23		3.43	3.22
124¼	Rugeley		10.28	11.27		3.37	3.17
127¼	Colwich		10.32	11.32		3.32	3.12
133½	**Stafford**	**arr**	**10.40**	**11.40**	**dep**	**3.23**	**3.3pm**
	Norton Bridge						
	Standon Bridge						
	Whitmore						
	Madeley						
	Basford						
158¼	**Crewe**		11.19	12.19		2.45	2.25
0	**Crewe**						
3¾	Worleston						
8¼	Calveley						
11	Beeston						
	Beeston Coal Siding						
15½	Tattenhall						
17¼	Waverton						
	Waverton Coal Siding						
21¼	**Chester**	**arr**	**11.48am**	**12.48am**	**dep**	**2.25am**	**1.55pm**

Miles	Stations		Down Trains			Up Trains	
0	**Chester**	**dep**	**11.58am**	**12.58am**	**arr**	**2.5am**	**1.45pm**
	Saltney Junction						
3	Bett's Siding						
3¼	Mold Junction						
5¾	Sandycroft						
6¼	Dundas's Siding						
7	Queen's Ferry		12.8				
9	Connah's Quay						
11½	Hunter's Siding						
12½	Flint					1.50	1.26
12¾	Muspratt's Siding						
14½	Bagilt						
15¼	Dee Bank						
16¾	Holywell		12.23			1.40	1.20
	Llanerchymor Siding						
	Eyton's Siding						
19	Bychton Siding						
20	Mostyn						
24¾	Gronant						
26	Steele's Siding						
26¼	Prestatyn						
30	Rhyl		12.43			1.20	1.0
31¼	Foryd						
34¼	Abergele		12.49				
37¾	Llysfaen						
40¼	Colwyn						
	Llandudno Junction						
45¼	Conway		1.4			12.58	12.38
48½	Pendyffryn						
49¾	Penmaenmawr						
50½	Wright's Siding						
52¼	Llanfairfechan						
54¼	Aber						
58	Pen Lan						
59¾	Bangor		1.25			12.37	12.17
61	Menai Bridge						
63¼	Llanfair						
66	Gaerwen						
72½	Bodorgan		1.44				
75¼	Ty Croes						
81	Valley						
	Ticket Stage		2.2				
84½	**Holyhead**	**arr**	**2.5pm**	**3.5am**	**dep**	**12.0am**	**11.40am**

Engine classes: Nos. 1 and 561, and *Star* - 'Problem' 2-2-2s.
Engine mileages: In December 1861 'Problem' No. 561 ran 3686 miles - and so did Thomas Baron!

Plate 42: *Technically a poor picture but one of great interest, since it shows the second of Ramsbottom's 'Problem' 2-2-2s, No. 229 Watt, at the north end of Stafford station. In the background is Railway Street, which still looks much the same today. In 1862 this engine made a high-speed run from Holyhead to Stafford with the 'Trent Special', which was then taken on to Euston by a Southern Division 'Bloomer', and it could well be that this photograph was taken after the run, as there are streaks of dirt from the slots in the driving splasher. If so, the engine has turned before returning to Crewe, presumably at the shed on the down side north of the station. Compared with the photograph at Preston, page 13, the safety valves are now the standard Ramsbottom type with tail rod but the engine still seems to have the same 2000-gallon tender, which would have been essential for such a non-stop run. Perhaps even the men are the same as in the picture at Preston.*

Plate 43: *Another Ramsbottom 'Problem', No. 291 Prince of Wales, at Stafford - Railway Street is beyond the engine tender - but this time the engine is on the shed. Compared to* Watt, *there are three noteworthy differences. First and most obvious is that the tender is a standard 1500-gallon type, recognisable by the fact that the engine side sheet is higher than the tender tank. Second, the engine has an injector; a control wheel for it is visible above the side-sheet and much of it is visible below, in front of the trailing wheel. Third, the nameplate is the later standard type with the subsidiary inscriptions 'CREWE WORKS, L&NWR Co', and the date, whereas that on No. 229 has the name only* Watt. *The enginemen seem to be the two on the right but who the other two men are, on the left, can only be speculated.*

Plate 44: *The original print from which this photograph is reproduced was sent by F. E. A. Eades, well known locomotive historian, contributor to the SLS Journal and friend of S. S. Scott, to his friend, W. L. Harris, also a locomotive historian and friend of C. Williams of Crewe, with 'Best wishes for Christmas and the New Year' at Christmas 1970. Eades wrote on the back of the print: 'Small Bloomer No. 103' and then 'The original taken in 1860, a positive on glass, on which it was possible to read the inscription on the splasher plate "London & North Western Railway 103 May 1857. Manufactured at the Engine Works at Wolverton". The gentleman in the stove-pipe hat was Mr John Widdowson who was "pay clerk for the railway between London and Crewe". (Stafford? -EE) He was afterwards designated as "Cashier". He retired in the 1870s and died in 1881. I should imagine that the staff was paid fortnightly as they still were (all below "special grades") in the 1920s to*

my knowledge.' The location is always said to be Stafford, which seems correct, but although buildings are just visible on the right which could be Railway Street, they are too distant and faint to be identified with certainty.

More problematical is the engine livery, which seems most likely to be dark green but is possibly 'Brunswick' or 'light Brunswick' or 'bright green'. A light-coloured line that could be white or cream or yellow is on the left and top of the panels on the tender and engine side-sheet, and on the flare of the tender top, so presumably a corresponding line on the right and bottom of these panels is a colour which is not recorded on the emulsion of the film, possibly red or reddish brown. This style of lining is known as 'offset shadow lining' and is designed to give the effect of a raised area in the centre of the panel.

Date		Name of Engine	Name of Driver	Number of Miles	Remarks
1862					
Feby 6	Thurs	Star	J. Tesdale	156	to Preston & Stafford.
Feby 7	Fri	Star	J. Tesdale	156	to Stafford & Preston.
Feby 8	Sat	Star	J. Tesdale	156	to Preston & Stafford.
Feby 9	Sun	Star	J. Tesdale	156	to Stafford & Preston.
Feby 10	Mon	Star	J. Tesdale	156	to Preston & Stafford.
Feby 11	Tues	Star	J. Tesdale	156	to Stafford & Preston.
Feby 12	Wed	Star	J. Tesdale	156	to Preston & Stafford, L. Mail.
Feby 14	Fri				Moved Family to Crewe.
Feby 15	Sat	Star	J. Tesdale	156	to Stafford & Preston.
Feby 17	Mon	Star	J. Tesdale	135	to Liverpool & Stafford.
Feby 18	Tues	Star	J. Tesdale	135	to Liverpool & Stafford.
Feby 19	Wed	Star	J. Tesdale	135	to Liverpool & Stafford.
Feby 20	Thurs	Star	J. Tesdale	135	to Liverpool & Stafford.
Feby 21	Fri	Star	J. Tesdale	135	to Liverpool & Stafford.
Feby 22	Sat	Star	J. Tesdale	135	to Liverpool & Stafford.
Feby 24	Mon	Owl	J. Tesdale	156	to Preston & Stafford.
Feby 25	Tues	Owl	J. Frost	156	to Preston & Stafford.
Feby 26	Wed	Owl	J. Frost	156	to Preston & Stafford.
Feby 27	Thurs	Owl	J. Frost	156	to Preston & Stafford.
Feb 28	Fri	Owl	J. Frost	156	to Preston & Stafford.
Mch 1	Sat	Owl	J. Tesdale	156	to Preston & Stafford.
Mch 3	Mon	Atalanta	J. Tesdale	168	to Liverpool & Preston.
Mch 4	Tues	Atalanta	J. Tesdale	168	to Liverpool & Preston.
Mch 5	Wed	Problem	J. Tesdale	168	to Liverpool & Preston.
Mch 6	Thurs	Problem	J. Tesdale	168	to Liverpool & Preston.
Mch 7	Fri	Mazeppa	J. Tesdale	168	to Liverpool & Preston.
Mch 8	Sat	Mazeppa	J. Tesdale	168	to Liverpool & Preston.
Mch 9	Sun	Mazeppa	J. Tesdale	131	to Preston & Stafford.
Mch 10	Mon	Mazeppa	J. Tesdale	131	to Preston & Stafford.
Mch 11	Tues	Mazeppa	J. Tesdale	131	to Preston & Stafford.
Mch 12	Wed	Mazeppa	J. Tesdale	131	to Preston & Stafford.
Mch 13	Thurs	Mazeppa	J. Tesdale	131	to Preston & Stafford.
Mch 14	Fri	Mazeppa	J. Tesdale	131	to Preston & Stafford.
Mch 15	Sat	Mazeppa	J. Tesdale	131	to Preston & Stafford.
Mch 16	Sun	Mazeppa	J. Tesdale	131	to Preston & Stafford.
Mch 17	Mon	Mazeppa	J. Tesdale	131	to Preston & Stafford.
Mch 18	Tues	Mazeppa	J. Tesdale	131	to Preston & Stafford.
Mch 19	Wed	Mazeppa	J. Tesdale	131	to Preston & Stafford.
Mch 20	Thurs	Mazeppa	J. Tesdale	131	to Preston & Stafford.
Mch 21	Fri	Mazeppa	J. Tesdale	131	to Preston & Stafford.
Mch 22	Sat	Mazeppa	J. Tesdale	131	to Preston & Stafford.
Mch 24	Mon	Mazeppa	J. Tesdale	135	to Liverpool & Stafford.
Mch 25	Tues	Mazeppa	J. Tesdale	135	to Liverpool & Stafford.
Mch 26	Wed	Mazeppa	J. Tesdale	135	to Liverpool & Stafford.
Mch 27	Thurs	Star	J. Tesdale	135	to Liverpool & Stafford.
Mch 28	Fri	Star	J. Tesdale	135	to Liverpool & Stafford.
Mch 29	Sat	Star	J. Tesdale	135	to Liverpool & Stafford.
Mch 30	Sun	Star	J. Tesdale	135	to Liverpool & Stafford.
Mch 31	Mon	Star	J. Tesdale	156	to Preston & Stafford.
Apl 1	Tues	Star	J. Tesdale	156	to Preston & Stafford.
Apl 2	Wed	Star	J. Tesdale	156	to Preston & Stafford.
Apl 3	Thurs	Star	J. Tesdale	156	to Preston & Stafford.
Apl 4	Fri	Star	J. Tesdale	156	to Preston & Stafford.
Apl 5	Sat	Star	J. Tesdale	156	to Preston & Stafford.
Apl 7	Mon	Mazeppa	J. Moor	168	to Birmingham & Rugby.

21st April. The entry for No. 979 is the earliest known record of a Southern Division engine with its number having been increased by 600, this renumbering having occurred sometime in April. The letters 'mc' beside 979 perhaps mean 'McConnell'.

1st June. It seems that through the night of 1st June, without ever having been over the road before (there was clearly no provision for 'road-learning' at that time), Baron drove 'Crewe Goods Tank' No. 141 to Hereford. There he would have another surprise, as the railways in the Hereford area were then mixed gauge, the Great Western Railway being laid to broad gauge.

2nd June *et seq.* Baron works on ballasting for King, the 'concractor' (Lancashire dialect again). The firm of Greene & King did the work on the Abergavenny-Brynmawr section, presumably sub-contracted from Wm McCormick MP, who had the contract. The LNWR leased the MT&A for 1000 years by agreement of 8th November 1861, confirmed by Act of 7th August 1862.

The MT&A was dissolved on 30th June 1866 and was absorbed by the LNWR.

5th June. 'Slept at Llanfoist Inn' (near Abergavenny). Baron's ditto marks are a bit vague, so it is not clear how many nights he slept there.

Engine classes.
Hurricane, Pilot, Quail, Sirius, Snipe, Starling, No. 63 - all 'Crewe Goods' 2-4-0s.
No. 141 - 'Crewe Goods' 2-4-0 tank.
Meteor - 'Crewe Passenger' 2-2-2.
Nos. 125, 547, 574, 576, 581, 582 - all 'DX' 0-6-0s.
No. 475 - Fairbairn 0-4-2 built for North Eastern Dvision in February 1854 - see pages 104-5.
No. 879 - Goods 0-6-0 by Fairbairn for Southern Division in April 1854 - see pages 104-5.
No. 979 - 'Small Bloomer' 2-2-2 built at Wolverton in October 1861 - see pages 104-5.
Atalanta, Mazeppa, Owl, Problem, Star, Wellington - all 'Problem' 2-2-2s.

Plate 45: *This view is often described as 'the first train on the opening day of the Kirkburton branch on 7th October 1867', and that idea is certainly supported by the posed photograph, apparently of civic digitaries and contractor's men. However, Neil Fraser, a knowledgeable local historian, was certain that it was taken in 1868. The train is standing just north of Kirkburton station, near Huddersfield. The engine is Trevithick 2-4-0 tank No. 37 Hawk, which was built originally as small firebox 'Crewe Goods' 2-4-0 No. 240 Bee, in May 1850; it was converted to a side tank in October 1859 and sent to work on the North London Railway as its No. 31 before returning to the LNWR in late 1860 as No. 37 Hawk. The carriages are all four-wheelers. The leading one is 3rd class No. 41, which has luggage rails on the roof, a feature which was discontinued in 1851 and reinstated for a short time in 1863, luggage on the roof, of course, being vulnerable to sparks from the engine. There are two oil lamps which are centred over the partitions so as to be shared by the compartments, and destination board brackets are fitted on the upper panel between the inner doors. The second carriage is a compo, with two 1st class compartments in the centre, a 2nd class coupé or half compartment in the near end (with end window) and a 3rd class compartment at the far end. The door handles are the older style of commode handle, pre-dating the snake pattern of 1871. The brake van has four panels either side of the luggage doors. At the end is a large ogee or ducket, with destination-board brackets, and on the roof is a side lamp.*

Thomas Baron set off from Crewe on No. 141, of the same class of engine as No. 37 here, without any 'route learning' at all and eventually reached Abergavenny where he worked ballast trains and later passenger trains on the branch to Brynmawr. The 'Opening of the line' was on 1st October. Whether there was an opening ceremony is unclear, but certainly he worked the branch train for many weeks with the same engine, and quite possibly the train looked very similar to the one here with No. 37.

Date		Name of Engine	Name of Fireman	Number of Miles	Remarks
1862					
Apl 8	Tues	*Mazeppa*	J. Moor	158	to Birmingham & Rugby.
Apl 9	Wed	*Mazeppa*	J. Moor	168	two trips to Liverpool.
Apl 10	Thurs	*Mazeppa*	J. Moor	158	to Birmingham & Rugby.
Apl 11	Fri	*Mazeppa*	J. Moor	168	two trips to Liverpool.
Apl 12	Sat	*Mazeppa*	J. Moor	158	to Birmingham & Rugby.
Apl 14	Mon	*Mazeppa*	J. Moor	191	Liverpool & Preston.
Apl 15	Tues	*Mazeppa*	J. Moor	150	to Rugby.
Apl 16	Wed	*Mazeppa*	J. Moor	191	Liverpool & Preston.
Apl 17	Thurs	*Mazeppa*	J. Moor	150	to Rugby.
Apl 18	Fri	*Mazeppa*	J. Moor	106	to Preston, Good Friday.
Apl 19	Sat	*Mazeppa*	J. Moor	150	to Rugby.
Apl 21	Mon	No. 979 mc	W. Mold	150	to Rugby.
Apl 22	Tues	No. 979	W. Mold	106	to Preston.
Apl 23	Wed	No. 879	W. Mold	150	to Rugby.
Apl 24	Thurs	No. 879	W. Mold	106	to Preston.
Apl 25	Fri	No. 879	W. Mold	150	to Rugby.
Apl 26	Sat	No. 879	W. Mold	106	to Preston.
Apl 28	Mon		T. Baron		in Shed 1st Engineman.
Apl 29**	Tues	*Wellington*	J. Tortington	158	to Birmingham & Rugby.
Apl 30	Wed	*Mazeppa*	J. Rose	168	two trips to Liverpool.
May 1	Thurs	*Mazeppa*		158	to Birmingham & Rugby.
May 2	Fri	*Mazeppa*		168	two trips to Liverpool.
May 3	Sat				in shop, Turning.
May 4	Sun	No. 582	Breaton	106	to Preston.
May 5	Mon	*Pilot*	W. Beach	42	Excursion to Chester.
May 5	Mon	*Hurricane*			Back to Works.
May 6	Tues	*Snipe*	J. Pigot	24	to Winsford.
May 7	Wed	*Quail*	J. Pigot	62	to Manchester.
May 8	Thurs	*Sirius*	B. Backer	63	to Shrewsbury, to leave her.
May 9	Fri	*Meteor*		50	Cattle to Stafford.
May 10	Sat	*Starling*	W. Beach	63	Assisting to Salop.
May 11	Sun	No. 547		106	to Preston.
May 12	Mon				Relieving.
May 14	Wed	No. 63		106	to Preston.
May 15	Thurs	No. 576		106	to Preston.
May 16	Fri	No. 125		150	to Rugby.
May 17	Sat	No. 574		232	to Carlisle.
May 21	Wed	No. 475		106	to Preston.
May 22	Thurs	No. 475		106	to Preston.
May 23	Fri	No. 581		106	to Preston.
June 1	Sun	No. 141		95	Sunday from Crewe to Hereford all night. Uncoupled
June 2	Mon	No. 141			and then to Pontypool Road to turn and back to Abergavenny branch to ballast for King, contractor.
June 3	Tues	No. 141			Coupled & got ready for Ballasting.
June 4	Wed	No. 141	W. Baker	59	Ballasting.
June 5	Thurs	No. 141		39	Ballasting. Slept Llanfoist Inn.
June 6	Fri	No. 141		40	Ballasting. Slept Llanfoist Inn.
June 7	Sat	No. 141		66	Ballasting. Slept Llanfoist Inn.
June 8	Sun	No. 141			Sunday. Washed out.
June 9	Mon	No. 141		77	Ballasting.
June 10	Tues	No. 141		100	Ballasting.
June 11	Wed	No. 141		30	Ballasting.

** Henceforth in the diary, 'T. Baron' is entered under 'Name of Driver' and the fireman's name is shown occasionally under 'Remarks'. Here, 'Name of Driver' is now replaced with 'Name of Fireman' and 'Remarks' retains the same function as previously.

9th June. 'Robinson came to see us' probably means 'to see me', but who was Robinson? There was a dinner on the opening of the Abergavenny-Brynmawr section on 29th September 1862, which was attended by Geo Findlay and 'Mr Robinson, Loco Supt of the LNWR' (newspaper report). So perhaps that was the 'Robinson' and perhaps he discussed Baron's impending permanent move to Newport/Abergavenny.

22nd July: Baron records 'to Crumlin viaduct, off work', which presumably means that he went to the viaduct just to see it, that is, as a sightseer. The following day he went to Crewe 'for orders' and then worked from there until late August when he went to Shrewsbury and Hereford, and finally to Newport, from where he worked to Hereford until the end of September when he finally moved his family from Crewe to Abergavenny.

Engine classes.

No. 141 - 'Crewe Goods' 2-4-0 tank.
Vandal - 'Crewe Passenger' 2-2-2.
588 - 'DX' class 0-6-0.

Richard Henry Bleasdale was a professional photographer with a particular interest in railway subjects, whose superb photographs, often with the engine crew and other people carefully posed in the picture, are almost instantly recognisable as his work. He was born at Chipping, twelve miles north of Preston, in Lancashire. In the 1870s he lived for a time at Crewe, then at Derby and in the 1880s in Birmingham. A photograph by him, mounted on card, of Webb '17in Coal Engine' No. 2429, carries the inscription 'R. H. Bleasdale, Photo(grapher), 136 Park Road, Aston, Birmingham'. He died in Birmingham in 1897. His son, Reginald E. Bleasdale, 1872-1947, had a photography business in Warwick for many years. He did not take railway photographs himself but sold prints of his father's pictures.

Bleasdale is perhaps best known nowadays for *Spooner's Album,* forty-one pictures of the Festiniog Railway which he took in 1887, on commission by the long-time manager of the Festiniog, Charles Easton Spooner. The album was reproduced and published in 2003. Overall, however, Bleasdale's achievement was his wide coverage of the Britsh railway scene in the second half of the nineteenth century. His negatives are now in the National Railway Museum at York.

Plate 46: *One of the engines Thomas Baron worked on was 'Crewe Goods' 2-4-0 No. 337* Snipe, *posed here at Monument Lane shed in 1877 for the camera of Richard Bleasdale. The records of F. E. A. Eades show that No. 337 was fitted with a new boiler and cylinders in October 1871 and lost its nameplates in 1874-5. Apart from Webb chimney, black paint and a lamp socket at the top of the smokebox (introduced in 1872), it appears much the same as when built. Richard Bleasdale took at least two exposures of No. 337 on this occasion without camera or engine being moved. This one seems to show a typical engine crew of the time, probably the men rostered to work the engine that day.*

Plate 47: *Another view by Richard Bleasdale of 'Crewe Goods' 2-4-0 No. 337 Snipe at Monument Lane shed in 1877. The man standing on the ground by the tender is perhaps the running shed foreman but the two gentlemen posing on the footplate are hardly typical Victorian enginemen. So who are they? Friends of Richard Bleasdale perhaps.*

Plate 48: As pretty a Victorian tank engine as could be imagined, and superbly photographed by Richard Bleasdale at Walsall shed despite what would now be considered primitive equipment and methods. 'Crewe Goods' 2-4-0 No. 46 Medea was built in April 1848 with small firebox and curved frames and rebuilt as a tank engine in 1870. In June 1875 it was put on the duplicate list as No. 1966 and withdrawn in June 1888. The date is in the 1880s, as the boiler bands seem to be in the later style - a red line on either side, rather than a central red line with cream and grey on either side. The beautifully shaped numerals '6' and '9' on the numberplate are well shown. From 1915 these numerals were somehow wrongly interchanged on new numberplates made in Crewe Works, upside down versions of both being used with noticeably bad aesthetic consequences!

Plate 49: *Not all 'Crewe Goods' 2-4-0s converted to tank engines had side tanks. Some had saddle tanks, perhaps because Crewe Works had scrapped some old saddle tank engines and had some surplus saddle tanks that could be put to good use. No. 145, which was originally built as a large firebox straight frame 2-4-0 in October 1853 and named Crow, poses for the official photographer alongside the paint shop in 1884, probably shortly before it was renumbered 1815 on the duplicate list. It was withdrawn in September 1890.* Crewe OS52

Plate 50: *The first of the Large Firebox 'Crewe Goods' 2-4-0s, No. 310 Isis was built in May 1853 and rebuilt as a saddle tank in April 1874. This picture of it at Manchester London Road station, when it was Longsight carriage pilot, must have been taken after March 1884 when it was renumbered 1924 on the duplicate list and before June 1889 when it was renumbered 3064 in the 3000 series duplicate list. It was scrapped in September 1891. A number of men have gathered to have their pictures taken. On the right is the yard shunter, with his warning hooter in his right hand. Beyond him is a Manchester, Sheffield & Lincolnshire Railway carriage. Another shunter seems to have joined the enginemen on the footplate, a platform inspector or perhaps assistant station master is peering through the gap between the engine and carriage, while two more men are posed on the left. There is a tool box resting on the front bufferbeam, doubtless the only place for it - there is no space on the footplate, even when there are only two men on it, or anywhere else. There is a rope hanging down from the water filler on top of the tank for use by the fireman when taking water. It provides something for him to hold on to when he climbs up, using the footstep on the tank, to stand on the hand rail and guide the 'bag' into the tank. It is a long way down if he falls off!*

Date	Name of Engine	Name of Fireman	Number of Miles	Remarks
1862				
June 12 Thurs	No. 141		20	Ballasting.
June 13 Fri	No. 141		82	Ballasting.
June 14 Sat	No. 141		48	Ballasting.
June 15 Sun	No. 141			Sunday. Washed out.
June 16 Mon	No. 141		42	Ballasting.
June 17 Tues	No. 141		56	Ballasting.
June 18 Wed	No. 141		26	Ballasting.
June 19 Thurs	No. 141		18	Robinson came to see us.
June 20 Fri	No. 141		52	Ballasting.
June 21 Sat	No. 141		66	Ballasting.
June 22 Sun	No. 141			Sunday. Washed out.
June 23 Mon	No. 141		38	Ballasting.
June 24 Tues	No. 141		56	Ballasting.
June 25 Wed	No. 141		71	Ballasting.
June 26 Thurs	No. 141		64	Ballasting.
June 27 Fri	No. 141		42	Ballasting.
June 28 Sat	No. 141		40	Ballasting.
June 29 Sun	No. 141			to Crewe home. Washed out.
June 30 Mon	No. 141		66	Ballasting.
July 1 Tues	No. 141		80	Ballasting.
July 2 Wed	No. 141		77	Ballasting.
July 3 Thurs	No. 141		71	Ballasting.
July 4 Fri	No. 141		80	Ballasting.
July 5 Sat	No. 141		7	Ballasting.
July 6 Sun	No. 141			Washed out.
July 7 Mon	No. 141		38	Ballasting.
July 8 Tues	No. 141		34	Ballasting.
July 9 Wed	No. 141		40	Ballasting.
July 10 Thurs	No. 141		78	Ballasting.
July 11 Fri	No. 141		27	Ballasting.
July 12 Sat	No. 141			Wet. Washed out.
July 13 Sun	No. 141			Sunday. To church.
July 14 Mon	No. 141		16	Ballasting.
July 15 Tues	No. 141		24	Ballasting.
July 16 Wed	No. 141		24	Ballasting.
July 17 Thurs	No. 141		24	Ballasting.
July 18 Fri	No. 141		22	Ballasting.
July 19 Sat	No. 141		26	Ballasting.
July 20 Sun	No. 141			Washed out.
July 21 Mon				to Crumlin Viaduct, off work. [Presumably, to see it.]
July 22 Tues			103	to Crewe for orders.
July 23 Wed				Waiting orders.
July 24 Thurs				Waiting orders.
July 25 Fri				Waiting orders.
July 26 Sat				to Wigan & Preston, pleasure.
July 27 Sun				to Wigan & Preston, pleasure.
July 28 Mon				to Crewe.
July 29 Tues				in Shed Standing Spare.
July 30 Wed				in Shed Standing Spare.
July 31 Thurs	*Vandal*		42	to Chester special.
Aug 1 Fri				Relieving.
Aug 2 Sat				Relieving.
Aug 4 Mon	No. 588	T. Taylor	212	to Holyhead.
Aug 5 Tues	*Vandal*		162	Excursion to Bangor all night.
Aug 6 Wed	*Vandal*		81	from Bangor Excursion.

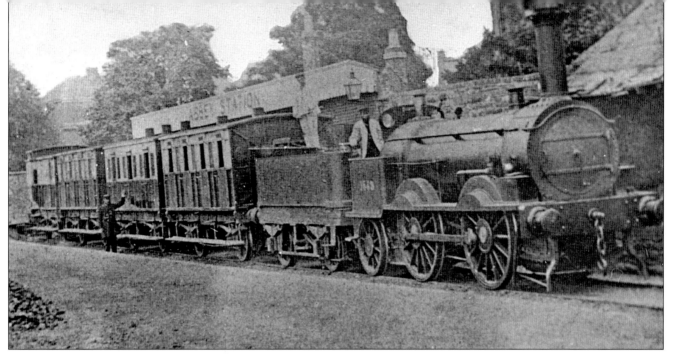

Plate 51: *Scene at Shrewsbury Abbey station of the Potteries, Shrewsbury & North Wales Railway in about 1873, as a train hauled by Bury, Curtis & Kennedy 0-4-2 No.1859 (its old LNWR number before sale to the PS&NW) awaits departure.*

Plate 52: *'DX' No. 49 posed at Coleham shed, Shrewsbury. It was built in June 1871, and this photograph was quite possibly taken shortly after completion, though what the occasion was, with top-hatted gentleman and three others standing by the engine, the driver at the regulator and the fireman beside him, is something of a mystery. Surely a 'DX' at Shrewsbury was hardly something new at that late date, so perhaps the presence of the 'top hat' was the reason for the photograph being taken. Whatever the reason was, however, we must be grateful for an excellent picture.*

Engine classes.
Fury - 'Crewe Goods' 2-4-0.
Nos. 141 and 256 - 'Crewe Goods' 2-4-0 tank engines.
Columbine, Vandal - 'Crewe Passenger' 2-2-2s.
Ambassador, Nos. 448 and 582 - 'DX' class 0-6-0s.
No. 430 - Sharp Bros Goods 0-6-0 built in July 1846 and rebuilt as a saddle tank in March 1858 - see page 105.

No. 465 - Sharp Bros Goods 0-6-0 built January 1849 and rebuilt as 0-6-0 saddle tank 11.1860 - see page 105.

9th August. 'Took her to Birkenhead', but does he mean the engine *Fury* - if so, he gives no mileage - or does he possibly mean his wife?

Date		Name of Engine	Name of Fireman	Number of Miles	Remarks
1862					
Aug 6	Wed	Ambassador		150	to Rugby.
Aug 7	Thurs	Vandal		150	to Rugby with Mail.
Aug 9	Sat	Fury			took her to Birkenhead.
Aug 11	Mon	No. 582	J. Rose	286	to Carlisle.
Aug 12	Tues	No. 582	J. Rose	286	to Carlisle.
Aug 16	Sat	No. 582	J. Rose	286	to Carlisle.
Aug 18	Mon	No. 449		42	Special to Chester.
Aug 19	Tues	No. 590		86	to Liverpool Excursion.
Aug 20	Wed	Reynard	Goff	102	to Rhyl, Goods.
Aug 21	Thurs	No. 318	Goff	212	to Holyhead.
Aug 23	Sat	Ostrich	Goff	102	to Rhyl.
Aug 25	Mon	No. 582			Birmingham.
Aug 26	Tues	No. 582		106	to Preston.
Aug 27	Wed	No. 582		286	to Carlisle.
Aug 29	Fri	No. 582		286	to Carlisle.
Aug 30	Sat	No. 448		62	to Shrewsbury.
Aug 30	Sat	No. 49		31	to Shrewsbury all night.
Aug 31	Sun	No. 448		53	Shrewsbury to Hereford all night.
Sept 1	Mon	Columbine		41	to Newport.
Sept 2	Tues	Columbine		82	Newport to Hereford & Back.
Sept 3	Wed	Columbine		82	Newport to Hereford & Back, 3.30pm.
Sept 4	Thurs	Columbine		82	Newport to Hereford & Back.
Sept 5	Fri	Columbine		82	3.30 Newport to Hereford & Back.
Sept 6	Sat	Columbine		82	3.30 Newport to Hereford & Back.
Sept 7	Sun				Sunday at Newport.
Sept 8	Mon	Columbine		82	8.0am to Hereford & Back.
Sept 9	Tues	Columbine		82	8.0am to Hereford & Back.
Sept 10	Wed	Columbine		82	8.0am to Hereford & Back.
Sept 11	Thurs	Columbine		82	8.0am to Hereford & Back.
Sept 12	Fri	Columbine		82	8.0am to Hereford & Back.
Sept 13	Sat	Columbine		82	8.0am to Hereford & Back. Home at night to Crewe.
Sept 14	Sun				Crewe to Newport to work.
Sept 15	Mon	Columbine		82	to Hereford & Back, 3.30pm.
Sept 16	Tues	Columbine		82	to Hereford & Back, 3.30pm.
Sept 17	Wed	Columbine		82	to Hereford & Back, 3.30pm.
Sept 18	Thurs	No. 430		19	Government Inspector to Brynmawr.
Sept 19	Fri	Columbine		82	to Hereford & Back.
Sept 22	Mon	Columbine		82	8.0am to Hereford & Back.
Sept 23	Tues	No. 465		105	to Crewe to leave Engine.
Sept 24	Wed	No. 256		105	Crewe to Abergavenny.
Sept 25	Thurs	No. 256		22	Trying Engine.
Sept 27	Sat				Crewe to Abergavenny. Wife and furniture.
Sept 29	Mon	No. 141		38	two passenger trains to Brynmawr.
Sept 30	Tues	No. 141		40	Ballasting.
Oct 1	Wed	No. 141		57	three trips to Brynmawr: 9.30am, 12.55, 6.00pm. Opening of Line.
Oct 2	Thurs	No. 141		57	three trips to Brynmawr.
Oct 3	Fri	No. 141		57	three trips to Brynmawr.
Oct 4	Sat	No. 141		57	three trips to Brynmawr.
Oct 5	Sun				Sunday. Washed out.
Oct 6	Mon	No. 141		57	three trips to Brynmawr.
Oct 7	Tues	No. 141		57	three trips to Brynmawr.
Oct 8	Wed	No. 141		57	three trips to Brynmawr.
Oct 9	Thurs	No. 141		57	three trips to Brynmawr.
Oct 10	Fri	No. 141		57	three trips to Brynmawr.

Plate 53: *6ft 'Crewe Single' No. 1192 Lazonby sometime between 1873 and 1879. It was built by Rothwell for the Lancaster & Carlisle Railway in 1857 and is seen here as No. 1192 after it was restored to the capital list in December 1871. The location is the LNWR shed at Hereford, which was built originally for the Shrewsbury & Hereford Railway in the 1850s. This photograph was submitted to the LNWR Society with a request for information and was put on the Society's Webbsite as 'mystery photograph' No. 77. The caption here has been based on the information later published on the site, which came mainly from Harry Jack.*

Date		Name of Engine	Name of Fireman	Number of Miles	Remarks
1862					
Oct 11	Sat	No. 141		57	three trips to Brynmawr.
Oct 12	Sun				Sunday. Washed out.
Oct 13	Mon	No. 141		57	three trips to Brynmawr.
Oct 14	Tues	No. 141		57	three trips to Brynmawr.
Oct 15	Wed	No. 141		57	three trips to Brynmawr.
Oct 16	Thurs	No. 141		57	three trips to Brynmawr.
Oct 17	Fri	No. 141		57	three trips to Brynmawr.
Oct 18	Sat	No. 141		57	three trips to Brynmawr.
Oct 19	Sun	No. 141			Sunday. Washed out.
Oct 20	Mon	No. 141		57	three trips to Brynmawr.
Oct 21	Tues	No. 141		57	three trips to Brynmawr.
Oct 22	Wed	No. 141		57	three trips to Brynmawr.
Oct 23	Thurs	No. 141	J. Thomas	57	three trips to Brynmawr.
Oct 24	Fri	No. 141		57	three trips to Brynmawr.
Oct 25	Sat	No. 141		57	three trips to Brynmawr.
Oct 26	Sun				Sunday. Washed out.
Oct 27	Mon	No. 141		57	three trips to Brynmawr.
Oct 28	Tues	No. 141		57	three trips to Brynmawr.
Oct 29	Wed	No. 141		57	three trips to Brynmawr.
Oct 30	Thurs	No. 141		57	three trips to Brynmawr.
Oct 31	Fri	No. 141		57	three trips to Brynmawr.
Nov 1	Sat	No. 141		57	three trips to Brynmawr.
Nov 2	Sun	No. 430			Sunday. Washed out.
Nov 3	Mon	No. 430		19	Engine failed.
Nov 4	Tues	No. 141		57	Leading wheels changed.
Nov 5	Wed	No. 141		86	Brynmawr & Llanfingel.
Nov 6	Thurs	No. 141		76	Brynmawr & Llanfingel.
Nov 7	Fri	No. 141		57	Brynmawr & Llanfingel.
Nov 8	Sat	No. 141		57	Brynmawr & Llanfingel.
Nov 9	Sun	No. 141			Sunday. Washed out. Blocks.
Nov 10	Mon	No. 141		67	Brynmawr & Llanfingel.
Nov 11	Tues	No. 141		57	Brynmawr & Llanfingel.
Nov 12	Wed	No. 141		76	Brynmawr & Llanfingel.
Nov 13	Thurs	No. 141		76	Brynmawr & Llanfingel.
Nov 14	Fri	No. 141		76	four trips Brynmawr & Llanfingel.
Nov 15	Sat	No. 141		76	four trips to Brynmawr.
Nov 16	Sun	No. 141	J. Thomas		Sunday. Washed out.
Nov 17	Mon	No. 262		57	three trips to Brynmawr.
Nov 18	Tues	No. 262		57	three trips to Brynmawr.
Nov 19	Wed	No. 262		57	three trips to Brynmawr.
Nov 20	Thurs	No. 262		57	three trips to Brynmawr.
Nov 21	Fri	No. 262		57	three trips to Brynmawr.
Nov 22	Sat	No. 262		57	three trips to Brynmawr.
Nov 23	Sun	No. 262			Sunday. Washed out.
Nov 24	Mon	No. 262		57	three trips to Brynmawr.
Nov 25	Tues	No. 262		57	three trips to Brynmawr.
Nov 26	Wed	No. 262		57	three trips to Brynmawr.
Nov 27	Thurs	No. 262		57	three trips to Brynmawr.
Nov 28	Fri	No. 262		57	three trips to Brynmawr. New Blocks.
Nov 29	Sat	No. 262		57	three trips to Brynmawr.
Nov 30	Sun	No. 262			Sunday, washed out.

Abergavenny Branch L & N W Railway
Driving on this same branch from this date up to April 24 1877 and commenced
being Night Foreman April 25 1877 at Abergavenny Engine Shed.

3rd November.
Despite the primitive state of the steam locomotive in the 1850s and 60s, this is the first time in the whole diary that Baron records 'Engine failed'. Primitive they may have been, but on this evidence the engines of that time were not unreliable.

5th November *et seq*. 'Llanfingel' is presumably the modern 'Llanvihangel'.
Engine classes: No. 141 and 262 - 'Crewe Goods' 2-4-0 tank engines; No. 430 - Sharp Bros Goods 0-6-0 built in 1846 and rebuilt as a saddle tank in 1858 - see page 105.

Plates 54: *This Sharp 0-6-0 saddle tank, photographed outside Crewe Works paint shop, is not No. 430 on which Thomas Baron worked, as the openings in the coupling-rod arches are smaller than those in other photographs, but possibly it is one of seven Sharp 0-6-0s built for the North Eastern Division in 1857 and later converted to saddle tanks (British Locomotive Catalogue Part 2A, pages 123-4). Whatever its origins, it has acquired a Webb chimney and other Crewe boiler fittings - or does it in fact have a Ramsbottom boiler?*
LGRP 15125

Plate 55: *'Old Crewe' 6ft Single No. 42* Sunbeam *became* Engineer Northampton *in April 1895. Here the cleaners seem to have done a good job on it, possibly at Northampton shed in the late 1890s.*
C. J. Alcock

At the back of Baron's diary are what appear to be simply personal notes of things he wished to remember. They are transcribed below, retaining his spelling, with explanations of some words and phrases in square brackets.

Recept for Stomak and Hapatite 5 New Egs.
[Recipe for stomach and appetite]

Robert Worsley. Painter House Decorator, Worsley Terrace, Standishgate Wigan. Also House Agent.
Joseph Howard. Brick layer and concractor Greenough Street Wigan.

Adresses
Mr Charles Harris. Engineman.
Kilburn Street Hill, Shepton Mallet, Somercet.
Mr P. Slater, Thomas Buildings, Wharfe Road, Soho, Birmingham
Revd. T. Leech, Foxdale, Sent Jomes, Isle of Man.
['Sent Jomes' - Saint Johns? as below]
Mr James Lawson, 64 Cromptons Terrace, Warrington Lane, Wigan.
Mr Kermode, Foxdale, St Jons, Isle of Man.
Mr Thomas Lowe, No. 9 Rodney Street, House Agent, Wigan.
Took Springfield Cottage Cantrif October 11 1872.
Came in October 22 1872.
Mr T. Lowe, 3 Brethertons Row, Market Place, Wigan.
Mr Thomas Lowe, Brethertons Row, Market Place, Wigan, Lancashire.

Certifate of Marriage of Robert Baron & Betty Mackinson at the Parish Church of Bolton le Moors on the 12th day of Sept 1830 by Thos Logg, Curate

Richard Hargreaves	)	
James Liptrot	) Witnesses	
Henery Powell present - Vicar		
	Cost	5s 2d

[The date 1879 is enclosed in a box near the first line above and seems to indicate the date when the certificate was sent for.]

Thomas Baron is son was Baptized at Standish Church April 19 1835 and was born at Adlington.
Thomas Marsden Curate
Cost   3s 7d

Deth regester of Father cost 2s 7d
	Postage	10d
	Total	12s 2d

Ages of Robert Barons Children
April 17 1831	Margret	Born
March 6 1833	Sarah	Born
April 5 1835	Thomas	Born
Jany 23 1838	Mary	Born
Dec 25 1840	Jane	Born
Apl 14 1843	Elizabeth	Born
Oct 30	John	Born
June 30 1849	William	Born

Betty ther Mother Died Sept 8 1849 and was Buired at Standish Church Lancashire.
Robert there Father Died April 7 1874 and was Buired at Standish Church Apl 10.
No. of Book 71 & 72 1387.
No. of Patent Lever watch Esplin Wigan 650.
No. of Ded Beat watch Yates maker 2945.
June 6 1873 Mrs Smith came to live with us from Preston.
Jane Smith Died April 17 1874 and was Buired at the cemetry Abergaveny.

74755 No of Mrs Barons Gold Watch.

Reciepts
One gallon of water. 1/2 oz of Ginger 1/2 oz of Cream of Tarter 4 oz of Sugar when nearly cold put in a little Barme and bottle it.
[Apparently, this is a recipe for ginger beer; barm - yeast, in Lancashire.]

A Reciet for Sores on gathered Brests
one pennyworth of Venus Terpintime.
[Venice turpentine.]
one pennyworth of Honney the yoak of one Egg a little Lard and Flower mix into a Salve

A Reciet for the Yellows
Boiled Ormric and goos greace
[Ormric - turmeric; 'goos greace' - goose grease.]
Aply it on a plaster on the Crown of the Head.

Quoit Club Commenced February 9 1872 2d per week.

M A H F Ends M. Mr S. Piark B.

Adresses
Mrs Robinson at Mesr Smalwood & Sons Lower Priory Birmingam.
Mr S. Hill; Gate Street Oswestry Salop.
Mr S. Hill No 1 Darby Place High Street Gosport Hants
Mr G. Ramsey Engine Driver Nantwich Road Crewe
Mr Robert Baron, 52 Lower Morris Street, Schoels, Wigan, Lancs
Mrs S. Prowe Shop Keeper Ince Near Wigan Lancashire
Mr G. Lewis 60 Nelson St Preston
Mr Robert Nevin Ince Old Hall Nr Wigan
Mr John Clements Engine Driver 20 Albion Street Pill Newport Monmouthshire

Thomas Baron -1835-1910
Harry Jack

Born in the days of King William IV and Queen Adelaide, Thomas Baron lived right through the long reign of Queen Victoria, then most of that of Edward VII, and died a few weeks before the accession of George V. He was two years old when the Grand Junction Railway opened, and eleven when the London & North Western Railway was created; the Crimean War broke out just before his 19th birthday, the American Civil War ended just after his 30th. In his last years, only a century ago, he could have been known by people who were known to many of us. But his life was very different from ours.

His parents, Robert Baron and Betty Makinson, came from the village of Adlington in Lancashire and were married in 1830. Robert was described as an 'engineer', and later as an 'engine tenter' in a cotton mill, so he was probably a maintenance mechanic looking after stationary engines and other machinery such as looms and spinning-mules; Betty Makinson (or Mackinson) was a farmer's daughter. Adlington was in the parish of Standish, but Makinson's farm was just over the boundary in Bolton-le-Moors parish, so it was at Bolton that they were married on 12th September. This was just three days before the opening of the Liverpool & Manchester Railway, although by that time Bolton already had its own railway, which ran for almost ten miles to the site of its planned junction with the Liverpool & Manchester at Kenyon. The Bolton line had been worked by some famous pioneer locomotives: Timothy Hackworth's Rainhill Trials entrant *Sans Pareil*, Robert Stephenson's *Lancashire Witch*, Edward Bury's *Dreadnought* and *Liverpool*. Omens, perhaps, of Thomas's future career?

Thomas was born in Adlington on 5th April 1835, and was baptised in the parish church at Standish a fortnight later. By the time he was six, the family had moved to Lady Lane in the hamlet of Goose Green, which sounds like a rustic idyll, but by that time it had become surrounded by coal pits. In the 1840s, probably when Robert Baron's work took him to another factory, they moved into Wigan, to the Scholes district, which was then rapidly filling up with industry and rows of streets; their new address was Eccles Mill Yard. Thomas was the third of at least eight children, but when he was fourteen, and shortly after the birth of her last child, his mother died.

His father Robert remained with the rest of the family in Wigan, but Thomas was sent away to his widowed grandmother's to work as a 'farmer's errand-boy' on her small farm on Adlington Common. What his schooling had been and what else he may have worked at are unknown, but at the age of twenty in June 1855 he started work on the railway, as a cleaner at Preston engine shed. Six months later he began occasional trips on the footplate as a stoker, and was promoted to a full-time fireman in 1857. He was then lodging in Water Street West, overlooking the curve on the railway just north of Preston station.

On Christmas Eve in that year, in St John's church, Preston, he married Grace Smith. She was a 21-year old weaver, living with her widowed mother in a small terraced house in Bow Lane, midway on the short walk between Preston station and the engine shed. His diary does not mention his marriage, being mostly an account of his work, but he was on the footplate the day before his marriage and the day after it.

Grace's father, Joseph Smith, had been a flax-dresser in a nearby mill, but had died twenty years before, leaving his wife Jane to bring up their four infant children. They lived in a series of tiny dwellings in Spring Street, Marsh Lane and Bow Lane in the same small area of Preston among textile mills.

After their marriage Thomas and Grace moved into 3, Lodge Street, taking his mother-in-law with them. This street was just next to Preston engine shed. They had a daughter, Elizabeth, born in 1858, followed by a son, Robert, in 1860. Sadly Robert had *spina bifida* and was hydrocephalic; he suffered from fits and only lived for nine months. All Thomas put in his diary was the stark entry on 12th December 1860: 'Burying Child'.

He was transferred to Crewe in October 1861, and moved his wife and daughter there in the following February. Perhaps they were glad to go, for the 'Cotton Famine' created by the Northern blockade of Confederate ports during the American Civil War was beginning to cause acute distress in the cotton towns of Lancashire; eventually almost half the work force of Preston was unemployed and on meagre parish relief.

Thomas was promoted to driver in April 1862, and worked away from home, driving ballast trains for the contractor of the Abergavenny branch in June and July, while living at the Llanfoist Inn. He then returned home to Crewe but was soon transferred permanently to Abergavenny and moved his family 'and furniture' there on 27th September 1862.

In 1864 their daughter Elizabeth caught scarlet fever and died, aged 6, leaving them childless, but seven more children were born later and survived - perhaps helped by being brought up in healthier surroundings than industrial Lancashire. At first they lived in Grofield in Abergavenny, then moved to Chapel Road, Cantref, near Brecon Road station and the new Abergavenny engine shed which opened in 1867. In 1871 they were living at a public house, The Cantref, but the following year they moved into nearby Springfield Cottage. Thomas was a regular driver on the Merthyr, Tredegar & Abergavenny branch until his last promotion, to Night Foreman at Abergavenny shed, on 25th April 1877.

Thomas's father Robert had remained in Scholes, Wigan, and died there aged 64 in April 1874; he was buried at Standish church, where he had buried his wife twenty-five years before. Grace's mother Jane Smith, after thirty-five years of widowhood in Preston, moved in 1873 to live with her daughter and son-in-law at Abergavenny, but she died just ten days after Thomas's father.

By the 1890s Thomas and family were living at Prospect House in North Street, Cantref. In his retirement he has been described as having a big beard, and was often to be seen standing by his garden gate. He died of influenza, aged 74, on 13th January 1910. Three weeks later his widow, a chronic asthmatic, had a stroke and died.

Baron's Engines
Harry Jack

Locomotives at Preston shed.

In the early period of Baron's diary the line north of Preston belonged to the Lancaster & Carlisle Railway, but it was worked by the LNWR, so in addition to working south over LNWR tracks, engines from Preston shed also took trains north through Lancaster over Shap to Carlisle, and on the Kendal & Windermere branch from Oxenholme; Baron records firing on an excursion to 'Cendal' on 9th September 1856. Then it was arranged that the L&C would provide its own motive power from 1st August 1857, and to help out, forty LNWR engines were sold to them. Of these forty, Baron worked on fifteen during 1856 and the early months of 1857.

Meanwhile, beginning in January 1857, engines were built at Crewe to replace those about to be sold, bearing the same names and numbers. Baron mentions four engines before the date of the sale, which had already been replaced by new engines: *Canning, Starling, Redstart* and *Friar*; but the engines he refers to must be the engines sold to the L&C, rather than the newer engines built in January, February and May of that year. Presumably the new engines were kept in store and had not yet entered traffic.

He worked on another curious L&C engine, one of that company's first two, *Spitfire*, which was a mysterious 0-6-0 built by Jones & Potts in September 1846; the L&C then sold it to a somewhat reluctant LNWR in November 1847. Baron fired on it on 6th and 10th November 1856, on trips to the Victoria colliery, Standish, just a few days before an offer from the colliery owner, John Taylor & Co, was accepted and the engine went to them for £590.

Something similar happened with *Ribble*, with which he went to Parkside on a ballasting job on 3rd March 1856. It was recorded on 9th May as having been sold, 'with its tender', to James Cross of the St Helens Railway for £500. This was another mysterious engine. Originally from the Preston & Wyre Railway, it had come to the LNWR in April 1850, after a spell on the Lancashire & Yorkshire. It is believed to have been an 0-4-0 or 0-4-2 built by Bury, Curtis & Kennedy, perhaps in 1846-7.

The others he worked on from Preston were mostly standard 'Old Crewe' types, half a dozen of them dating back to Grand Junction days, and a couple built at Edge Hill, but in this period he also mentions three nameless engines, Nos 2, 5 and 14, which were probably from the Ballast Engine stock.

Originally the maintenance of Northern Division track had been in the hands of private contractors, but in November 1852 LNWR engineers took over and some old engines were set aside for the work. These engines seem to have lost their names but were given numbers, and by 1858 they comprised Nos. 1 to 25. Their identities are unknown, with one exception. Ballast engine No. 14, which seems likely to be the engine Baron fired to Carlisle and back on 6th June 1857, was the famous ex-Liverpool & Manchester Railway 0-4-2 *Lion*, now preserved, which featured in *The Titfield Thunderbolt* and other films.

He also fired to Carlisle and back on No 2 (1st February 1857) and went four miles to Broughton and back with No 5 'trying engine' (14th January 1857) before going with it to Carlisle on a goods train the following day. Of course, it could be that these were running numbers of Crewe engines, but if so it is odd that apart from these three he always gives the engine's name at this period, and none of the names of traffic engines Nos. 2, 5 and 14 - *Hecla, Falcon,* and *Witch* - are ever mentioned by him.

The ballast engine stock seems to have been discontinued shortly after this; Nos 9, 10 and 21 were sold in August 1858, and No 14 was sold 'out of stores' in May 1859.

In Baron's last year at Preston he had more modern engines: his first 'DX', No 450 *Banshee* in November 1860, followed in March 1861 by No 548, apparently his first encounter with the then new injector, and his first 'Problem', *Tantalus*, in June. He also worked on two of the newer L&C engines, *Newby* and *Wennington*, which had come to the LNWR with the other L&C stock after that company was leased to the LNWR in August 1859. Both were based on the 'Old Crewe' design: *Newby*, built by Rothwell in 1856 was a 2-4-0, while *Wennington* was a Fairbairn 6ft 2-2-2 of 1859.

Locomotives After Preston.

Baron's transfer to Crewe brought him into immediate contact with more of the standard 'DX' and 'Problem' classes, but also with some oddities - Fairbairn 0-4-2, No. 475 from the erstwhile North Eastern Division, and two of McConnell's engines from Wolverton, No. 879, a Fairbairn Goods 0-6-0, and No. 979, a 'Small Bloomer'; they had evidently been transferred to Crewe for trial immediately upon the takeover of the Southern Division. His first mention of 979, on 21st April 1862, is the earliest known record of an engine with its new number after the renumbering of the entire SD stock by the addition of 600, which occurred at some as yet undiscovered date in that month.

There was also an 'Old Crewe Goods' which had been rebuilt as a 2-4-0 tank engine and had spent some time on the North London Railway before its return at the end of 1860 when the LNWR renumbered it 141 and, perhaps at some later date, named it *Pheasant*. This engine took him to Monmouthshire, where it was hired for £4 4s per day to Mr King, the contractor for the Abergavenny to Brynmawr section of the Merthyr, Tredegar & Abergavenny line. On the ceremonial opening day, 29th September 1862, Baron drove No. 141 with two trains up to Brynmawr and back, and in the next two months, to the end of his diary, this engine and another Crewe Goods tank, No. 262 *Liver*, worked the branch passenger trains.

Other engines he drove from Abergavenny included two more from the old North Eastern Division, Sharp 0-6-0 saddle tanks Nos. 430 and 465. With 430 he took Colonel William Yolland on his official inspection of the new line from Abergavenny Junction to Brynmawr on 18th September 1862 - the colonel expressed himself 'fully satisfied'. The other Sharp saddle tank, No. 465, had seen service on all three LNWR divisions: it was originally built for the SD, transferred to the NED, then taken over by the ND.

Curiously, at least one and probably two of Baron's engines have survived: No. 49 *Columbine*, now in the Science Museum in its 1870s guise as No. 1868, and the famous *Lion*, which has recently been put on show at the new Museum of Liverpool.

The list which follows identifies each of the engines Baron records, as they were at the time he worked on them, and gives information such as the class, wheel arrangement, builder, date and so forth but for the most part excludes the complexities of their subsequent history; firstly it lists in alphabetical order the engines he records by name and then in numerical order those he records by number.

The information is generally based on *British Locomotive Catalogue 1825-1923 Parts 2A and 2B London & North Western Railway and its Constituent Companies* compiled by Bertram Baxter and edited by David Baxter and published by Moorland Publishing Company, Ashbourne, Derbyshire, and supplemented by additional information from the work of D. H. Stuart, W. L. Harris, Ted Craven, Brian Reed and Harry Jack.

Name	No.	Details
Adjutant	159	'Crewe Goods' 2-4-0 built 1.1857.
Admiral	172	'Crewe Goods' 2-4-0 built 10.1847, rebuilt 7.1858.
Albion	76	'Crewe Passenger' 2-2-2 built by GJR 9.1845, rebuilt 2.1858.
Ambassador	216	'DX' 0-6-0 built 10.1860.
Ant	300	'Crewe Goods' 2-4-0 built 1.1853.
Atalanta	97	'Problem' 2-2-2 built 5.1860.
Banshee	369	'DX' 0-6-0 built 6.1859.
Baronet	101	'Crewe Goods' 2-4-0 built 2.1847.
Bela	89	'Crewe Goods' 2-4-0 built 8.1846, rebuilt 12.1857.
Booth	308	'Crewe Goods' 2-4-0 built 4.1853. To L&C 8.1857.
Cadmus	256	'Crewe Goods' 2-4-0 built 3.1850.
Canning (i)	110	'Crewe Passenger' 2-2-2 built 6.1847. To L&C 8.1857.
Canning (ii)	110	'Crewe Passenger' 2-2-2 built 1.1857.
Caradoc	246	'Crewe Goods' 2-4-0 built 10.1849.
Castor	199	'Crewe Goods' 2-4-0 built 3.1848. To L&C 8.1857.
Cerberus	18	'Crewe Passenger' 7ft 2-2-2 built 6.1857.
Chillington	243	'Crewe Goods' 2-4-0 built 5.1849.
Clarendon	264	'Crewe Goods' 2-4-0 built 5.1851.
Colossus	66	'Crewe Goods' 2-4-0 built 10.1851.
Columbine	49	'Crewe Passenger' 2-2-2 built by GJR 7.1845, rebuilt 1856.
Commodore	175	'Crewe Goods' 2-4-0 built 11.1847, rebuilt 8.1858.
Dalemain	80	'Crewe Passenger' 2-2-2 built by GJR 3.1846, rebuilt 10.1857.
Delamere	228	'Crewe Goods' 2-4-0 built 12.1848.
Dromedary	168	'Crewe Passenger' 2-2-2 built Edge Hill 8.1847, rebuilt 11.1859.
Eagle	20	'Crewe Goods' 2-4-0 built 11.1854. To L&C 8.1857.
Eden	87	'Crewe Goods' 2-4-0 built 8.1846.
Elephant	113	'Crewe Goods' 2-4-0 built 6.1847, rebuilt 11.1857.
Elk	299	'Crewe Goods' 2-4-0 built 11.1852.
Ellesmere	245	'Crewe Goods' 2-4-0 built 8.1849.
Falstaff	358	'Crewe Goods' 2-4-0 built 3.1855. To L&C 8.1857.
Fame	197	'Crewe Goods' 2-4-0 built 3.1848.
Fly	302	'Crewe Goods' 2-4-0 built 2.1853.
Friar	178	'Crewe Passenger' 2-2-2 built 11.1849. To L&C 8.1857.
Fury	307	'Crewe Goods' 2-4-0 built 3.1853.

Name	No.	Details
Goldfinch	151	'Crewe Passenger' 7ft 2-2-2 built 8.1857.
Hardwicke	292	'Crewe Goods' 2-4-0 built 11.1852.
Helvellyn	94	'Crewe Passenger' 2-2-2 built 11.1846.
Herald	263	'Crewe Goods' 2-4-0 built 2.1851.
Hurricane	330	'Crewe Goods' 2-4-0 built 3.1854.
Ingestre	85	'Crewe Passenger' 2-2-2 built by GJR 5.1846, rebuilt 8.1857.
Ixion	232	'Crewe Goods' 2-4-0 built 12.1848.
Jason	40	'Crewe Passenger' 2-2-2 built 5.1847. To L&C 8.1857.
Liver	262	'Crewe Goods' 2-4-0 built 11.1850.
Loadstone	288	'Crewe Goods' 2-4-0 built 8.1852.
Marquis	102	'Crewe Goods' 2-4-0 built 3.1850.
Mazeppa	234	'Problem' 2-2-2 built 11.1861.
Megatherion	212	'Crewe Passenger' 2-2-2 built Edge Hill 5.1848.
Menai	206	'Crewe Goods' 2-4-0 built 6.1848.
Mercury	371	'Crewe Passenger' 2-2-2 built 7.1855.
Mersey	77	'Crewe Passenger' 2-2-2 built by GJR 11.1845.
Meteor	115	'Crewe Passenger' 2-2-2 built 5.1849, rebuilt 1.1858.
Minotaur	271	'Crewe Goods' 2-4-0 built 8.1851. To L&C 8.1857.
Newby	378	Goods 2-4-0 built by Rothwell 1857 for L&C (No. 2), LNWR 378 12.1859.
Ostrich	133	Goods 0-6-0 built by Beyer Peacock 1859. To LNWR 1.1860.
Owl	134	'Problem' 2-2-2 built 5.1860.
Pilot	181	'Crewe Goods' 2-4-0 built 11.1847, rebuilt 7.1857.
Pollux	200	'Crewe Goods' 2-4-0 built 3.1848. To L&C 8.1857.
Prince Ernest	313	'Crewe Passenger' 2-2-2 built 6.1853. To L&C 8.1857.
Problem	184	'Problem' 2-2-2 built 11.1859.
Quail	335	'Crewe Goods' 2-4-0 built 5.1854.
Redstart	156	'Crewe Goods' 2-4-0 built 3.1856. To L&C 8.1857.
Reynard	318	'Crewe Goods' 2-4-0 built 9.1853.
Ribble	258	Goods 0-4-0 (?) built by Bury (?) for Preston & Wyre Railway 1847 (?), LNWR ND No. 258 from 4.1850. Sold to the St Helens Railway for £500 in 5.1856 and seems to have kept its name. The St Helens Railway already had a *Mersey*, and the two were soon joined by *Tyne, Forth, Dee, Shannon* and so on. When the LNWR acquired the St Helens Railway in 1864, *Ribble* was allocated No. 1376 in 8.1864, but was scrapped the following month.
St George	203	'Crewe Goods' 2-4-0 built 4.1848.
Saddleback	84	'Crewe Passenger' 2-2-2 built by GJR 4.1846, rebuilt 8.1857.
Salopian	248	'Crewe Goods' 2-4-0 built 10.1849.
Scorpion	7	'Crewe Passenger' 2-2-2 built 4.1852.
Sefton	285	'Crewe Passenger' 2-2-2 built 5.1852. To L&C 8.1857.
Sirius	30	'Crewe Goods' 2-4-0 built 1.1855.
Snake	373	'Crewe Goods' 2-4-0 built 8.1855. To L&C 8.1857.
Snipe	337	'Crewe Goods' 2-4-0 built 5.1854.
Snowdon	227	'Crewe Goods' 2-4-0 built 9.1848.
Spitfire	215	Jones & Potts 0-6-0 built 9.1846 for L&C, No. 2. Sold to LNWR 1848, No. 215. Sold to John Taylor & Co, £590, minuted 14.11.1856; Taylor owned the Victoria Pit, Standish.
Star	165	'Problem' 2-2-2 built 11.1860.
Starling (i)	154	'Crewe Goods' 2-4-0 built 11.1854. To L&C 8.1857.
Starling (ii)	154	'Crewe Goods' 2-4-0 built 2.1857.
Stentor	6	'Crewe Goods' 2-4-0 built 11.1854.
Tantalus	60	'Problem' 2-2-2 built 3.1860.
Terrier	357	'Crewe Goods' 2-4-0 built 2.1855. To L&C 8.1857.
Tiger	117	'Crewe Passenger' 2-2-2 built Edge Hill 5.1849, to traffic 5.1850.
Vampire	43	'Crewe Goods' 2-4-0 built 10.1848, rebuilt 6.1857.
Vandal	59	'Crewe Passenger' 2-2-2 built Edge Hill 7.1848, rebuilt 7.1859.
Vulture	47	'Crewe Passenger' 2-2-2 built 5.1847, rebuilt 4.1857.
Wasp	241	'Crewe Goods' 2-4-0 built 5.1850, rebuilt as 2-4-0 tank 12.1858.
Wellington	218	'Problem' 2-2-2 built 2.1862.
Wennington	533	Passenger 2-2-2 built by Fairbairn 1859 for L&C (No. 70), LNWR No. 533 12.1859.
Wordsworth	82	'Crewe Goods' 2-4-0 built by GJR 4.1846.

No.	Details
1	'Problem' 2-2-2 built 11.1861, later named *Saracen*.
2	Ballast engine, details unknown.
	Possibly: *Hecla*, 'Crewe Goods' 2-4-0 built by GJR 10.1844.
5	Ballast engine, details unknown.
	Possibly: *Falcon*, 'Crewe Goods' 2-4-0 built 9.1855.
14	0-4-2 built by Todd, Kitson & Laird 7.1838 for L&M *Lion*; 'Ballast Engine No. 14' from 1857.
	Possibly: *Witch* 'Crewe Passenger' 2-2-2 built by GJR 6.1846.
49	*Columbine*, 'Crewe Passenger' 2-2-2 built by GJR 7.1845, rebuilt 1856.
63	*Herod*, 'Crewe Goods' 2-4-0 built 9.1855.
125	*Soho*, 'DX' 0-6-0 built 11.1861.
141	'Crewe Goods' 2-4-0 tank, built as 2-4-0 *Ellesmere* No. 245 in 8.1849, rebuilt as tank engine 11.1859, to North London Railway (No. 35) 2.1860. Returned to LNWR, in 12.1860 numbered 141 and named *Pheasant* then or shortly after. Hired to Mr King, contractor on Merthyr, Tredegar & Abergavenny line 8.1862.
256	*Cadmus*, 'Crewe Goods' 2-4-0 built 3.1850, rebuilt to tank engine 8.1862.
262	*Liver*, 'Crewe Goods' 2-4-0 built 11.1850, rebuilt to 2-4-0 tank engine in 9.1860.
318	*Reynard*, 'Crewe Goods' 2-4-0 built 9.1853.
430	Sharp Bros 0-6-0 Goods built 7.1846, NED 30, renumbered 430 in 8.1857, rebuilt 0-6-0 saddle tank with 17in cylinders 3.1858.
448	'DX' 0-6-0 built 7.1859.
449	'DX' 0-6-0 built 7.1859.
450	'DX' 0-6-0 built 9.1859.
465	Sharp Bros Goods 0-6-0 1.1849, SD 238, to NED 65 in 10.1849, LNWR 465 8.1857, rebuilt as 0-6-0 saddle tank 11.1860.
475	Fairbairn 0-4-2 built 2.1854, NED 75, renumbered 475 in 8.1857, rebuilt 1862.
547	'DX' 0-6-0 built 1861.
548	'DX' 0-6-0 built 2.1861.
561	'Problem' 2-2-2, built 5.1861, named *Prince Oscar* 5.1862.
571	'DX' 0-6-0 built 8.1861.
574	'DX' 0-6-0 built 9.1861.
576	'DX' 0-6-0 built 9.1861.
581	'DX' 0-6-0 built 9.1861.
582	'DX' 0-6-0 built 10.1861.
588	'DX' 0-6-0 built 3.1862.
590	'DX' 0-6-0 built 4.1862.
879	Goods 0-6-0 built by Fairbairn 4.1854, SD No. 279, 879 in 4.1862.
979	'Small Bloomer' 2-2-2 built at Wolverton 10.1861, SD No. 379, 979 in 4.1862. *Wasp* in 1872.

Ballast Engines

In one or two places, Baron describes the work he did simply as 'ballasting'. Until 1852 practically all the ballasting work on the Northern Division was done by the contractors, but from 1853 a group of engines separate from the working stock was numbered in its own series as 'Ballast Engines'. These almost certainly were old Northern Division engines which had been replaced in the capital list.

A list of 31st May 1854 shows where the following Ballast Engines were stationed

No.	Station
3	Warrington
4	Birmingham
5	Crewe
9	Chester
10	Chester
11	Bangor
12	Birmingham
13	Edge Hill

Another list of late 1857 or early 1858 shows:

No.	Station
5	Stour Valley line, Birmingham
9	Manchester
10	Bangor
16	Bolton
21	Bangor

In 1858 Ballast Engines carried numbers 1 to 25. Only one of them can be identified, No. 14. This was the ex-Liverpool & Manchester Railway 0-4-2 No 57 *Lion* which was renumbered as LNWR 116 in 1846, and replaced in 8.1857 - so presumably put into ballast stock as No. 14 at that time, or not long before. It was reported on 25th May 1859 as 'Ballast engine *Lion* No. 14 sold out of stores to Mersey Dock Committee for £400'. It became quite famous later!

Plate 56: 'DX' class No. 1651, which was built at Crewe in January 1868, in original condition about 1870. The location is unknown but quite possibly the photograph was taken at Rugby on the same occasion as Plates 45-7, as S. S. Scott states that the class was allocated to sheds in blocks of numbers and that 1600-99 were stationed at No. 8 shed, Rugby, 'at that time and for many years subsequently'. Furthermore, Harry Jack was once told by C. R. Clinker about a Rugby photographer, who took these pictures, so this may also be the work of the same man. Although a crane, a pile of pipes and some trees is not much to work on!

These engines has only two lamp sockets, one at either end of the bufferbeam, the socket at the top of the smokebox being introduced only in 1872-3, while the lamps themselves are of a little-known type with lenses on three sides if not all four. The crane on the left seems to have a hexagonal jib. The upper line of inscription seems to read: 'No. 1 TO LIFT 5 TONS'; and the lower line 'WHEN LIFTING ROUND TIMBER 2½ TONS' (or ROUGH? TIMBER).

Plate 57: 'DX' 0-6-0 No. 578, which was built in September 1861, only seven months after No. 548, the engine which provided Thomas Baron's first experience of an injector. No. 578 has an injector, as the wheel controlling the steam supply is prominent on the side of the firebox. The injector itself is hidden by the footplate side-sheet but the water feed-pipe can be traced easily from below the side sheet, past the firebox behind the centre driving wheel to the clack valve. Apart from this injector, the engine seems to be in much the same condition as No. 355 Hardman, the first of the class, when introduced in September 1858. Both date and location of this photograph are unknown, although it is thought to have been taken at Crewe. No. 578 is quite clean and well cared for, but seems far from new, as its paintwork, especially on the cab side-sheet has been well scuffed and marked by enginemen's boots as they made their way along the running plate.

Plate 58: Lion at the Liverpool & Manchester Railway celebrations in 1930, for which it was restored to working order at Crewe Works.
W. Leslie Good

Plate 59: *In 1859 the old Liverpool & Manchester Railway engine* Lion *was sold by the LNWR to the Mersey Docks & Harbour Board. Shortly before that it had become Ballast Engine No. 14, so may be the engine* Thomas Baron *worked on in June 1857 (see page 24 for details). The MD&HB used it as a stationary engine driving pumps in Prince's Dock, Liverpool, where it was discovered still at work some seventy years later. In 1929 it was removed from the engine house and displayed at Lime Street station in Liverpool, but eventually was taken to Crewe Works and restored by the LMS so that it could perform in the 1930 celebrations of the centenary of the Liverpool & Manchester Railway. This photograph shows it after removal from the pump house. It lacks coupling rods, boiler lagging and any sort of cover on the boiler and firebox.*

Figure 11: *Drawing of* Lion *as first built by Todd, Kitson & Laird for the Liverpool & Manchester Railway in 1838. It was one of two Luggage Engines supplied by that builder at the time, the other being* Tiger. *This drawing was produced at Crewe Works in 1928 and was one of a series depicting the original engines on plaques fitted below the nameplates of 'Royal Scot' class engines named after old locomotives.*

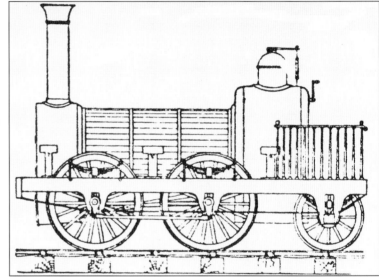

Figure 12: *Drawing of* Lion *prepared by Crewe Works drawing office and signed by Hewitt Beames, who was then divisional mechanical engineer, Crewe, on 9th September 1930.*

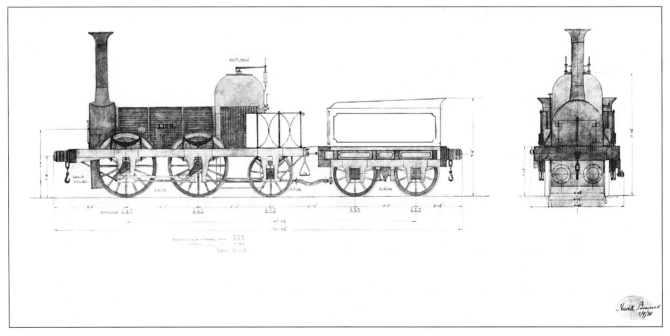

Plate 60: *Crewe Works made an excellent job of restoring Lion, posed here for photography in the traditional place for ex works engines on the Old Line to Chester. It has acquired a brass cover over its firebox durng restoration, which purists are entitled to criticise as non-authentic, but others may forgive this addition as it is at least stylish. Over the years since 1930 the engine has been steamed several times, perhaps most notably starring in the film The Titfield Thunderbolt. During its time at Dinting, it was driven by Mike Bentley, who describes at as 'a lovely little engine'. Who could disagree?*

LNWRS Collection

Plate 61: *'Old Crewe Single' 2-2-2 No. 49* Columbine, *which Thomas Baron worked on at Abergavenny, was renumbered 1198 on the duplicate list in June 1871, to make way for a 'DX' 0-6-0 to take its place in the capital list as No. 49. It was renumbered again as 1868 in December 1871 and became* Engineer Bangor *in November 1877. Here in a photograph by H. S. Shedden (whose notes show the exposure was 1/50sec at f11) it heads along the up line near Abergele in 1897.*

Plate 62: *Another view of* Engineer Bangor *at about the same period. This time it is posed on the six-span lattice-girder viaduct crossing the valley of the Dee north of Corwen, probably in the 1890s.*

Plate 63: *By great good fortune* Engineer Bangor *was preserved (in the mistaken belief that it was the first engine built in Crewe Works) and is now displayed in the Science Museum, South Kensington; its tender is in store at Wroughton near Swindon and the cab, fitted in its later life, is in the Heritage Centre at Crewe, still with the plate stating - incorrectly - that it was the first engine built at Crewe Works in 1843. Its cab was removed when it was prepared for display in its present form, in the first Webb black livery as used in the 1870s with full lining on the boiler, and with its first duplicate number, 1868.*

Plate 64 left: *Close up view of the 'pet cock', operated by the driver twisting the handle on the boiler hand rail at the footplate end. This moved the lever seen here (the pin seems to be missing) which opened or closed the cock at the base of the clack valve and allowed water, steam and air to escape along the polished copper pipe over the side of the engine, indicating to the driver what was happening at the valve.*

Plate 65 below: *Lamp socket on the wooden front bufferbeam with a space between the beam and the front of the inside cylinders. This was the traditional arrangement of many LNWR engines right up to the end of Mr Webb's tenure as chief mechanical engiiner, and lamp sockets were the standard traditional fitting on all LNWR engines until the company ceased to exist in 1923. Only the 'Claughtons' introduced in 1913, were an exception to this rule - for some reason unknown.*

Plate 66: *As first built, No. 1868 had two axle-driven pumps to supply the boiler with water but at some stage the pump on the right-hand side was replaced by an injector mounted on the side of the firebox, as seen here. The pipe curving up from behind the trailing wheel on the left is the water feed from the tender, controlled by a hand wheel on the front of the tender, while the pipe curving away behind the driving wheel on the right leads to the clack valve on the right-hand side of the boiler. Two pipes bring steam from the top of the firebox. The one on the right is the main steam supply to the injector. The other blows steam back into the tender to clear a blockage or melt ice in freezing weather, the large polished overflow pipe allowing steam and water to escape.*

Plate 67 left: *The footplate. The reverser is on the left, the driver's side, and near it is the handle operating the black rod running below the coffee plate to work the sanders on both sides. The four long levers on the back of the spectacle plate operate, left to right: the blower; the whistle; the steam supply to the injector; and steam supply to blow back (by diverting the injector steam supply). The water gauge is a 'modern' addition.*

Plate 68 below: *close up view of the right-hand side of the firebox, showing the two try-cocks, used to check the water level before the fitting of the water gauge, the two steam supply pipes from the top of the firebox and the black rod operating the sanders.*

Plate 69: *No. 1868 in the hall at the Science Museum, photographed from the balcony. The restorers did a superb job of polishing brass and copper fittings, though whether any of the class was ever turned out so well on the LNWR is doubtful. Indeed, safety valves and domes seem to have generally been painted. The copper pipe emerging from behind the dome/safety valve on the firebox is the steam supply to the injector. The pipe branching off it is the 'blow back', diverting steam from it into the tender to clear any blockage.*

Plate 70: *Right-hand cylinder of No. 1868 with drain cocks that could not be operated from the footplate but only by hand, by a man standing on the ground beside the engine.*

All the models on the next four pages, Plates 71-78, are by David Viewing to Gauge 1, 10mm scale 1¾in gauge. David also kindly supplied the captions.

Plate 71 above: *'Crewe Goods' 2-4-0* Mastodon *at the LNWR Society Open Day at Kidderminster Railway Museum in 2015. It has a Ramsbottom chimney and original four-wheel tender as modified about 1860. It is recorded in 'Locomotives in Profile' as built at Crewe in 1849. Some of these engines survived into the 20th century and a photograph shows one of them out of use in a siding in the 1920s.* Mastodon *is in the green livery used by the LNWR until 1873. The exact shade is in doubt, but the colour used here is that recommended by Kenneth Wood, who has studied the subject extensively. The model is built from a kit of parts supplied by John Dale of 'Old Originals' in the late 1990s using etched nickel silver and lost wax castings. It is a working model with helical drive gears and LiPo battery with radio housed in the tender, giving up to four hours running time. There are plans for this model to be made available once more by Mercian Models. The name with a natural history theme was chosen as reflecting the spirit of the age and intended to partner sister engine 2-2-2* Megatherium.

Plate 72 below: Mastodon *on the G1MRA track at Warley exhibition in 2015*

Plate 73: Megatherium *is a 'Crewe Passenger' 2-2-2 very similar to the surviving* Columbine, *presently on display in the Science Museum, London. The original engine was built by the LNWR at Edge Hill, Liverpool, not at Crewe, but the intention in the model is to show it as a Grand Junction Railway engine might have appeared. So it is portrayed 'as built', as closely as possible, with flared chimney cap and horse-hair stuffed buffers. An LNWR minute of the period mentions boilers being clad in canvas sheets and painted. So rather than varnished wood the model shows cladding sheets, which could be either canvas sheets as in the minute or thin iron sheets! The model also incorrectly shows the engine number on the chimney in Southern Division style, even though it is a Northern Division engine. The builder makes no apologies for this, since it looks good, but an alternative chimney is available. The name* Megatherium *(a type of extinct South American giant ground sloth) was chosen to complement* Mastodon *and itself is a subject of contention, being so spelt by authorities such as* Locomotives in Profile, *while others such as Baxter give the spelling* Megatherion. *The model uses components supplied by John Dale and like* Mastodon *is a working model with the same drive and control equipment and with several hours running time. The chassis is fully sprung (essential for a single wheeler) and the engine can operate as a 'double header' with her consort as in Wishaw* Railways of Great Britain.

Plate 74: *LNWR four-compartment composite carriage about 1865 in the original livery, as established by Kenneth Wood from scrapings taken from a surviving door found on a grounded body at Wappenham, near Towcester. It has a rack for luggage on the roof, although there is some doubt about how long this practice persisted. The lining shows an allusion to the 'stage coach' style of earlier Firsts, but in most respects this is a 'modern' carriage of a style that persisted into the 20th century. The model is built from a John Dale etched brass kit, which is now available from Mercian Models.*

Plate 75: *London & Birmingham Railway break van, based on an engraving discovered in the Great Northern Railway archive by Tadeusz Opyrchal. This might be the first break van used on a main-line railway and is attributed to J. Wright & Co, London. Wrights had moved to Birmingham by 1845 and this van may date from the opening of the railway in 1838. A puzzle at first is the lack of cut outs in the side for the guard to look out along the train, a question that resolves itself once it is realised that the ballast for the van is held in a large water tank under the floor. As a result, the floor level is raised by about 18in, meaning that the guard could easily see over the van roof. Headroom inside the van body would have been very limited and it is not known if the now ubiquitous coal stove was provided. The water ballast may not have been satisfactory because a similar but later LNWR van illustrated by Clark in* Railway Machinery *published in 1855 has iron weights and a lower floor level, complete with cut-outs in the sides for the guard to look over. In common with other early L&BR vehicles, the break van has sprung buffers at one end only. It's believed that the sprung buffers faced the front of the train and that vehicles were turned on the ubiquitous wagon turnplates found in every station to face the direction of travel. Brake application is by means of the large lever which must have required considerable force to operate. All later break vans seem to have a screw arrangement.*

Plate 76: *Brown, Marshalls & Co. coaches. This three-compartment First and matching Third are based on drawings in Daniel Kinnear Clark's seminal work* Railway Machinery, *published in 1855, which contains exquisitely detailed engravings of vehicles like the ones illustrated here, apparently reproductions of original works drawings made by Brown, Marshalls & Co. The drawings were traced directly from an original copy of* Railway Machinery *into CAD, and then printed in 22thou etched brass for soldered construction. The models are fitted with ball bearings to enable haulage by single-wheeler locomotives like* Megatherium.
Although not dated, the drawings represent late 1840s practice. The First has glazed windows and even droplights in the doors. The Third is very similar to the surviving LNWR 'Wappenham' coach (see below) and the window openings in the side panels are probably a later modification. It is unlikely that the 'windows' were glazed at the time, although wooden boards might have been supplied to allow passengers to block out some of the weather (and the light!).
Clark does not attribute these carriages to any particular railway, although Brown, Marshalls built vehicles for many lines. Since they were located in Saltley, Birmingham, it is reasonable to suppose that these particular carriages at least crossed LNWR metals and they are shown here in LNWR colours recommended by Kenneth Wood.

Plate 77: *This Brown, Marshalls & Co First was also built from a drawing in* Railway Machinery. *It is finished in a deep blue which is based on the colour of a very similar First at the Swedish Railway Museum in Gavle, Sweden. Although that particular coach is attributed to the railway works at Trollhatten, Sweden, it is known that Brown, Marshalls also supplied coaches in the early days of the Swedish Railways, so the choice of this colour for the model is not entirely fictional. Anyway, it looks nice!*

Plate 78: *This Brown, Marshalls & Co Brake Van is based on another of Clark's illustrations in* Railway Machinery. *Once again, the exquisite detail in Clark's engravings allows a model to be produced incorporating every detail of the prototype, and as with the other models based on Clark, the drawing was traced directly into CAD from the original engraving and reproduced in etched brass. It is not known which lines this brake (or 'Break', as it was spelled then) was sold to but it is hoped that one day a photograph will come to light showing one in service, somewhere. As an aside, it is a particular problem with producing models in the period between the beginning of railways and the end of the 1860s that very few photographs exist, and that most early rolling stock had already disappeared before, as author David Halfpenny puts it, 'The light of photography fell upon the world'.*
The model shows a prominent birdcage, or 'lantern', and a similar arrangement can be seen in a contemporary engraving of the terrible 1865 crash on the South Eastern Railway in which Charles Dickens was involved. Clark's drawing shows 'sledge' brakes that bear directly upon the rail, a very effective type of brake that was outlawed by the 1860's because it tended to tear up the track! These breaks are reproduced in working form in the model and the author was warned by the secretary of the local model engineering society that 'sledge brakes are not permitted in the society's rules', which indeed they are not, in 5in gauge

An Engineman's Point of View
Michael Bentley

The discovery of this valuable and enlightening document and its subsequent copying by Ted Talbot, has created a most interesting subject for me as an ex-footplate man and ASLEF member, who has studied the working conditions of locomen for many years.

Two books have been written about the formation of the various railway trades unions, *The Lighted Flame* and *Engines and Men*, but very little early material is contained in them, certainly not much before 1870.

The importance of Thomas Baron's diary is that it takes us back to the very early days of a rapidly expanding railway system and shows just what was expected and demanded of the work force.

Miscellaneous personal notes at the back of the diary show that Thomas Baron was born on 5th April 1835. So he was twenty years of age when he was set on as an engine cleaner at Preston depot in June 1855, and yet just six months later, on 5th December, he has his first firing turn, on No. 243 *Chillington*, a 'Crewe Goods' 2-4-0, firing for Driver Booth on a local trip job with coal for a Mr Smith.

What his occupation was before becoming a cleaner is unknown, as is the training he had before his first firing trip, but doubtless it was purely 'on the job' experience rather than training as such. He had no doubt spent a great deal of his six months cleaning and so forth, but he also must have watched, and probably helped with, the never-ending performance of filling engine boilers and maintaining an adequate water level in the boilers of engines in steam on the depot. Without injectors the only means of putting water into a boiler in steam was the axle-driven pump. So every engine would either have to be run up and down the yard to actuate the pump or be allowed to slip gently on greased rails, either against stop blocks or 'leaning' on another engine. Tender engines might also be slipped with the tender hand-brake hard on, but obviously that was not possible with tank engines. These methods were used all over the system, sidings being provided at main stations, so that engines could keep their boilers topped up as necessary.

With, no doubt, a great number of engines having leaking tubes and seams, the depots must have sounded very busy indeed, with engines panting away and not going anywhere.

A great deal of this work would be carried out by the 'Shed Turner', the LNWR name for the men employed on shed shunting and similar duties.

Thomas Baron's second firing turn on 12th December was much more exciting, a trip to Crewe on 2-4-0 No. 299 *Elk* with a cattle train, a total mileage of 108. This must have given him a real insight into what he was to expect. There was no 'passing out' by locomotive inspectors, as occurred on BR in my day; promotion on the LNWR was always governed by the 'requirements of

Plate 79: *Small firebox 'Crewe Goods' 2-4-0 No. 284* Harbinger *was built with a small firebox and direct action in April 1852 and rebuilt as a tank engine in October 1867. This official picture of it with a Webb chimney and numberplates must have been taken after 1878. The wall of the paint shop, which was opened in that year, has been painted out from roughly above the level of the buffers.*

the service', which rather loose way of working continued until the formation of the LMS.

Baron's firing turns in 1856, fifteen of them, mostly at the end of the year, show some interesting items. On 3rd March he goes on a ballast train with Driver Booth, the engine being Preston & Wyre Railway *Ribble* just before its sale out of service. On 2nd December he is on 'Crewe Goods' No. 20 *Eagle* assisting in snow conditions - what fun that must have been on a completely open footplate with no protection at all from the elements! LNWR engines only had a rudimentary spectacle plate until F. W. Webb began to fit cabs in the early 1870s. On Christmas Day he was assisting at Winwick Quay, where the night mail had come to grief - not the last accident at that place.

The year 1857 dawns and Baron now has regular employment as a fireman. Probably the expansion of the railway system required more drivers, and so the senior firemen were promoted to drivers' positions elsewhere (whether they wanted to be moved or not), creating what we used to call a 'put up' lower down the chain. The details of the engines he worked on reveal the fascinating collection of motive power allocated to Preston. At this time the timing of the last trains from Preston to Lancaster and Kendal entailed the engine and men staying all night at those places so as to be able to work the first train back on the following day. As small depots began to be provided at such points, this way of working no doubt altered, but at this time for Baron and his driver it meant at least 15 hours on duty.

Another interesting fact that can be gleaned from the diary is the mileage and availability of these early 2-2-2 and 2-4-0 engines. I was once told by a storeman at Buxton, whose father had been a fireman on 'Crewe Goods' 2-4-0s at Ladmanlow, that this type of loco would 'run for ever'. These engines look fragile and primitive, even feeble, but Baron's records show just what the availability of them was day after day in service. Their capacity for work is amazing. The 2-4-0 *Loadstone* works unbelievably long sessions. If these records show correctly what Baron's engine was doing, and apply equally to other engines at the depot and throughout the system - and there is no reason to suspect that they do not - the depot and the company must have been covering immense mileages with these 'Crewe Goods' engines.

On 11th March 1861 he took the new 'DX' goods No. 548 to Coppull to try her out and to learn how to use an injector. This gives a good idea of when injectors began to be fitted to replace axle pumps. It was probably a Giffard type injector as is still fitted to *Cornwall*. Baron must have got very used to No. 548 as he and Driver Brown had the engine for many miles.

The requirements of the service dictated that on 8th October 1861 he reported for duty at Crewe and fired for Driver Worthington on a new 'DX' goods, mainly going north to Carlisle, lodging and returning the following day. The only record of him being sick and off

duty appears here, from 10th to 12th November 1861. No doubt the rain and freezing winds over Shap had taken their toll.

It was not until 12th February 1862 that he managed to move his family to Crewe. So as well as working long hours and living in lodgings, he still has to travel to Preston to visit his home.

On 28th April 1862 he notes 'Shed 1st Engineman', in other words, he has reached the stage of senior fireman, the next to be promoted to driver. Even so he fires the following day to Driver Tortington on the 'Lady of the Lake' *Wellington*. The following day, 30th April, no doubt equipped with *Rule Book*, lamp and overcoat, he became a driver. No sooner had he commenced in his new grade on 1st June than he is sent to Hereford, and thence to Pontypool Road and Abergavenny, where he seems to remain for a while, being employed on ballasting the new line to Brynmawr. His engine is No. 141, a 'Crewe Goods' 2-4-0 tank engine, which was first on the Northern Division, then sold to the North London Railway and returned to the LNWR in 1861. On 22nd July he is back at Crewe awaiting orders. Various jobs are given to him until 31st August when he heads towards Hereford again and on 1st September has No. 49 *Columbine* to work between Newport and Hereford. His experience on this line must have been a factor in his transfer to Abergavenny with wife, family and furniture on 27th September 1862. He uses 2-4-0 tank No. 141 on many trips to Brynmawr, washing out the boiler each Sunday and also 'blocking', replacing the engine's wooden brake blocks if necessary; if conditions at Buxton, another hilly area, are any guide, No. 141 would get through brake blocks very quickly working from Abergavenny, especially on the Brynmawr road.

What a pity the diary ends here. But we must be grateful for what has survived. How did these men manage trains over roads they had never seen before, without even knowing what gradients to expect? And having to bring a train back from Stafford after the death of his driver? Although the train was double-headed, there is no mention of another driver or fireman being assigned to help him from Stafford, so it seems that depot was already stretched to the limit for crews. The age-old railway foreman's answer would be, 'Do the best you can.'

Another interesting item is the entry for 8th February 1861. The management, obviously satisfied with the way he conducted himself on the occasion of his driver's tragic death, realised he was to be trusted, gave him No. 66 *Colossus* and told him to shunt the yard, which he obviously did well, as he was told to do the same again on 8th, 9th and 10th of that month, and on the last day he was banking trains as well as shunting. Two further driving turns came on the 14th and 15th of that month, shed turning plus banking.

This all proves the old saying once very popular on the LNWR, 'men of iron and blocks of wood', perhaps the opposite of today!

Plate 80: *'Bloomer' No. 887 Knowsley in immaculate condition at Monument Lane shed in 1877. It is in the first version of Mr Webb's lined black livery with the boiler bands lined in grey. There is a Giffard injector secured to the side of the firebox below the cab side, the water control being visible above the front part of the cabside sheet. The man holding the regulator is probably the driver but the other two seem likely to be friends of Richard Bleasdale, who took the photograph.*

Engine Driving Life
Michael Reynolds

Engine Driving Life by Michael Reynolds has good descriptions of the various work done by enginemen and of the operation of steam sheds, with explanations of several of the terms used in this diary such as 'shed turner', 'bank' engine and so forth. A short extract in which these terms are covered is reproduced below, retaining the spelling and punctuation of the original.

In general the book makes fascinating reading for anyone with an interest in the early days of railways. But it was written more than twenty years after Thomas Baron started to keep a daily record of his work, and during that period considerable development must have taken place. So although many of the terms were clearly unchanged from the early days of railways, it should be remembered that the book may not always be a reliable guide to the way things were done in Baron's time.

Engine Driving Life is thought to have been published by Lockwood in 1880; Ottley gives 1881. The extract below is from one of the 'eighth thousand' copies printed in 1882. It was reprinted by Hugh Evelyn in 1968.

Drivers are drivers; their engines are selected for them, like their positions, by the foreman, who has under him a staff of men and sub-foremen to prepare the engines for the road, and to have them in steam for the drivers to work.

In the running shed there are gangs of men told off for certain work, and no other, with a foreman over them. There are the fitters, who do all repairs - temporary repairs; there are the coal-men, who coal the engines; there are the washer-outs, who wash the boilers inside; there are the cleaners, who clean the boiler outside; there is the turner with his men to light up, and raise steam by the time the driver is booked on duty.

When the driver went off duty, he told the coal-men how much coal to put on the tender, and what kind of coal, if there were several kinds at the coal-stage; and if Welsh coal was amongst them he would be sure to ask for some, whether he got any for asking or not. If the supply was rather limited, and the driver one of those straightforward men who never 'tip', the chances are he would get none. The ganger of coal-men writes down in a book the amount of coal he delivers to each engine, and this is compared with the number of miles run by the engine, and the weight of coal consumed by each engine in a month, divided by the miles run, gives the weight of coal in pounds consumed per mile, and by this means the superintendent finds out *the man* who is the heaviest in fuel and *the man* who is the lightest in fuel.

A monthly sheet is made out and posted up in the running shed, setting forth the various shades of good and bad enginemanship, by informing all and sundry how much coal each man burned per mile. It is fair work to get on and keep time with Welsh coal at 25lb per mile; with Derbyshire coal at 28lb per mile. A standard is fixed by which the men's work is estimated. On some lines the drivers are allowed 14lb of coal per mile per engine, 1½lb of coal per mile for a carriage, and 1¼lb of coal per mile for a waggon. So that if a driver makes a run of fifty miles with eighteen carriages, on the above standard scale, he would be allowed in total, for engine and carriages, 2050lb, or 18¼cwt of coal; and if he performed the journey with 12¼cwt, he would obtain six pence or one penny per cwt.

After an engine is coaled, it is taken into the shed and cleaned inside by the washers twice a week, and outside every night or every day by the cleaner. About three hours before the engine is required, the bar-boy comes along with a torch-lamp, steel broom, and fire-bar lifter, and enters the firebox to clean it of clinkers, to sweep down the tube-plate, and to re-arrange the bars. After him follows the fire-lighter with a short shovel and hammer: he breaks a few lumps of coal up on half a dozen engines, and then goes to the furnace, where about a ton of coal is all on a blaze, and shouts out 'Fire, fire'. The foreman cleaner hears this, and dispatches half-a-dozen youths to carry fire in long shovels on their shoulders to the engines. This done they go to their cleaning again. The fire-lighter adds fresh coal to that which is now just put into the firebox - about 1½cwt - and after he has assured himself that it is lighted, he, in his rounds, looks in on it occasionally, and takes stock of what steam the engine is making. If an engine is too forward, he lowers the damper, and if another is too slow, he exerts himself to forward the fire, either by putting wood on or getting the engine under the 'blower' - a contrivance that has cracked many a boiler. It consists of a piece of tubing (¾ inch), having one end in the chimney of an engine and the other attached to a boiler containing steam, which is allowed to escape by means of a cock through an orifice. As the steam issues from the orifice of the pipe, it induces a current of air to ascend through the fire, the tubes and the chimney - in fact, it blows up the fire. The same effect, though in a different manner, is produced by running an engine about in reversed gear by means of another engine

Following the firelighter is the shed turner, who is responsible for the engines being in steam; he now and again pays each engine a visit, and casts his eye at the steam-gauge. More than once, since railways started, the turner has looked and looked for steam in vain, and then found the boiler red-hot, having been lighted up without water in it. Such cases are rare, but when they do happen there is the 'sack' for the firelighter, a fine for the turner, and the postponement of an increase of salary for the foreman. Again, there is the fitter; he contrives, if possible, to do all the little repairs required before the time is due to leave the shed.

All the repairs which the drivers think are necessary, to work their engines and trains with punctuality, are entered in a book kept for the purpose, in charge of the foreman fitter, who, under a printed heading, writes down opposite each case the name of the fitter he has chosen to do such and such work. Amongst his men he finds those who can let a big-end together better than others, and nearly every one has an aptitude for some special work, on which he is mostly employed. One man is noted for making joints, another for lifting and putting in a brass, another for valve-setting, while some are of no note or likelihood.

When the driver arrives, his engine is ready for him - coaled, cleaned, repaired, and in steam; and he takes possession at once, about an hour before train-time. The engine-men are in what are called 'links;' that is, groups of from eight to a dozen, as may be required, to work the expresses. Then follow second express-men; then men for fast passenger-trains, which make several intermediate stops at stations, past which the above 'fly' by; then men for slow passenger-trains; then men for slow trains. On the goods-trains the like order prevails - express, slow or pick-up goods, and short trains. There is an auxiliary 'link', consisting of engine-men who are ready with engines to go and do anything - 'banking,' 'piloting,' and 'shunting.' The 'bank' engine-men wait with their engines in steam, coaled, and watered, near to the passenger-station; and should an engine-man come up who finds, owing to a heavy train, he is losing time, he obtains the assistance of the 'bank' engine, taking it with him in front as far as he likes. He will not take the bank engine if he can avoid it, because an engine in front smothers the one behind it with dust or slush, which is apt to get into the machinery and start it heating. A bank engine-man must know his way about the line. The pilot engine-men assist other engine-men who are strangers to the part they are about to pass over; but the term piloting is generally applied to engines which assist the goods engines as the 'bank' engine does the passenger engines. The shunting engine-men marshal the waggons and carriages about the yards and stations, and get them ready for the main-line engines to be attached to them as soon as they come out of the shed. The shunting engines reduce the hours of the main-line men, which allows them more time for rest; and besides, it enables the train engine to get away with a fire intact. When the train engine is messing about and shunting, it pulls the fire about and causes the slag in the coal to run, which, meeting with no blast, settles upon the bars, and clinkers them over.

There is a class of engine-men who have no engine, but carry a shovel and gauge-lamp, and their firemen carry two lamps. These are relievers. Some half-dozen of them occupy a cabin at the end of the passenger-platform, and in their turns they take charge of the engine from the main-line enginemen, who get straight off their engines, and walk to the steam-shed, where they enter the repairs they require in the book, and talk for a few minutes with other drivers of what they have seen and heard on the road. It is not an uncommon thing for two drivers to meet in this way, who, four hours previously, were three hundred miles apart, having come one hundred and fifty miles from opposite directions. The relief men take charge of the engine, and put their own lamps on. The lamps and tools belonging to the engine are locked up by the fireman before he leaves it; otherwise, the next time he comes on duty he would find that somebody had taken them. The relief engine-man and his mate - they don't call him a fireman - take the engine to the turn-table, and turn it round. These men return to the cabin and take their turn in relieving other engine-men.

Boiler Explosion at Edge Hill

In May 1857 the boiler of 'Crewe Goods' 2-4-0 St Patrick exploded at Edge Hill, Liverpool. The event is related here in extracts from the Liverpool Mercury, *which reported it in several issues, as did other newspapers. Thomas Baron passed through Edge Hill on 4th and 7th May, two days before and one day after the fateful day.*

From the Liverpool Mercury, *Wednesday 6th May 1857.*
Terrific Boiler Explosion at Edge-Hill, and Loss of Life

Yesterday forenoon, a fearful explosion took place of the boiler of one of the locomotive engines belonging to the London & North Western Railway company, causing the immediate death of one man, and frightfully wounding two others.

It appears that the engine *St Patrick*, which is chiefly used for assisting trains in and out of the station, was standing on one of the goods sidings at the Edge Hill station, having attached to it a train of four wagons loaded with sand, which was about to be taken down the line. The engine driver and fireman were both at their posts, and the engine was about to move on, when suddenly the boiler burst, accompanied by a loud report resembling a clap of thunder. The effects of the explosion were felt all over the station, which was much shaken, and between 20 and 30 panes of glass were blown out of the windows. The engine driver, Joseph Ford, was blown into the air almost to the height of the large chimney adjoining, which is 80ft high, and he fell about twelve yards from where the explosion took place. He was fearfully scalded all over his body, and shockingly bruised about the head and face. He was conveyed to the Tunnel Hotel. Mr Pennington, surgeon, was almost immediately in attendance, and on seeing the body pronounced life to be extinct. The body now lies at the Tunnel Hotel awaiting the coroner's inquest. The fireman, whose name is Seth Foulkes, was blown from the tender, and thrown over two of the same wagons, alighting on the last but one. On examining the poor fellow, he was found to have received several bruises, and was dangerously wounded. One of his legs was nearly blown off, and broken in three or four different places. He was dreadfully cut on the head, bleeding profusely from the crown, which was laid entirely open. He was also very much scalded all over the body, and presented a shocking spectacle. He was conveyed to the Royal Infirmary with all possible speed, and his wounds attended to, and he now lies there in a precarious and almost hopeless state.

Another man, Henry Harrison, a 'line foreman', was injured by the accident, but not dangerously. At the moment when the explosion took place, Harrison was passing the engine, and was blown across the line to a distance of from 15 to 20 yards. When picked up, he was found to be insensible, but no limbs were broken. He was, however, much scalded in various parts of the body, and severely bruised about the head and face. He was conveyed to the Royal Infirmary, along with Foulkes, the fireman, where he now remains.

The engine and boiler were shattered to pieces, and various portions were scattered about on the line. The tender was completely turned over and laid across the line. The engine had but recently undergone examination, and was considered in good working condition.

From the Liverpool Mercury, *Friday 8th May 1857.*

The Boiler Explosion at Edge Hill Station

Yesterday an inquest was held upon the bodies of Joseph Ford, engine driver of the *St Patrick* locomotive, 31 years of age residing at 13 Back King Street; and Seth Foulkes, aged 23, a fireman, who resided in Botanic Street, the two unfortunate men who were killed at Edge Hill station by the bursting of the boiler of the engine on Tuesday morning last, about half past eleven o'clock.

James Worthington, fireman of the engine *Ptarmigan*, said he had been nine years in the service, and the engines used for jobbing were quite as good as those used for goods trains. He had been with the *St Patrick* engine, and had never heard any complaint, as the foreman on duty generally examined the engines to see that all was right. There were two foremen at the Edge Hill station, Bartholomew Martin and William Eaton.

John Reach, an engine-driver for twelve years, had charge of the engine *St Patrick* on Monday last from six in the morning until four in the afternoon. In the fore part of the day he discovered a leakage from the box, which he observed proceeded from one of the stays, but not of such importance as to report to the foreman. He reported it to the deceased man Ford and he himself would not have hesitated to take charge of the engine on the following day.

Sampson Evans, boilermaker for 20 years, had heard no complaints of the *St Patrick* engine since the month of August last, at which time he examined the firebox, and found a part defective, which he cut out and replaced with new copper, and it was placed in a thorough working state. After what occurred on Tuesday he examined the firebox, and found the surface thin, but not particularly so. The piece which

he had put in was still on the side, and he had observed some scales on the upper surface of the box, but these could not be discovered before the explosion took place, unless by taking off the dome and removing the regulator. He could not say that the dome was off when he repaired the firebox in August last, as that was not in his department, but that of the fitters. Mr Marshall superintended the repairs at that time. He should have thought that the engine was fit to run for twelve months after the over haul. In reply to the foreman of the jury, witness observed that the new piece he had put in, was attached by $\frac{7}{8}$in copper staves, 5½in in length, which extended from the inside across the water space of three inches, and were riveted on each side.

Edward Ross, engineer, who had made an examination of the engine and boiler since the accident, found that the explosion had taken place at the top of the firebox, over the fire-door, between the first and second rows of stays. A quantity of scale had collected at the top and down the side. Heard that the thickness of the plates was originally $\frac{7}{16}$th, but found near the spot where the patch had been put by the witness Evans that the plate was only a ¼in, and the top less than *that*, which was not sufficiently strong for safe working. Many of the copper stays had not a full thread; the holes were too large and a great many of the plates had stripped themselves off the stay bolts without stripping the threads, which was a proof that the holes were too big. He attributed the cause of the explosion to three reasons, all helping each other. First, the scale having collected, and consequently prevented the water touching the plate, which would be softened thereby; second, the thinness of the firebox plates; and third, the copper stays not having sufficient thread to support the plate. There was no indication to show that the boiler was short of water. If the engine boiler and firebox were thoroughly cleaned and put into working order in August last, witness would not have deemed it necessary to examine them so soon as far as the scales were concerned. He was decidedly of opinion that the plates of the firebox were too thin for safe working at a pressure of 90lb; and the more so as the copper stays had not sufficient thread. When he looked in the firebox he saw that a great many of the stays had been leaking. Looking at what had taken place, and after the examination of the engine, firebox and stays, he did not think there had been any negligence on the part of anyone as regarded the work done or what ought to have been done. If there was any blame at all, it was from want of forethought; the greatest blame was on the part of the man who put the stays in, but from the lapse of time, nine years, since the engine was made, it was impossible to find out the workman who did it. The thickness of the scale which he found could not have accumulated since August last.

The Coroner then said that the latter answer conveyed an idea that the engine had not been properly overhauled, and the jury, in order that the parties might be brought forward who made the repairs in August last, adjourned the inquest until Saturday morning next.

The Harrow Accident,
26th November 1870

From The Staffordshire Advertiser, *Saturday December 1870*

Calamitous Accident on the London and North Western Railway: Seven Lives Lost

An appalling and fatal accident occurred to the express train leaving Euston Station at five o'clock on Saturday afternoon. In the first part of the train were three or four Manchester carriages, and behind them the carriages for Liverpool. At Harrow a dense fog prevented the drivers from seeing any signals, while the fog signalman had not been able to get up the line. The result was that, about fifty yards beyond the station, the express, which was going at fifty miles an hour, ran into some goods vans which, in consequence of an accident, were standing on the main line. The driver of the train seems to have shunted as usual; but, unknown to him, some of the vans broke away before they had passed on to the siding, and were left on the main line, the other part of the train proceeding on its way. The signalman immediately telegraphed the next point, Wimbly Cutting, to block the line. The man at Wimbly promptly turned on the danger signal and also displayed a hand signal; but owing to the fog the drivers of the express did not see these signals, and the train rushed on and dashed with terrific force into the goods trucks.. The crash was fearful, and it was heard some miles off. The first engine was smashed to pieces, and its tender utterly ruined. The second engine, the Clyde, was greatly damaged. The first two or three Manchester carriages were smashed, portions of them being thrown some distance, and the sides and roofs of the others were torn away. All these, and the debris of the goods trucks, were piled up across the line, as they had been thrown by the force of the collision. The Liverpool carriages and the rest of the train escaped without much injury. The crash and shrieks of the passengers at once attracted the railway officials and people from the houses near the line, and they set to work to extricate the passengers. Some were found to be dead, while others were buried beneath a mass of the wreck, from which it required great labour to extricate them. Many were only shaken, or so slightly hurt as to be able to render assistance to the injured.

The driver of the first engine, William Shelvey of Bletchley, was killed at once. He was a man of great experience and courage, and invariably travelled with a favourite dog – a half-bred fox. When Shelvey's remains were discovered under the dome of his engine, his dog, which had escaped unhurt, was found watching near the body.

From The Morning Advertiser, *6th January 1871*

The Late Fatal Accident at Harrow
The Adjourned Inquest on Mr Lamb of Manchester

Yesterday Dr Lankester, coroner of Central Middlesex, resumed, at the Euston Hotel, his adjourned inquest on the body of Mr John Lamb, aged 36, coach proprietor of Manchester, who had died at the hotel from the injuries received by the late collision on the London & North Western Railway at Harrow.

Mr Blenkinsopp, solicitor, again represented the London & North Western Railway. Mr Cawkwell, general manager; Mr G. P. Bruyeres, general superintendent, and other officials of the company, were also present.

The coroner having explained the circumstances under which the enquiry has been opened and adjourned, Mr Blenkinsopp suggested, with a view to facilitate the proceedings, that he should read the depositions of the witnesses taken on the occasion of the coroner's investigation at Harrow, and then the jury could re-examine them upon any points they might think of importance to enable them to arrive at a conclusion.

This course was assented to, and James Walker, the signalman at Harrow, was first called and had his evidence read over. He was re-examined as to what was the state of the signals at the time of the occurrence. He said the 4.37 from Euston left Harrow at 5.9, and the next train, a goods, at 5.12. At that time it was foggy, but the signal was at danger. In foggy weather the distance signal was kept on for three minutes. He had himself put it on as well as the caution signal, which remains up until the road is signalled clear by telegraph. He told the driver of the goods train to shunt, and did not notice at the time that the train had become divided. Heard someone call out that the train had broken loose, and immediately he did so he blocked the line. That was at 5.18. The Wembley signalman had repeated the six beats to him, indicating the leaving of the train. At this time he could not see beyond 100 yards for the fog. When he heard the goods train had broken he sent the porter White up the line with fog signals, and called out for help. Directly after, he heard the express train coming. Being aware that the goods train had not shunted and had broken, he became alarmed and so flurried that he did not then know what to do. Heard one of the fog signals go off. Had been six years signalman, but had never had an increase of wages.

The evidence of White, the porter, was next taken, and was in the main corroborative of that of Walker. He heard Walker call for help when he heard the goods train had broken. Walker sent him up the line to place fog signals. He had placed the first about sixty yards from the Harrow station on the down line, and a second about forty yards beyond it, when he heard the express coming upon him, and had not time to lay any more signals.

Charles Robinson, the signalman at Wembley, who was censured by the Harrow jury, was first examined and then requested to remain in the court to hear the evidence of the driver and fireman of the express train. He said the goods train passed his box at six minutes after five, although it should have been at Harrow at that time, and he stopped it until the preceding train had passed at 5.23. He kept the danger signal up from the time he received the block signal as he did not receive the clear signal, and a train which followed the express stopped in obedience to that signal. That was about eight minutes after the express had gone past. For this train he had laid down fog signals, although he considered it was not too foggy for the danger signal to have been seen.

Robert Stone, engine-driver of the second engine to the express train, stated that the express left Euston at its usual time. They approached Wembley at 5.21. Both he and his mate were on the look-out for signals, as it was foggy. He noticed the white signal up at Brent, which is on the London side of Wembley. It was foggy at the time. They approached Wembley at about the rate of 37 miles an hour. The usual express speed was about 42 miles an hour. Did not see that the red signals were up at the post at Wembley, but at the time the steam was blowing across their faces from the first engine. William Shelvey was the driver of the first or pilot engine, and it was his duty, upon seeing a danger signal, to have blown his whistle as a signal to the driver of the second engine to pull up. Had he done so witness would at once have shut off his steam.

Mr Blenkinsopp: It is equally the duty of a driver, if any circumstance occurs by which he does not see the signals at a station to treat it as a danger signal and act accordingly. Witness would have done so had he been in charge of the first engine of the express, and not seen the signals on passing Wembley.

Robinson: in answer to questions by the jury, said he was on duty 12 hours at a time, and his wages were 19s per week.

Thomas Ruith, fireman to the second engine of the express train, corroborated the driver's evidence that they could not see the signals at the Wembley station on account of the fog and the steam from the first engine blowing across their faces. At the time they were approaching that station from London. Had the driver of the pilot engine seen the red signal or not seen any signals, he ought to have blown his whistle, which he did not do, or the witness must have heard it. Heard the fog signals as they approached the Harrow station. Saw the white light at the signalman's box at the Wembley station, but not the post signals.

Mr Cawkwell, the general manager, produced the *Regulations*, and No. 206 showed it to be the duty of a driver when he cannot see the signals at a station to treat the fact as a danger signal, and pull up his train in as short a distance as possible.

After some conversation, in the course of which the coroner remarked upon the possibility, as it was admitted to be a foggy evening, of a driver being unable to see signals, he at the time being on an engine with a train going at the rate of 37 miles an hour.

The court was cleared of strangers, and after a consultation of nearly three-quarters of an hour the Jury delivered the following special verdict:

'We find that the deceased John Lamb died of "pyaemia" produced by injuries received in a collision between an express passenger and good train on the London & North Western Railway on the 29th November last, and that the said death arose from misadventure.

'The Jury, however, desire to add to their verdict their opinion:-

1st. That the driver of the pilot engine, William Shelvey, neglected to comply with clause 206 of the *Rules and Regulations of the LNWR Company* for the conduct of the traffic, as it was imperative on his part to have stopped the engine if he could not distinguish the signal at Wembley.

2nd. That they regard the hours of duty of men engaged as signalmen and pointsmen as excessive.

3rd. They are also unanimously of opinion that the safety of passengers travelling by railway cannot be secured until a separate line of rails is provided for all goods trains on lines of so much traffic as that of the LNWR.

Signed: 'Jonathan Salter', Foreman. Edwin Lankester, Coroner.

Mr Blenkinsopp assured the coroner and jury that their views would be fully represented, and would no doubt receive the earnest and attentive consideration of the LNWR Company. The Inquiry then terminated.

From The Watford Observer*, 7th January 1871*
Reviews – *The Animal World*

This month the 'monthly advocate of humanity', issued by the Royal Society for the Prevention of Cruelty to Animals, has as a frontispiece a picture of poor Shelvey's (the engine-driver who was killed at Harrow) dog and children. We copy it for our readers, while we recommend the *Animal World* to their notice. There is a great deal of valuable information in it regarding the treatment of animals which all ought to see.

'The Engine Driver's Dog'
A touching story is told in connection with the late fatal railway accident at Harrow. 'Duke', as poor Shelvey was called, owing to his Roman nose resembling that that of the late 'Iron Duke', never travelled without his dog on the engine, who was there at the time of the collision alluded to. More fortunate than his master, he turned up without a scar after the shock and crash was over. By permission of the railway authorities, a gentleman of high family has seen this affectionate animal, and writes to me as follows: 'Snatchburry' is a little rough-haired dog, of a yellowish colour; pretty small head, most intelligent eye, with a good deal of the rough terrier breed in him. He was originally a stray dog, and was picked up on the platform at Euston-square about ten years ago by the unfortunate engine-driver Shelvey, and accompanied him on his daily journeys ever since. He generally rode, no matter how high the wind was, on the tool-box of the tender. Although he always barked when the train approached a station, he would do so most furiously if they went over a fog signal, and rush

frantically round and round the tender. When the body of his master was discovered, he was found standing by his side, and followed the corpse to the goods shed, where he was temporarily placed, and could only be removed by force. When his master's body was placed in the coffin, he moaned and cried most piteously. On the day of the funeral, two black rosettes were attached to his plain but neat collar, and he was led by George Craffe, who was formerly three years stoker and mate with his former master. Twice, in his efforts to reach the coffin, did he break away, and at last Craffe was obliged to carry him in his arms. This man took charge of him when he was sent home on the night of the accident; but he is now in charge of William Green, an engine driver, and an old friend of the deceased, who seems to have taken great care of him, as he is in excellent condition. When Green has done his work, he takes 'Snatchburry' to his late home, where his moans after his late master recommence, and he can only be quieted by some of the clothes of the deceased, especially his boots, being placed on each side of the fire, where poor Shelvey used to place them after he had done his work. He will then lay down near them and watch for hours.

On the death of his master one of the committee of the Home for Lost and Starving Dogs at Holloway offered him an asylum for life, but received a most courteous reply from one of the principal officers of the LNW Railway Co, saying that hundreds of Shelvey's fellow workmen would be only too glad to have him if his widow could not support him. Such proved to be the case, as on the arrival of the train on the 12th instant, at Euston-square, he was surrounded by numbers of porters, mechanics and labourers, all anxious to caress their favourite; and this was repeated in the presence of the writer, who accompanied the engine to Camden town, everyone holding out their hands to pat the dog.

I cannot conclude this story without alluding to the praiseworthy conduct of the driver, William Green, and the stoker, George Craffe, to whom the writer is indebted for the above particulars. When offered a small remuneration for their loss of time, they both firmly and respectfully refused to receive anything, and when pressed to do so only consented on the condition that the money should be added to the subscription which is being made for Mrs Shelvey and her four fatherless children. W. F.

The Harrow Accident,
G. P. Neele

Railway Reminiscences by G. P. Neele contains two references to this accident, firstly a factual account of what happened and the impression it made on him when he visited the scene, and secondly the consequences it had in bringing about a thorough revision of the arrangements for signalling in foggy weather. In Neele's words, 'it was one of a long catalogue of accidents affecting' the LNWR in the autumn of 1870. This included one at Carlisle when a North Eastern Railway mineral train cut through a night express on a crossing and one to the up 'Irish Mail' at Tamworth when a signalman thought it was a coal train approaching and turned it into the platform line.

The accidents culminated in one at Harrow on Saturday 26th September, when in dense fog the 5pm express ran into the tail of a coal train, 128 yards north of the down main signal. Six persons were killed on the spot and forty-one injured. In this case, as the coal train was being moved forward to shunt, a coupling snapped, the wagons separated, and the rear portion of the train remained on the line; the signalman at Harrow blocked the line by telegraph to Wembley Cutting; there was an inexperienced man on duty there, and he had no distant signal; the express passed his box without observing any main line signal. The fogmen from Harrow were not ordered out until the foreman heard the break away, and in the fog the distant signal at Harrow was not sighted by the driver of the express, who came on at high speed.

The journey down to Harrow with Mr Cawkwell (the General Manager; Neele was Superintendent of the Line), in the chilling fog that evening, will not easily be forgotten. The wrecked train, the blazing fitful light by which the men worked amid the 'debris' and the dead, forms a ghastly reminiscence; it was 2 o'clock in the morning before any traffic could pass up or down.

The accident at Harrow led to a thorough revision of the arrangements for fog signalling generally. The instructions in the old rule books were very vague. The existing regulations are the outcome of this accident. Special circulars were issued to the line defining very closely the duties of the fogmen, their instructions as to coming on fogging duty, the post each man was appointed to serve; and in subsequent years, as fogs still proved sources of danger to travelling trains, and flaws or weak points developed, lists were drawn up of the various signalling posts requiring fogmen, the names of each man specified, and the name of the man to replace the former should the fog prove of long continuance; in addition, lower arms, repeaters of the higher signals, were arranged to be placed on any posts considered too lofty for observation by drivers during fogs.

At the Clearing House the question naturally appeared, and led to some debate as to the performance of the duty of 'fogging' at junctions with foreign lines - a difference of opinion existing, one party contending that each company should find its own fogmen, the other that the company owning the junction should find the fogmen; the latter was adopted as the standard rule, it being left to the owning company to settle in all cases with its neighbours. The correspondence entailed in obtaining definite settlements with surrounding companies was very considerable, there being much difficulty in making sure of fogmen and relief fogmen at country junctions.

Driver Shelvey's Dog
Michael Reynolds

> *But the poor dog, in life the firmest friend,*
> *The first to welcome; foremost to defend;*
> *Whose honest heart is still his master's own;*
> *Who labours, fights, lives, breathes for him alone,*
> *Unhonoured falls, unnoticed all his worth;*
> *Denied in heaven the soul he had on earth.*

Engine Driving Life by Michael Reynolds also contains, as well as factual accounts of the work of enginemen, the organisation of engine sheds and such like, this touching story of an engine driver's dog and of the driver's death in an accident at Harrow on 26th November 1870.

A homeless dog in London, choking with emotion, stiff with tramping, and hungry, entered the handsome porch at the grand entrance to Euston Square railway station, which was full of excitement - all bustle, activity, and variety. Within the vast fabric, between the piles of luggage of wraps and bags, between the high, low, rich and poor, the poor 'doggie' tremblingly alive, trusting in his character for honesty, passed by the colossal pillars, waiting rooms, and booking-offices on to the platform. There he looked searchingly about him, trying to find, amongst the many faces, one that he could recognise, or to find a voice addressed to him, when - unexpected happiness - he was saluted and carressed by the kind-hearted driver, who was no other than Driver Shelvey, who led the grateful animal on to the engine. He found him to be a little rough-haired dog, of a yellowish colour; with a pretty small head, a most intelligent eye, and a good deal of the rough terrier, and while piles of luggage were being brought into the vans, and before departure-bell began to ring lustily, the 'doggie' had been placed on the back of the tender, the circumference of which was to prove his world. Suffering had done much to quench all hopes of his ever becoming a carpet-dog. Whether he ever had any idea of being an engine-driver's dog is not known, but at all events he soon made himself at home, and he took an intense interest in signals. And so, in the easiest way in the world, by catching the swing of circumstances, he passed at a bound from the condition of a forlorn cur, with eyes dim and temper soured, into a position which no other dog occupied, and one in every way likely to make him good-natured and popular. But there is no telling how many nights in the streets, lying on stones huddled up, half-frozen, he had experienced; how many times he had been caught, kicked and beaten from square to terrace, before he was crushed by the ponderous car of neglect, until the pulse of his little heart beat with joy to find a home and refuge on the back of the tender of an express engine - a perfect stranger amidst so much that was passing strange, and yet content with present good, finding in his new berth, upon the tool-box of an engine, a world of wealth and keen enjoyment.

The 'Duke', as Driver Shelvey was called owing to his Roman nose resembling that of the Duke of Wellingon, never afterwards travelled without his dog, whom he named Snatchbury. For years this intelligent creature made daily trips with his master between Bletchley Junction and London, running fast express trains in foggy weather, in the darkness of the night as well as in the sunlight of day. Now trotting about Euston platform, impatient for the right-away signal, now going at sixty miles an hour, with a strong breeze blowing all the shaggy hair back from his pretty face, disclosing a set of beautiful white teeth, now on Bletchley platform, hopping about on three stilts as proud as Punch, and priding himself that they had kept time. He would give 'Duke' a look which was full of expression, as much as to say: 'Well done our side'. Every day he was gaining intelligence by culture, and he came to know the code of signals, so that when he saw a red light, indicating danger, he would call attention to it. He knew also, after a little experience, the route his master took every day. He could distinguish his own engine from others, although there were many others of the same class, of the same size, and painted in every particular the same.

Wonderful stories are told of dogs, which teach us that dogs are not inferior animals, that their powers can be developed and their natures raised, so that the idea of the animals being mere machines filled up with instincts, as an engine is filled with steam, is absurd. A dog's intelligence is developed by culture, the same as that of the two-legged dogs. Let us not, however, be dogmatical, but stick to our subject. Master Snatchbury was for a period of ten years 'on duty' every day. He sometimes found his arrangements all behind his master's in a morning, and so he had to follow him to the shed, where he could cock up his bright eye first at one engine and then at another, as he ran down the roads between engines, and having found the right one, and some time to spare, he would take a look round and see if anybody was about to offer him a toothful. If he was very late, and he could not just find the engine, his anxiety would increase and intensify his earnestness, until it had worked him into a state of almost convulsive frenzy, making a series of leaps over pits, to cut off the corners, accompanied by a whining cry developing into a sharp shrill bark. He would sometimes arrive just in time to join the engine when it was leaving the shed for the passenger station; but if he considered the time was too short to join the engine at

Plate 81: *'Large Bloomer' No. 992, which was built at Wolverton in 1862. It now has a Ramsbottom castellated chimney cap and screw reverser, so the date is probably about 1870. Lying on the tender toolbox is a dog, which is quite possibly Snatchbury with Driver Shelvey and his fireman on the footplate. Shelvey's engine in the Harrow accident, however, was not this 'Bloomer' but Ramsbottom 'Problem' No. 833* Clyde.

E. Pouteau No. 290

Plate 82: *6ft 'Crewe Single' No. 365* Vesta *in Webb black livery with the boiler bands edged in red, the later standard scheme, rather than the red, cream and grey used originally. The photographer was Bleasdale and the date 1879. Prominent on the tender tool box is a dog, which seems to be paying close attention to the photographer. In later prints of this photograph the dog has been removed.*

the shed, he would go direct to the station. On one occasion he arrived just in time to see his master going away; but seeing it was a hopeless case, he made no fuss or cry about it, but walked into a quiet spot and dropped down, with his two fore-feet straight out before him, indicating health, strength, and happiness; and there he lay, taking stock of the trains running in and out of the station, until one came up which was going *his* way, the way that would enable him to join his own engine. He would jump on the engine and work his way to London or Rugby, after Driver Shelvey; and, on the engine arriving at the platform, he would take a smart run over the yard from engine to engine until he found his engine, for Shelvey had been sent out before his time after arriving at the shed, and it so happened he was in a contrary direction to that which he had been accustomed to run. Snatchburry, when he came to the shed, thought he must have been mistaken, and that Shelvey could not have left home; so he went down home, and put his head into each room, and gave a good sniff or two, and was satisfied his master was gone. He ran off to the station again and took the first train for Rugby Junction; not finding Shelvey there he came back to Bletchley, and not seeing anything of him there, he went back to London and searched the yard over, but with no better effect, and so he came home again, tired out, to find his master at supper. How much of this intelligence he owed to instinct, how much to culture, or how much to brain, is a problem. It is one of those 'things which no fellow can understand'. But it is enough that he had affections, loving and remembering, and thinking; and, further than that, when once properly housed, fed, and cared for, he never made the least sign of dishonesty, or any desire to return to London life. Snatchburry loved engines, and his career must have picked up an acquaintance with a good many other dogs *en route*.

The reflection tempts us into speculation. They would see he was a smart young chap, rather rough, but good-hearted fellow, with the smell of engine-oil about him, and with an unaccountable amount of cheek to be running into vans and asking every dog where he was bound for; but their courage would be raised by his kind speeches about his 'being on duty', and he could assure them that the oscillation and noise they could feel after starting was simply a way the iron horse had when he was scampering away as fast as he could be made to do so, and the best thing for them to do was drop into a nap until he barked for the driver to stop; and so to their great joy travelling dogs would remember the good services rendered gratuitously by the good-natured driver's dog. Snatchburry had to distinguish colours; and he distingished stations from residences. On seeing a red light he would bark, and also approaching a station; but he also knew that a fog-signal indicated extreme danger, and when the wheels of the engine went over some, followed with a *bang*, he would rush frantically round and round the tender, no matter how high the wind was or the speed, or how cold and bleak the air was, in hurricanes of snow and in the midst of perils he called aloud *his* warning high into the air. Driver Shelvey possessed all the knowledge which renders a man fit to run fast and important trains. There were no intricate questions concerning railway working but what he held the thread of; nothing unapproachable, all easy of access, from leaking of a belly-stay in the boiler to an undeniable breakdown. He ran the most important trains; he ran every trip with success - day after day, for months, for years. His enginemanship was unquestionably sound, and men everywhere knew it - men of authority and experience. Still, on a dark November afternoon, within half an hour after leaving Euston Station with the five o'clock express, his engine was hurled from the iron track right across the other line, over which the engine fell on her side. Shelvey was killed and Snatchburry was saved. As soon as possible search was made for Driver Shelvey among the debris, and he was found with the dog standing by his side, and following the corpse to the goods-shed, where it was temporarily placed, Snatchburry could only be moved by force.

When his master's body was placed in the coffin he moaned and cried most piteously. On the day of the funeral, two black rosettes were attached to his plain but neat collar, and he was led by poor Shelvey's fireman, who fortunately was spared. He succeeded in breaking away from the mourners, and ran along to the coffin, and at last Craffe was obliged to carry him in his arms to the grave side. For some time after the funeral the mourner felt the loss of that friend who befriended him when he was only a poor homeless cur, and could be quieted only by kindness. Driver Green, an old friend of the 'Duke', would sometimes take him to his late home, when his moans after his old master would recommence, and he could not be pacified until some of the deceased's clothes were placed near him. Nothing could stay his cries and lamentations so effectually as bringing out his late friend's boots and placing them on each side of the fire where poor Shelvey used to place them after he had done his work. He could then lie down by them and watch for hours, evidently expecting the return of the owner. Alas! He was no longer in the busy throng; he had travelled life's railway, all stations were past, and he had been stopped in death by an unfortunate mistake. A goods train was standing at Harrow Station; and, with the signal in his favour and the darkness of the night preventing his seeing the danger, he went right into the train. After Shelvey's death, Snatchburry was taken charge of by Driver Green, who took great care of him until poor little 'doggie' entered into his rest, when all that was mortal of him was scrupulously attended to; and he is now in a little glass case, anxious-looking as ever.

Plate 83: *The last 'Crewe Types' were shedded at Buxton and sub-shedded at points on the Cromford & High Peak line. A 'Crewe Goods Tank' was regularly stationed at Ladmanlow and used for shunting the local quarries and tripping to Bunsall incline. Here, No. 3097 is performing these duties and is fitted with a cab, a welcome luxury on the C&HP.*

Plate 84: *A 'Crewe Goods' 2-4-0 was also regularly stationed at Ladmanlow for working the line to Middleton Top. Here, No. 3074 is on this job, in charge of Driver Townley - the fireman's name is not known. The engine still has no cab, the only protection from the elements being weatherboards on both engine and tender. The photographer is thought to have been C. M. Doncaster, who also took photographs of the engine at Gotham Curve and Dowlow.*

Plate 85: *'Crewe Goods' 2-4-0 No. 3032 on the old depot at Buxton with the ticket platform in the right background. The driver was known as 'Sticky Buxton' and was a boxer of some renown.*

Further Reading

The London & North Western Railway: A History, by M. C. Reed, Atlantic Transport Publishers, Penryn, 1996.

British Locomotive Catalogue, 1825-1923, Vol 2A, London & North Western Railway and its constituent companies, by Bertram Baxter edited by David Baxter, Moorland Publishing Co, Ashbourne, 1978.

The Locomotives of the LNWR, by H. F. F. Livesey, The Railway Publishing Company, London, 1948.

'Locomotives Built at Crewe Works', based on the records of S. S. Scott, Stephenson Locomotive Society *Journal* serial publication January 1953 to February 1958, with many comments and corrections from readers. Covers engines built up to 1867.

Locomotives in Profile No. 15 Volume 2, The Crewe Type, by D. H. Stuart and Brian Reed, Profile Publications, Windsor, 1972.

'The First 182 Engines Built at Crewe', by W. L. Harris in *Premier News*, the journal of the London & North Western Railway Society, December 1992.

An Illustrated History of LNWR Engines by Edward Talbot, Oxford Publishing Company, Poole, 1985.

Locomotives of the LNWR Southern Division, London & Birmingham Railway, London & North Western Railway and Wolverton Locomotive Works, by Harry Jack, published by the Railway Correspondence and Travel Society, 2001.

LNWR Liveries by Peter Davis, George Dow, Philip A. Millard and Edward Talbot, the Historical Model Railway Society, 1988.

'The Iron "Lion", Locomotive, Pump Engine, Film Star' by C. W. Reed, Stephenson Locomotive Society *Journal*, Volume 33, 1957, page 312.

The Chronicles of Boulton's Siding, by Alfred Rosling Bennett, The Locomotive Publishing Co 1927, new edition by David & Charles in 1971.

The London & North Western Railway, A Selection of 7mm Locomotive Drawings, compiled by M. Sharman, The Oakwood Press,1986.

L&NWR Locomotive Names, by John Goodman, published by the Railway Correspondence & Travel Society, 2002.

'Locomotive Sheds, Part 1: the London & North Western Railway' by 'Perseus' (Leslie W. Jones), Stephenson Locomotive Society *Journal*, May 1957 to April 1960.

LMS Engine Sheds, Volume One, The L&NWR, Chris Hawkins and George Reeve, Wild Swan Publications, 1981.

Crewe Locomotive Works and Its Men, by Brian Reed, David & Charles, Newton Abbot, 1982.

The Railways Around Preston - an Historical Review, by Gordon Biddle, Foxline Publishing, 1989.

The Industrial Railways of the Wigan Coalfield, by C. H. A. Townley, F. D. Smith and J. A. Peden, Runpast Publishing: part one 1991; part two 1992.

Furness and the Industrial Revolution, An Economic History of the Furness (1711-1900) and the Town of Barrow (1757-1897), With an Epilogue, by J. D. Marshall, Barrow-in-Furness Library and Museum Committee, 1958.

Griffiths Guide to the Iron Trade of Great Britain, first edition 1873, introduction and notes to the new edition by W. K. V. Vale, published by David & Charles, Newton Abbot, 1967.

The Locomotive Engine, A Rudimentary Treatise, by G. Drysdale Dempsey, John Weale, London, 1857, reprinted by Kingsmead Reprints, Bath, 1970.

Loco Motion, The World's Oldest Steam Locomotives, by Michael R. Bailey, published by The History Press, Stroud, 2014.

The Railway-Engine Driver's Guide, by E. Flachat and J. Petiet, Ward & Lock, London, 1856.

Engine-Driving Life, Stirring Adventures and Incidents in the Lives of Locomotive Engine Drivers, by Michael Reynolds 'The Engine-Driver's Friend', Lockwood, 1880, reprinted by Hugh Evelyn, London 1968

John Ramsbottom - Victorian Engineering Giant, by Robin Pennie, The Lancashire & Yorkshire Railway Society, 2008.

Robert Pateson, a Scientific Philosopher. The Life and Work of an Early Photographer, by Emma Heslewood and John Garlington, Harris Museum, Preston, 2004.

Perceptions of Great Engineers, Fact and Fantasy, edited by Denis Smith, published by the Science Museum for Newcomen Society, National Museums and Galleries on Merseyside and the University of Liverpool, 1994.

Early Railway Prints, A Social History of Railways from 1825 to 1850, Gareth Rees, Phaidon, Oxford, 1980.

A Regional History of the Railways of Great Britain, published by David & Charles, Newton Abbot: *Volume 7 The West Midlands* by Rex Christensen, 1973; *Volume 10* The North West by Geofrey O. Holt, 1978; *Volume 11 North and Mid Wales* by Peter E. Baughan, 1980; *Volume 12 South Wales* by D. S. M. Barrie, 1980.

Victorian Railwaymen, The Emergence and Growth of Railway Labour 1830-1870 P. W. Kingsford, Cass, 1970.

Waterways Journal 'Sea Routes to Wolverhampton: The iron ore traffic ... Cumbria to ... the West Midlands' by Peter Sandbach, Volume 17 pages 12-27, The Boat Museum Society, Spring 2015.

The Industrial Canal, Volume 2, The Railway Interchange Trade, Tom Foxon, The Heartland Press, 1998.

Plate 86: *When the last 'Crewe Goods Tank' was withdrawn from service in 1905, the Crewe Works official photographer was moved to record the occasion and travelled to Buxton to photograph the engine, No. 3054, on Buxton shed with Mr Needham, the shedmaster posed beside it and with a Whale 4-4-2 'Precursor Tank' in the background, doubtless as an example of progress over the years. Despite having worked for many years in the High Peak, the engine still has no cab, and still has a water pump driven off the crosshead and no means of operating the cylinder drain cocks from the footplate. Although the class was no longer used by the LNWR, several examples continued in industrial service, having been sold to collieries and similar railways. Likewise, No. 3054 was not scrapped but sold to a colliery in North Staffordshire, where some of its predecessors had gone. So more than forty years after Thomas Baron had first set off from Crewe to make his way to Shrewsbury, Hereford and eventually Abergavenny on 'Crewe Goods Tank' No 141, and more than thirty years after F. W. Webb had first fitted a cab to an LNWR engine, the last of the class was withdrawn by the LNWR in much the same condition as No. 141 had been and continued to work in industrial service for several more years yet.*

LNWR Society collection

Epilogue
As Michael Bentley has quoted elsewhere in this book,
the use of wooden brake blocks and the general conditions faced by the men on the footplate,
as exemplified here in the record of Thomas Baron's daily work,
gave rise to the old saying in reference to the London & North Western Railway:
'Blocks of wood but men of iron'.
A race of heroes indeed!